Little Symp

A Phil Spector Reader

Edited by Kingsley Abbott

First edition published in 2011 by
Helter Skelter Publishing
PO Box 50497, London W8 9FA

Cover design by Chris Wilson
Typesetting and layout by Graeme Milton
Printed in Malta by Progress Press Company Ltd

A CIP record for this book is available from the British Library.

ISBN 978-1-905139-01-9

www.helterskelterpublishing.com

Little Symphonies
A Phil Spector Reader

Edited by Kingsley Abbott

**Helter
Skelter**
publishing

For Sean Body – a wonderful man

Contents

Foreword by Richard Williams

Once upon a time just about everybody in the music business had a Phil Spector story, and many of them are to be found within these covers. Those stories usually contain an account of a piece of weird behaviour that was designed to get up someone's nose, and they were passed down to posterity by observers who would roll their eyes in astonishment at the thought that he could get away with it in the climate of his era. Most often, he did.

The real story, however, is that no one ever made better pop records than Spector, and that's the alpha and omega of the matter. To know him is to love him? Well, maybe. The jury is still out on that one, although the defence has no shortage of witnesses prepared to testify to the warm and generous nature of a man also notorious for his habit of taking a handgun into the recording studio, and for his resistance when pursued by those believing themselves to be owed royalties on his hits. Purely in terms of the music, however, his achievement is beyond dispute. Forty years have passed since his greatest hits burned up the airwaves. But play them now, and hardly any one of those records shows a trace of rust.

Yes, fashion moved on and he was left behind, nursing a degree of resentment as he faded into the shadows. But try the test right now. Play 'You've Lost That Lovin' Feelin'', the most audacious and perfectly executed of all orchestral pop records. Try something a little more obscure, such as the Ronettes' 'Born To Be Together', the Crystals' 'Little Boy', Ike and Tina Turner's 'I'll Never Need More Than This', Dion's 'Make The Woman Love Me' or Cher's 'A Woman Story'. None of them was even a hit, but any one of them packs a punch, musical and emotional, that makes the chart at the beginning of a new century look like a desert.

If you want, you can certainly blame him for inventing the 'manufactured' pop record, a phenomenon that, at the time of writing, appears to have destroyed almost an entire generation's enthusiasm for music. He was, after all, the first to see the A-side of a 45rpm as a canvas on which he, the producer, could paint his dreams and visions; using singers, musicians and record techniques as colours on his palette. But the difference between Spector and all but his earliest and most genuine disciples remains a matter of soul. Spector wanted people to go out and buy his records in large quantities, and he was certainly happy that the business made him a millionaire when he was 21. Yet it remains impossible, no matter how many layers of cynicism have obscured the perceptions of those who listened at first in a state of relative innocence, to believe that the primary purpose of the exercise was anything other than the drive to create something that had never been heard before, something that he described to me so charmingly – long ago, before the darkness began to close in – as 'little symphonies for the kids'.

An earlier generation sometimes looked on aghast at his bratty flamboyance, at the long hair and the velvet jackets and the imperious demeanour, but the craftsmanship he deployed was formidable. He had paid his dues in two ways, by learning how the men he admired did their jobs, and by trial and error. And what he created as a result was something almost unimaginable in the digital era: a finished artefact, not susceptible to revision. Although he rehearsed endlessly and put his session musicians through dozens of takes on the songs he considered particularly significant, the point was that when he was through, he was through. That was it. That was the work of art, and it was non-negotiable.

I once spent a few days in a New York studio, watching Spector and John Lennon putting together 'Happy Xmas (War Is Over)'. Both men revered the spontaneity of early rock and roll, but it was a lesson to observe the strategies with which Spector went out turning spontaneity into a record that retains its spirit and appeal more than 30 years later. They fell out eventually, of course, but while they were still enjoying each other's company it was impossible to miss Lennon's admiration for his temporary producer's very specific but quite undiminished skills.

Like Muhammad Ali (with whom he was once friendly), Spector is a gift of a subject to anyone who tries to make his living from words. Tom Wolfe was the first to spot the potential, and Spector was at his peak when, having secured the necessary access, Wolfe turned the material into 'The First Tycoon Of Teen', an essay which established the template. Most of those who followed Wolfe into Spector's presence came back with tales of gloomy mansions, darkened rooms, and a slight figure with a high, lispy voice living for the moment when his time might come again. Here the myth and the truth coincide, forming a remarkable story with, of course, an unbeatable soundtrack.

Introduction

Phil Spector's productions have been in my blood since my early days of record collecting when, without properly realising why, I sat playing 'He's A Rebel' over and over again. Then I played the B-side 'I Love You Eddie' over and over as well. There was something I couldn't quite put my finger on then, but something that I understood the following year when 'Da Doo Ron Ron' and 'Be My Baby' hit the shops. It was then that the power of the sound, the Wall of Sound, hit me. It demanded your attention in a way that no other records were managing at the time. Evidently I wasn't alone in my excitement as the records charged up charts all over the world, but few of us at the time would have stopped to think about how powerful a force for change Spector's work was to be for the record business. He was to change just about everything.

This *Phil Spector Reader* is the third part of a trilogy of Helter Skelter-published books that investigate groundbreaking US pop music from the sixties. Along with *Back To The Beach: A Brian Wilson & The Beach Boys Reader* and *Calling Out Around The World: A Motown Reader*, the book aims to tell the musical stories of some of the most influential pop music ever made. By re-visiting some of the best writing about each area and linking it with new pieces and fresh interviews, we aim to produce books that are both entertaining and informative. The past few years has seen an understandable media concentration on Spector in terms of his murder trial, but this *Phil Spector Reader* concentrates on the man as an influential producer and, whilst there are pieces herein that do illuminate some aspects of his personality that are impossible to totally divorce from the story, the focus of the book remains solidly on the music. As I look over the contents list of the great writers and musicians represented in this book, I feel particularly pleased because not only are they a veritable who's who of intelligent music writers, they are also among the people who have given me the most pleasure over the years whether it be through fanzines, magazines, records or books. Like my other 'Reader' books, this is intended to be a dip-into book, and is aimed at informing past, present and future musical students of Spector's work.

Assembling a book such as this inevitably means drawing on outside help, which is in itself one of the joys of the work. There are many who have provided help in putting it together. My thanks go to all the wonderful and knowledgeable people who have contributed at various times in different ways: Ronnie Spector, Hal Blaine, Carol Kaye, Mark Wirtz, Tony Hatch, May Pang, Phil Chapman, David Kessel, Ellie Greenwich, Spencer Leigh, Charles White, Peter Canvel, Richard Havers, Peter Doggett, Joe Foster, Martin Roberts, Mick Brown, Carole Gardner, John Reed, Rob Finnis, Joe Nelson, Claire Francis, Ted T who delved into his archives for me, and the great number of people who contributed their Spector top tens. My appreciation also goes especially to all the writers whose work is represented in this book. I extend my thanks to Richard Williams who was the first person to realise that Phil Spector was deserving of a book. His recently revised biography *Out Of His Head* is thoroughly recommended as a fine chronological telling of the story, and I was delighted when he consented to provide a foreword and a piece for this book. Very, very special thanks are also due to Mick Patrick for providing a great deal of help, both directly and indirectly, behind the scenes. Mick was the publisher of the wonderful *Philately* magazine that kept the Spector flame alive for many years, and is now actively involved with Ace Records compiling and annotating exciting and informative CD compilations. It would also be impossible for this book to happen without Helter Skelter Publishing, so my thanks go to managing director Graeme Milton, and to Michael O'Connell and Ali Clarke for their earlier help in bringing this to fruition.

It was originally hoped to publish this book in 2005, at which time I was working on it enthusiastically with Sean Body, the then managing director of Helter Skelter. His subsequent illness led this book and other Helter Skelter projects to be put on the back burner until now. Many of the renewed discussions about this publication have been in the light of Sean's approach and viewpoints, and I would like to think that the final emergence of the book would meet with his approval. During the period that Sean's health ebbed and flowed, up to the point when he lost his battle with his illness, the first and second murder trials of Phil Spector occurred, culminating in the eventual guilty verdict and his subsequent sentencing to many years in jail. At time of writing Spector's appeal has just failed, so it is safe to assume he will continue to serve some considerable time in detention.

The sixties was an incredible decade for musical development and invention, which will remain important for future generations to discover and evaluate. Phil Spector's work was then, and remains, amongst the very best, and subsequent events do not change that. It is my hope that the power and invention of the body of music that he was responsible for will remain worthy of discovery and appreciation, and that his undoubted influence on other producers will be understood.

Kingsley Abbott
May 2011

Part One

Little Symphonies – Big Sounds

01
Setting The Scene by Kingsley Abbott

That Phil Spector was to some extent a product of his time is unmistakable, and to explain the nature of the pop record business at the start of the sixties is therefore imperative. It is a time that is now subject to as much misinformation as it is to correctly documented facts. Just as Motown is now a catch-all term for all black sixties pop soul for some observers, the label Brill Building pop has been subject to a particular form of music writers' Chinese Whispers. The world that Phil Spector was trying to break into as he started out was in fact very particular and very localised, and this introductory piece attempts to paint the correct backdrop to his development.

Phil Spector got it right in one very particular way, and it was one over which he had no particular control. He was quite simply in the right place at the right time... actually several times in quick succession. Having been brought up in New York's Bronx, his family had moved to the promised land of Hollywood in 1953 following the death of his father. Although the LA music scene was embryonic at the time, it was here he caught the rock'n'roll bug along with thousands of other kids, though in Phil's case it was a British record, Lonnie Donegan's 'Rock Island Line' that had really excited him. He began dabbling with music whilst still at Fairfax Junior High, working with an embryonic group called the Sleepwalkers (featuring at various times the talents of Sandy Nelson and Bruce Johnston with the ubiquitous Kim Fowley also hanging out) before forming the Teddy Bears who gave Phil his first taste of success... and failure soon after.

After the Teddy Bears and the subsequent Spectors Three had each run their course, Phil returned to New York in May 1960 under direction from his mother who saw his future as a court stenographer and UN interpreter. It is likely that, even then, Phil had other ideas, as he had with him an introduction from record business man Lester Sill to Jerry Leiber (himself an ex-Fairfax student) and Mike Stoller who had themselves re-located to the Big Apple to bring a more commercial feel to some of the Atlantic label's output. Leiber and Stoller were already music business veterans, who had learnt at the school of hard knocks, having seriously lost out early on in their careers on the substantial royalties due to them for writing the massive hit 'Hound Dog'. They had set up Spark Records in Los Angeles, which ran for some twenty or so issues, hitting big with the Robins' 'There's A Riot Going On'. As writers, producers and now music businessmen, they had convinced a couple of the Robins to work with them as they formed the Coasters, who were to give them their first big New York successes. Leiber and Stoller were therefore attractive folk to get to know for the young Phil, eager to learn more about the business.

New York at this stage was the centre of the pop music world. Los Angeles by contrast was yet to get to reach cruising altitude, despite its healthy and exciting independent record scene. New York was where the majority of the major record companies were based, and it had a well-established role as a music town from its many jazz clubs, R&B activity and Broadway shows. The big theatre and variety houses had formed the spearhead for a constant demand for writers, publishers and producers who were mostly clustered around Times Square. Here was all the old guard of music business personnel, working feverishly from a variety of office blocks. Foremost amongst these was the Brill Building at 1619 Broadway, between 47th and 48th Streets, the main building on that particular block, flanked on either side by the Turf and Jack Dempsey's restaurant where many of the deals were done. The Brill, with its lavishly-decorated hallway leading to the elevators, was almost a self-contained music industry of its own with offices, writing cubicles and a studio on site. Anyone with aspirations to being in pop had to have links there, or better still an office on-site. However, the Brill, despite its ongoing reputation, was already arguably past its peak; that had been between 1942 and 1957. This is not to say that it didn't have its share of the action: Coed and Clock Records were there, Bacharach and David had an office, and so did Leiber and Stoller, though they would often work from their apartments.

Across the street, and some 200 metres north, with a side entrance on West 51st Street, was what became known as the Aldon building at 1650 Broadway, which like the Brill had the full gamut of companies and two in-house studios: Allegro (where, for example, the Chiffons' 'He's So Fine' was cut) in the basement and Adelphi on the 7th floor. This is where the real buzz and youthful enthusiasm was to be found from 1958: described by Al Kooper as the 'best university

I ever attended' as opposed to the 'dentist office vibe' of the Brill. With its lower rents, 1650 housed George Goldner's group of labels (Gone, End etc), Scepter and Belltone Records, as well as Aldon Publishing, and this was where you would have found Carole King, Gerry Goffin, Barry Mann, Cythia Weil, Gene Pitney, Neil Sedaka, Howie Greenfield and Irwin Levine all working as writers, with artists such as Maxine Brown, Chuck Jackson, Little Eva, Big Dee Irwin, the Jive Five, Bobby Lewis, Jimmy Radcliffe and hundreds more hanging out, often congregating in the in-house coffeeshop called B/Gs. This was the atmosphere that attracted anyone with aspirations to success in the music business at that time, especially writers: Al Kooper recalls, 'You'd go up to the top floor and walk your way down playing your songs at each publisher's office. If you had a good song, it would be sold before you hit the lobby!'

However, 1619 and 1650 Broadway didn't have all the market sewn up by any means. A bit further down the street at 1697, between 53rd and 54th Streets was another building that housed a number of other independent labels. Here at the turn of the decade were Old Town Records with Arthur Pryscock and The Fiestas, Glover Records with Titus Turner, and the Herald/Ember group who also distributed some of the smaller labels, and most significantly the ground floor of 1697 Broadway was where CBS broadcast *The Ed Sullivan Show* to the nation. The same studio is now used for *The David Letterman Show*. Not far away were Atlantic and Shad at 157 West 57th Street, with Jubilee, Top Rank and Hanover Records all at other addresses in the same street, and perhaps most significantly for the young Spector, Leiber & Stoller were set up at No. 40. Further uptown was the groundbreaking black-owned Fire and Fury labels run by Bobby Robinson at 271 West 125th Street in Harlem, close to the famed Apollo Theatre. Many others shared some of these premises or were set up in other buildings within the locality. However, as producer Stu Phillips points out, the pop music scene was not just built on the energies of these independent labels. The established major labels were also very active: 'Concerning the sixties, the Brill Building, Aldon Building etc., I think that we all should remember that, although many of the hit records of the sixties were a result of the writers, producers and record companies housed in those famous buildings, a very large percentage of NYC hits came out of RCA Records, Capitol, Mercury, Decca, Colpix, Columbia, Roulette and many others, whose offices were not in either of those two buildings.

Also, major publishers like Chappell, Robbins Feist & Miller, and other similar companies located around NY provided hit material for artists. The sixties was an exciting period in the development of pop music, and many people and places spread all over NY were major contributors.'

The whole youth music scene was ripe for development as the sixties began. The 45 RPM plastic disc had been introduced by RCA Victor as early as March 1949, but, despite immediate enthusiasm from record buyers, there was an inevitable time lag as all the majors gradually came on board (Columbia not until the later 50s), and hardware manufacturers realised that the new playing form was a success and set about introducing ranges of smaller disc players that effectively put playing control squarely in the hands of the teenagers. They could now play their own material in their own spaces. This burgeoning new youth market attracted music business entrepreneurs to supply the records. New York's music market had been partly supplying the needs of Broadway and the safe MOR fifties white market, and partly developing the R&B and doo-wop sounds that were initially aimed at the black market. The latter sounds had already been eagerly picked up on by the white youth market with many crossover hits during the second half of the fifties. The new young writers and producers, who had grown up amid this thriving activity, were now ready to take elements of the R&B sounds and recycle them into the new pop markets, as exemplified by Carole King and Gerry Goffin's early success with the Shirelles' 'Will You Love Me Tomorrow'. Spector caught this upsurge exactly at the right moment as he arrived with his introduction to Leiber and Stoller, two of the hottest young writers-producers in town. From them he was to build on his studio knowledge, his writing, and also learn an approach to business. After their 'Hound Dog' royalty problems they had sought to keep more control over what went on around them, and not putting all their eggs in one basket. Whilst working mainly for Atlantic and Atco, they also worked for United Artists and had negotiated a freelance production deal with Big Top to cut whatever they desired. From their particular local knowledge, Phil would have gathered a fine mental map of all the right places to get your name known, and it is well known that he trawled the buildings introducing himself wherever he could. It was during the New York sojourn that Phil met one of his key future players when he was introduced to saxophonist Nino Tempo at Leiber & Stoller's office. Nino was a few years older than Phil, and had been given the responsibility of minding Jerry Leiber's apartment during a vacation. Nino and Phil thus became roommates for a few weeks. Nino recalls: 'One weekend in New York back then, we had five dollars between us. The subway was fifty cents, so if two people get on the subway... Now you've got four dollars for breakfast, lunch and dinner and to get back on the subway. Phil said: "Wait a minute. I know this girl and she told me if I was ever broke she always had five dollars under the gargoyle on her terrace." So we made it to her place and climbed out on her terrace from the fire escape. "It's here!" Phil shouted. More money to live an extra day on. Great laughs, great times.'

Phil with April Stevens and Nino Tempo

Despite such uphill beginnings, Spector was successfully forging the links that he needed to get the chances to make records, and was variously playing guitar, writing and under-studying production techniques wherever he could. His early production work, dating from mid-1960, was actually in both New York and Los Angeles. In New York for Atlantic he cut tracks with the Top Notes, Ruth Brown, the Castle Kings, Jean Do Shon, and Billy Storm, and it was with the latter singer that he also worked in LA studios. Included in this batch of early work was the original version of 'Twist And Shout' by the Top Notes, although by common consent it is agreed that this was not

Phil's finest hour as the changes he instituted in the structure reduced the effectiveness of the song's feel. However, on other labels he was starting to get some Top 50 hits with successes during 1961 from Ray Peterson, Curtis Lee, Gene Pitney, the Paris Sisters and the first songs with the Crystals. His decision to cut some of the Billy Storm tracks in LA is interesting as it is on these sides, most specifically on 'When You Dance' that we hear the first stirrings of Phil's big sound with massed castanets, soaring strings and a distinctive lead voice clambering over the top. It is no coincidence that this sound expansion happened on the West Coast.

Los Angeles' music scene during the fifties had offices for all the majors, largely catering for the white middle-of-the-road markets that linked to the TV and film industries. Aside from these there were many small independent labels aiming at the healthy radio-promoted R&B market. Along with New York, it also had an established jazz scene that could provide a pool of potential session players. As befitted a fast growing city in the sunshine, the young players were open-minded. Whilst many New York players were used to working within the tried and tested structures of Broadway based work, their Californian counterparts came without preconceptions, which gave young producers like Spector the chance to try new ideas in a friendly atmosphere. Phil was attracted to this just as there was emerging a group of 'first call' players who were to form the backbone to his hit productions. Phil, perhaps through luck more than judgement, was learning his craft just as these players were in the right mindset for taking on expansive and rule-breaking production ideas. Having apprenticed himself and taken advantage of all the learning opportunities in the established city, he was smart enough to realise that his growth lay predominantly with the young hot-shots working in the city that was soon to become the new entertainment capital of the US.

Phil had returned to New York at the right time, had been active amongst key hit makers, and was alert enough to realise the growing worth of Los Angeles. This astuteness was to serve him well as he made his play for teen pop domination.

02

Nik Cohn Visits Mr Spector by Nik Cohn

Originally written for Creem *magazine #19 in December 1972, this piece appeared later in re-written form. It illuminates some of the problems that were then associated with attempting to gain insights into Phil Spector's world. Cohn is, of course, remembered for his seminal rock text* Awopbopaloobop Alopbamboom *from 1969.*

In Los Angeles I wore a white silk suit and stayed at the Chateau Mermont high above Sunset Strip. There was a grand piano and candelabra in the lobby; within an hour of my arrival persons unknown had sent me a Mexican hooker, name of Angel, who scrubbed my back and cooked me scrambled eggs.

For three days I sat in my room and waited for Phil Spector to contact me. Greta Garbo had once lived in this suite, Myra Brekenridge had looked out of these windows, so I sat and watched the sunsets, working my way through packet after packet of Lemon Jumble cookies, while the phone didn't ring.

Here was my Hollywood dream – I went to bed at dawn, rose in time for lunch and changed my underwear three times a day. On the third afternoon the phone rang at last. An unidentified voice asked me if I wished to speak to Mister Spector. I said that I did. There was a silence. Then the line went dead.

The chateau was full of corridors and dark corners, Filipino bellhops, aged courtesans, ghost white junkies. Soon I reached down behind the cooker and came up with a blood stained silk kimono. I hid it in the air-vent and went out to cruise the Strip. When I got back Angel poured me tequila and painted her toenails scarlet. Afterwards she called her mother, and her brother, and her best girlfriend in Tijuana. So she said, at any rate, but when I looked down from my window, there was a man with a black moustache, just standing there, motionless.

The phone rang again. This time it was George, Mister Spector's prime bodyguard. Twenty minutes later he arrived in a black Cadillac, three hundred pounds of ex-cop, bearded, beringed and heavily holstered. Together we drove off down the Strip, past all the great landmarks, the sacred shrines. Past Dinos and Schwabs and Cyranos, past the Whiskey, past Phil Spector Productions, and on up the hill to El Dorado.

Or perhaps it wasn't El Dorado, after all. At this distance, I can't be sure it wasn't called Sierra Madre instead, or perhaps Besame Mucho or even who knows La Paloma. In any case, what matter? It was a mock-Spanish mansion in the classic Hollywood style, all balconies and latticed windows, guard dogs and electronic gates.

Originally, like any other palace north of Beverly Hills, it had been built for Barbara Hutton, twenty or thirty rooms, with circular beds and polar bear rugs, infinities of stucco and gilt, the works all paid for in nickels and dimes. The only stroke she'd missed was the heart-shaped pool.

My own role was Philip Marlowe. As I stepped from the Cadillac, blundering in the dark, I looked up by chance and caught a sudden movement, something shifting behind a curtain. A flurry of pink; perhaps a face, nothing more. Wolfhounds snapped and snarled behind their fence. George pushed a sequence of buttons and buzzers, spoke into a mouthpiece, moved me through an electric eye. First one door, then another opened before us. At last we penetrated the mansion.

I was left alone in a very long and high, very cold and empty reception room. Overhead I could hear footsteps, moving relentlessly back and forth. Coloured lights flashed in the darkness; a door slammed far away. Everywhere I turned there were pictures of Phil Spector. On coffee tables, around the pool table, stretched across the mantelpiece – Spector with the Teddy Bears, with the Righteous Brothers, with Ike and Tina Turner, with basketball players and karate champions, with Minnesota Fats, with Herb Alpert, with businessmen, with his mother, in profile, full face, formal and at ease. With companions or, most often, alone.

By the sofa there were three copies of *Tangerine Flake Streamline Baby* each with a marker at the chapter on Phil Spector. Underneath there were cuttings from *Time*, *Life* and *Rolling Stone* each with a marker at the section on Phil Spector. So I sat on the sofa and was idly browsing, when I paused to scratch myself and suddenly there he was, Spector himself, at the top of a flight of three small stairs, watching me. At first he did not move. Then I stood up and he came towards me. In close up, he hardly reached past my shoulder and, even with his gold-rimmed shades, steel-studded wristband and wispy beard he seemed like a child, maybe ten years old. As unformed and as vulnerable as that – he looked past my left ear, not quite smiling, and bit his lip. 'Pleased to meet you', he said and, finally, shook my hand.

Clearly this wasn't enough. For a very first meeting, something stronger, something altogether more dramatic was called for. So he waited a moment, undecided, and then he gestured around the room, a random sweep that took in the walls, the mansion – the whole of Los Angeles. 'Welcome', said Spector, 'to Hollywood'.

A routine took shape. I sat in my hotel room and every couple of days the phone would ring. Then George picked me up and took me to El Dorado and Spector talked at me. After some hours, George drove me back to the Chateau and I settled down to wait for the next time.

The idea was that I would eventually write a book. Therefore I crouched over a tape recorder, looking earnest, and Spector kept up a flow of monologue. Footsteps echoed interminably above us, the wolfhounds howled outside the windows and George sat polishing his guns, peaceful in the kitchen. Once I heard a woman singing in another room. Presumably she was Veronica, originally lead singer with the Ronettes, now Spector's second wife – she hummed a few bars of 'Black Pearl', then cut off dead half way through a line, and I never heard her again, nor saw the least sign of her existence. A shadow behind a curtain, a voice in another room and footsteps overhead – she might have been a wronged Victorian gothic heroine, imprisoned in the attic.

Phil Spector meanwhile was all benevolence. Although we were entombed in this mausoleum, he could hardly have been more genial and he told me jokes, showed me snapshots, and kept me plied with drinks. One afternoon he fixed me a plate of lox and cream cheese on rye, prepared with his own hands, complete with pickles and side salad (blue cheese dressing). Then he sang me old songs, showed me trick shots at pool and almost beat me at pinball. I walked on my hands; he did impressions of Lenny Bruce. Everything was spiffy.

Nevertheless I was spooked. Something in Spector remained shadowy, remote beyond reaching. Hunched beside me, with his shades and small child's face, he made me think of a toy – his bones were so bird-like, his voice so shrill and he carried such an air of fragility that often I was tempted to lift him up bodily and bounce him on my knee, one hand up his back like some freaked out ventriloquist's dummy. This sense of puppeteering survived in his talk. Time and again, I'd catch a whiff of something mechanical, rehearsed. He'd rap for hours, sometimes quite torrentially, and jump up and down, wave his arms, flash his hands all over the place. In anecdotes his voice would swoop and cackle and shriek in wildest hilarities. He gasped for breath, he clutched his sides. But all of it was performance. Suddenly, without any warning he'd freeze; in an instance the show was shut down. His limbs set, his eyes went dead. Precisely the effect was like putting money in a seaside peep show – pull the lever and he jerked into action, went through his charades. Let it go and immediately he stopped.

When he spoke of the past, it was different. Turn him loose in New York or Philadelphia, in his golden age, and he flamed. Right away he took on true intensity, outrage and obscenity, wild invention; labyrinthine sagas came tumbling out by the megamot, unstoppable, and then he seemed special – obsessive, original, full of overwhelming energies. Here you could see exactly how he had come to be Phil Spector. But bring him back to the present, even for an instant, he dried.

On paper it was hard to explain, this congealment. He was now in his late twenties, with money, prestige and great talent, adored and protected at every turn, and he lived exactly as he desired. His future was full of new plans and projects; his freedoms, within human capacity, were absolute. He had a family, he was healthy, and yet his life was a blank. He seemed to have no great pleasures, passions or even hatreds, and no great desires. Sometimes he said he was happy; other times he shook his head and looked away, but most often he simply sat and let time pass.

What was wrong? At sixteen, at twenty, at twenty-four, his drives had been phenomenal. His rage and speed, his sweep of vision, his will – no one in rock had ever moved faster, or been more gifted, or had a more ferocious sense of his own potential. Once he had dared everything, now he seemed to dare nothing. Only the trappings were left – the mansion and the bodyguards, the gold-rimmed shades, a few gestures and throwaways. Cadillacs and wolfhounds and distant footsteps, the motions of mystique. Beyond all that, nothing.

So one night, when conversation had ground to a halt and it seemed like there was nothing to be lost, I asked him if he felt finished. Was he exhausted? Was there anything ahead? Or was his life, in essence, already over?

For a moment he prepared to lose his temper. His face scrunched up tight and his mouth opened wide. But then he paused, right on the brink, and drew back. With the first volley of abuse already halfway up his gullet, he teetered. Let a few seconds pass. Then drew his head in, like a hedgehog taking refuge.

'How', he asked, with utmost caution, 'exactly do you mean?'

'Finished', I said. 'Done with. Complete.'

He looked surprised, a bit baffled. With fine drama, he removed his shades and peered past my ear again, off into infinity, as if to signal deep thought. He pondered, reconsidered, took his time. In the end, however, he must have given up, for he only shrugged his shoulders and put his shades back on. 'I guess it is', he said, off-hand, and we talked about something else.

In the first place, more than anything, Spector was a saga of self-invention: a demonstration, on heroic scale, of the possible.

Conceive, as a basis, that every life is shaped by two crucial inventions. The first is imposed from outside, at birth, by environment, family, genes, God; the second is projected from within, as the life picks up momentum, by force of will and imagination. So we begin by being invented and progress, if we can, to inventing ourselves.

The decisive element is nerve – how much do we *dare*? If we have been invented as plain, dumb, insignificant, will we dare to re-invent ourselves as glamorous, brilliant, heroic? If we are meant to obey, will we dare to command? And if we are doomed in any case, will be dare to be blown sky-high, in magnificent technorama wipe-out, rather than drain away slowly, on our knees?

In ninety-nine cases from a hundred, of course, we dare almost nothing. We exist as we've been packaged and if we make even minor adjustments – change professions or lovers or countries say, or wave a few protesting banners – we think that we're being enormous. But who goes to the limit? Who scraps his first self totally and starts again from scratch, rejecting all guidelines? Who runs riot? Phil Spector did.

In his first invention, he could hardly have been less promising. He started in the Bronx, Jewish and undersized, twitchy, panic-stricken. His mother overpowered him, his father died when he was nine. Rootless, he was brought out west, to Los Angeles, and that isolated him even more. He was close to nobody, belonged nowhere, was good at nothing. By his teens he was completely withdrawn – girls terrified him, his mother was all-consuming and he dreamed he was being strangled.

At Hollywood High he sat apart, stuck away in corners, and

festered. Once he showed me a snapshot taken in his mid-teens, surrounded by a group of classmates, smiling in sunlight. Half a dozen kids in a loose semi-circle, crew-cut, golden-fleshed, archetypal Californians: they slouch and chew gum, take their ease, while Phil peeks out, half-hidden, from behind a silver surfer.

It is an image of absolute security. Everyone here has cars, pretty girlfriends, the simplest and safest of futures. But then you glance at Spector and immediately he belongs to a different universe. Bad hair, bad skin, bad posture. Focus on the eyes and all you can see is evasion. White flesh in a world of tan, mess in a world of smooth – everything about him is alien, awkward, discomforting, and the others are all looking elsewhere.

That was the platform he worked off. In the first invention, he had been inadequate, terrified, doomed; in the second, his own, he took revenge. Just like Tommy's campers, he wouldn't take it, no way, and he cast off the imposition. All his pent-up energy and rage, all his caged intensity broke surface. Deliberately, he obliterated the past, wiped out memory, began again from nothing. It was rather like one of those magic drawing pads, where you can draw and erase and draw again as often as you want. At a stroke, Spector rubbed out the accumulated doodlings of seventeen years. Then he drew for himself.

Rock'n'roll, in the late fifties, was the obvious testing ground: new and virgin territory, ripe for raiding. The first wild burst of euphoria had just begun to dampen down, there was a temporary hiatus. The natural force of the early rockers had been harnessed and contained by the industry, so that while the young made the music, it was the middle-aged who made the money. What was needed, was a champion, someone to take on the massed ranks of baldies and cigar-chewing fatties, wrest away or at least intrude on their control. Someone with so much force and hunger that he would recreate the whole context in which rock functioned. Release, both creatively and commercially, a true Teen music. And that, more or less, is what Spector achieved.

The actual process by which he did so hardly matters here. Once you accept the basic concept of his re-invention, the rest becomes inevitable. Only invent and the future is inescapable, as irrevocable as past or present – the inventor is controlled by the force of his own invention.

So with Spector: he was a rock'n'roll fan, had a good ear, could play guitar. Soon he started writing songs and his first was 'To Know Him Is To Love Him', the title inspired by his father's epitaph. He took a boy and girl from Hollywood High, called them the Teddy Bears, put them into a neighbourhood studio, sold the product to a local label and waited. When it became a hit, he went to Philadelphia and immersed himself in the industry, blew all his royalties and moved on to New York, where the Brill Building, stuffed to overflowing with Jewish songwriters, was just becoming the new centre of American Teen.

It was now 1960. Spector made tea, ran errands and slept on desks, until Atlantic gave in to him and let him produce some sessions. He had hits with Curtis Lee and Ray Peterson, and wrote 'Spanish Harlem' for Ben E. King. Next he found partners and backers to set him up with his own label, Philles, and flew to Los Angeles, where he cut 'He's A Rebel' on one Friday, 'Zip-A-Dee-Doo-Dah' on the next. Both were million-sellers.

He set up New York offices and surrounded himself with assistants, flunkeys, bodyguards. He got married and divorced and married again, and he cut maybe twenty hit records in two or three years. Not long after his twenty-first birthday, he became a dollar millionaire and moved west to Hollywood. His hair was long, his clothes outrageous and he wore his shades all the time. He bought El Dorado, an office block, on the Strip, a fleet of cars with smoked-glass windows, impenetrable, behind which he could hide, and he trapped the instant absolutely. The industry called him a genius.

The instant passed. After the Beatles, he ceased to be the newest and hottest sensation of all. He still made hit records, still got his picture in the papers but his impetus slackened and he drew back into shadow. When he released 'River Deep Mountain High', and it wasn't a hit, his very finest record and his first important failure, he retired.

He was then almost twenty-five. Within five years, he had exhausted the fullest potentials of Pop, as artist, businessman and image, as hustler and myth. Truthfully, what more was left? Nothing, except to lock the gates of El Dorado and disappear. His journey was completed; all that remained was time to kill.

I don't mean, of course, that he managed all this by invention alone, without intellect, gifts, tremendous resources of energy and vision. On the contrary, it was precisely because he had such reserves, unrecognised, that the invention was possible in the first place. With the single exception of Elvis, he was the sharpest and most original talent that Teen produced, and on three levels at least – industrial, artistic and style – his effect was quite enormous.

As a businessman, first of all, it was Spector who created the concept of independence. Before him, rock was controlled by a few major companies – an individual might start his own label and do well enough locally, or within a specific market, but if he wanted to be national, he either had to tag on to one of the majors or pass half his life in slow and squalid escalation.

Spector ripped right through this. Straightaway he was universal, autonomous, insatiable. After the first few months he controlled every detail of his enterprise – production, publicity and distribution, hiring and firing, dealing and scamming, artwork, letterheads, even the colour of the toilet paper. No one had ever moved so fast, hustled remotely so hard and, by all logic, he should have fallen flat on his face. The industry wasn't constructed for this; it should have squelched him.

How did he escape? He made good records, of course, and he understood money, but that was hardly enough to faze a whole entrenched establishment. In the end, one can only explain it by personal force: face to face, he must have carried such impact, such obsessive certainty in his own rightness that custom, prejudice, pettiness indifference simply crumpled before his onslaught. Hunger, fury and flat-out insanity must have dragged him through where reason would have taken him nowhere.

Afterwards, everything was simpler. Once Spector had made the first breach, it was possible for others to slip through behind him and the whole of rock became looser, less restrictive. Independents took root, began to dictate their own terms. Lou Adler and Andrew Oldham, Shadow Morton and Kit Lambert – indirectly, all of them were created by his precedent. At one remove he was responsible for founding every breakaway in rock and even now, each time that some new hustler emerges to prate about doing his thing, being free and letting it all hang out, Spector should cop a percentage.

That was finance. At the same time he was also rock's first flirtation with art. Previously there had been great performers and, there had also been a handful of artists by intuition – Chuck Berry, certainly, and Buddy Holly, Leiber & Stoller, maybe Don Everly. But Spector, was the first to rationalise; the first to comprehend precisely what he was up to. With him, there was a totally different level of sophistication, complexity, musical range.

This could have been tricky. Rock'n'roll, like all mass media, works best off trivia, ephemera and general game-playing, and the moment that anyone starts taking it. more solemnly, he's treading on minefields. As performance, it has been magnificent. Nothing has been better at catching moments, and nothing has carried more impact, more evocative energy. While it lives off flash and outrage, impulse, excess and sweet teen romance, it's perfect. But dabble in Art and immediately it gets overloaded.

Somehow Spector got away with it. On one hand, he created a total imaginative universe, which I take to be the test of any true artist; on the other, he never let go of foolishness. So he was subtle and raucous, bizarre and familiar, emotional and strictly commercial, all at once; he stole from every source he could – Wagner, Leonard Bernstein, dashes of early Stravinsky, a thousand or a million hit singles, Rogers & Hammerstein – and was still completely original. Simultaneously, he was pretentious and funky. Very clever indeed, and most beautifully dumb.

What he did, basically, was to combine the two great romances of rock – rebellion and the teen dream – into one. The first meant wild greasy rockers, the second pretty boys. The first was noise and fury and filth, orgy and musical assassination; the second was sweetest, most perfect innocence. No way for the two to intertwine, or so it seemed, until Spector upped and did it. Using the massed songwriting duos of the Brill Building – Goffin/King, Mann/Weil, Barry/Greenwich – he churned out the purest, the most aching and idyllic of all teen ballads.

Into his sound, meanwhile, he poured his rage and revenge. Three pianos, half a dozen drummers, rattlers and assorted thumpers, whole battalions of brass and strings, all crashing and smashing away as hard as they could go, in torrential deafening, murderous release. His songs might be pure romance; his sound was pure slaughter. Together they meshed into purest energy.

Finally, after money and music there was Spector as image, where his influence was greatest of all. Right from the outset he'd been a guerrilla, plunging headlong into riot. When rock was still stuffed full of crew-cuts and natty Italian suits, he grew his hair to his shoulders, draped himself in frills and satins, perched on top of six-inch Cuban heels, affected a high-pitched lisp, jangled and shimmered from a dozen gold rings, bracelets, baubles.

Then there were his bodyguards and limos and mansions. His tantrums and his unmitigated gall, for his invention didn't mean that he wiped out his neuroses and terrors, merely that he turned them to his own use. He was as isolated and odd, as screwed up as ever, but now he flaunted it. If he didn't like the plane he was flying, he grounded it; if he didn't like a face he had it pushed in. So he wasn't precisely a gentleman but he was unquenchable. He was indulgent, hysteric, downright nasty, but he enlarged the possible.

It wasn't that any one of his numbers was unique in itself. Other Americans had grown their hair, dressed in drag, been naughty before. Beats had been more extreme, faggots more decadent, film directors more tantrummed, bike gangs funkier, Trotskyites more radical, assassins more psychotic, gangsters more ostentatious and whores more pious. What was special in Spector was that he combined so many different provocations and dissents at once and still managed to make them work for him, in mass commercial terms. He was a walking talking V-sign millionaire: for the first time, odium equalled money.

If Lenny Bruce had been John The Baptist in this, Spector was the Messiah, and from him, the word passed first to Andrew Oldham and the Stones, then into the general currency of rock. Gradually weirdery became the norm. Rock'n'roll became the new home of the professional freak, medium of the malcontent. Leon Russell and Alice Cooper, Zappa, David Bowie, the Fugs or, at other levels, Dylan, Jimi Hendrix, the Who – soon gesture and offence were commonplace. A whole new middle class was spawned off them. Woodstock generation, so smug and so secure that it was hard to imagine a time, just six or seven years earlier, when outrage had taken balls.

Money, music, style: in each of them his breakthrough was absolutely basic. At the time, in the early sixties, he seemed phenomenal; in retrospect, he's more impressive than ever. To come out of such a vacuum and wreak such changes, at such speed, with such totality – even now, it's hard to conceive the force and self-belief it must have taken. 'Phillip Spector', as Bert Berns said, 'is a holocaust.'

After 'River Deep Mountain High' when Spector retired in his huff and went up the hill, the idea was not that he would stagnate but that he would develop into all kinds of new and scintillating areas. Perhaps he would produce movies, perhaps he would set up projects with Lenny Bruce, perhaps he'd invade Wall Street. He would relax and read and finish his education; he would travel, and shoot pool, and train the American karate team. He would go through psychoanalysis, above all, which would release him from all his traumas and set him up for anything and everything. Soon he would be healthier and happier than he'd ever been, and he could make a fresh beginning.

It didn't work; it scarcely could. The best of rock is that it traps the instant. The corollary, almost inevitably, is that it misses out on permanence – it's totally unequipped for abstraction, for any profundities or second thoughts. While he had existed in continuous motion, Spector had been invincible. The moment he was slowed down, he was stranded. Take away his speed and you take away everything.

He went through the motions. He made long and complex journeys with himself, his analyst, his family, his bodyguards, his environment, his soul, his past, his possible future. He watched basketball and might have produced *Easy Rider*. He contemplated and rejected a dozen new departures, and he spawned a son. At the end of it all, after thirty months, he was bored stiff.

One of the worst things in boredom is the panic it causes. People who stay quite calm through riot, tragedy, even death go berserk in tedium. So Spector, who had thrived under pressure, now cracked on ease. Simply, he lost his nerve; made a fatal surrender, which was to retrace his steps.

One of his favourite dictums, which he told me several times, always in alien contexts, was *never repeat*. 'You can always come back,' he used to say, 'but you've got to come back better. If you come back worse, or even the same, you're dead.' And promptly he came back worse, or the same.

Instead of using Philles, which was at least his badge of independence, he made a deal with A&M. Perhaps he needed the money, perhaps he only needed emotional support. Whichever, it meant that, for the first time since his teens, he became an employee; a hired gun.

Next he signed a group named Checkmates Ltd., a supper-soul act from Las Vegas, and cut a single called 'Love Is All I Have To Give'. By his own highest standards, it was average. That put it at least a class above any other single of its year (1969). The only trouble was that it wasn't new – it was archetypal Phil Spector, technically and musically magnificent, but it broke no fresh ground. Therefore, it wasn't a hit.

The follow-up, 'Black Pearl' was less imposing but more commercial and contained at least one classic teen dream couplet: 'You'll never win a beauty prize, no, they won't pick you / But you're my Miss America, and I love you'. As it turned out that was the last great touch Spector managed.

When 'Black Pearl' made the American top twenty, he went back into the studios, to cut the obligatory album. Around the same time I arrived at the Chateau and Angel began to scrub my back.

Thus far it wasn't yet clear what direction Spector's comeback would ultimately take. Perhaps the Checkmates were only a dummy run; perhaps he was biding time. At the proper moment, no doubt, he would leap forth from concealment and launch himself on something completely new, startling, overwhelming.

Admittedly, after I met him, I was bothered by his indifference and seeming exhaustion. Still, I tried not to jump ahead – Spector, after all, was famous for shifts and surprises. 'You can't never tell with Phil,' said George. 'The man is a mystery. The man is a bottomless pit.'

This was the summer of 1969. At the Aquarius, down the far end of Sunset Boulevard, the producers of *Hair* threw a party in the parking lot, late one hot afternoon, for all the rich and/or beautiful freaks of Los Angeles.

We were still in the Love Age then, and the lot was full of baubles, bangles, beads, Paraphernalia by numbers – robes and Indian silks, joints in American flag papers, zodiac jackets, patchouli and joss sticks, Soul handshakes, hand drums and unwashed feet. Kaftaned musicians tootled away on Arabic flutes and pipes, and girls with long, blonde hair kept falling over and giggling. So we milled and mumbled in circles, all smiling beatifically, and I was introduced to Scott McKenzie, who wore an embroidered bedsheet and asked me what sign I was. 'A whole generation with a new explanation', he said several times, and I nodded sagely.

The city was full of Icepack. By the end of an hour the air was thick with smoke, half the guests were horizontal and the hired guards, too stoned to focus, were goosing each other with their nightsticks. The pipes droned on interminably and Graham Nash embraced Cass Elliott, Mike Love embraced David Crosby, Eric Burdon embraced anyone who would let him. Silver spoons appeared. Grotesquerie commenced.

It was then that Phil Spector arrived from El Dorado, immured behind his smoked windows and thickest, most ornate shades. Cruising by, he told George to drive him very slow, rolled his window down six inches and, with most extreme caution, he peeked out through the gap, took in the tableau.

What he saw was girls in semi-undress, doing belly dances on a table full of health foods; cross-legged meditators in a circle; tootlers and thumpers leading an impromptu dance in procession around the lot, a kind of hip Bunny Hop; a couple fucking in a giant bowl of brown rice; acid freaks shrieking or laughing uncontrollably, clawing at their eyes, flapping their arms in attempted flight, expiring; the guards collapsed in a heap; and John Sebastian, standing on one foot, improvising a psalm for all humanity.

Spector did not run away. Instead, as though unable to trust his senses, he rolled down his window a couple of inches further and put his eye still closer to the gap. And this was his undoing, because he was recognised and everyone came towards him.

Here was a major Hollywood event. Since his retirement, Spector had scarcely ever appeared in public, had cloaked himself in the greatest secrecy, thus acquiring an almost mythic stature, a sort of rock'n'roll Howard Hughes. Elsewhere he might be forgotten but Los Angeles was still his town – he remained the biggest, hottest, mysterious number of all and, the moment he was spotted he was surrounded.

Jingling their bells, jangling their bells, the guests all waved salaamed, brought him their flowers and their joints. Some of them even stripped all their clothes off and did a dance of celebration. In a sense, after all, he was their creator and was entitled to every mark of obeisance.

Spector himself, meanwhile, seemed paralysed; gazed out at these hordes in a stupor, both motionless and expressionless, while they swarmed around his Cadillac and smeared their fingers all over the paintwork. It was only when some Laurel Canyon speed-freak in a loincloth actually put his hand through the lowered window and tried to touch him that he suddenly came alive and flung himself backwards across the seat, shaken by spasms. Frantically he tried to wind up the window again, trapping the speedoo's fingers as he did so.

The crowd began to shuffle and look uneasy. Hare Krishna chanting was heard. 'George, get me out of here,' shrieked Spector, in utter panic, and so they departed, dragging the wretched freak a few feet by his fingertips.

Spector collapsed in a corner, trembling, green-faced. Outside a funeral parlour, a couple of blocks downtown, George gave him a big red pill and gradually he began to subside, was still. In the distance the guests continued to caper and flaunt but he didn't look back. Eyes half-shut he seemed drained; absolutely exhausted. 'Who were they?' he asked at last, and shook his head slowly, as though shell-shocked. 'I mean, who were those *animals*?'

Sessions were like old-boy reunions. For his return Spector had reassembled the same technicians, musicians, arrangers and even, in a couple of cases, the same songs that he'd used in his days of glory and the atmosphere was heavy with nostalgia. In between takes, the rhythm section would burst into impromptu jams on old Philadelphian hits; on the playback of 'Spanish Harlem', the whole studio seemed to sing along. Many of these men were middle-aged, essentially jaded and disillusioned, but somehow reverence for Spector had managed to fire them up and there was a sense of mild jollification. Gags and catch-phrases from ten years ago were brought out of storage and dusted down. Backs were slapped, wrists pulled, cigars handed round. One of the trumpet section produced a yellow balloon. 'Party time,' said Larry Levine, the engineer. 'I'd forgotten that sessions could be such fun.'

And Spector himself? He was the centre naturally, and for most of the time seemed jubilant. His lines were the fastest, his put-downs the most outrageous of all and I could hear his squeaks and yells from right down the hall.

On good takes, when things began to cook, he was marvellous: first he shuffled and sang along in an undertone, then escalated gradually. Through whoops and shimmies and little leaps, until in the end he'd be falling about in delirium, arms flying, head flung back, shrieking with all his lungs. His shades fell off; his tiny feet flew out sideways, like sparks off an anvil. Ecstatic, he burned.

Not that such high jinks were continuous – every so often, without warning, his head went down and he sagged. Then he'd slump in a corner or lock himself in another room and nothing could make him react. Ten minutes would pass; fifteen, twenty, and all action was suspended. No more gags, no more old routines – everything hung fire until his return.

Sometimes the silence would be broken by a furious tirade, offstage. Torrential outpourings of abuse, uncontrollable, incomprehensible: one pictured him, like Rumpelstiltskin, growing more and more frenzied, until at last he screwed himself into the ground. At last his passion would exhaust itself. Then there would be another long silence. Everyone waited patiently. Most of them had been through all this before, countless times no doubt, and they played cards or smoked in corners.

Finally Spector would reappear, smiling, refreshed, with a new one-liner already on his lips. Right on cue, someone would answer back and Phil would top them, and the tension fell away. The rhythm section remembered some more old riffs, the horns remembered some more old anecdotes. Time restarted.

The music itself was problematic. Technically there was no question that Spector was still absolutely brilliant. His sharpness of ear, speed of reaction and precision, were all astonishing and so was his certainty. Each track was packed with ideas, fire; real beauty.

Still there was something missing. For all the fine moments, there was an absence of surprise, a lack of real creative need. Just like the singles, Spector had been here before, many times.

Possibly he knew it. At any rate, after sessions, he tended to go a bit glum. He left the studio quickly, got in to his limo and George drove him straight back home. Most nights he kept silence all the way, hunched in a ball. But once, just down the block from his office, we passed some cops beating up on hippies and Spector was enraged. For some minutes he lost himself in one of his harangues, a wild and hilarious Bruceian satire. Then he fell quiet and looked prophetic. Obviously he was preparing a final pronouncement, a clincher, but in the end he only sighed and shook his head. 'This city sucks,' he said, and pretended to fall asleep.

Perhaps this wasn't the most sparkling of all his epigrams. Still it triggered me. For no obvious reason, I was suddenly reminded of W.C. Fields and his deathbed. Feeling the end come upon him the comedian turned his face to the wall and said: 'I'd rather be in Philadelphia.' Less metaphorically, but no less whole-heartedly, Spector might very well say the same.

Our book came to nothing. After each meeting, I'd take the tapes back to the Chateau and painfully transpose them, while Angel sucked lollipops, but the results were uniformly dispiriting. Like the Checkmates' album, they were full of fine touches – perfect little phrases or tales, sudden flashes, razor-sharp punchlines – but when you added them up, somehow they were barren.

The moment had passed, that's all. Philadelphia would have been perfect, New York or even early Hollywood, any time up until his retirement. Then a book might have been alive and bizarre. To write it now however, was simply to act as obituarist and, as Kit Lambert once wrote, if Nik Cohn writes your obituary, you're better off dead.

Already it was impossible to mistake his future. Having once let go of Philles and let himself be hired, he must automatically lose his uniqeness. As an employee, he ceased to be his own creation and acquired a context, a limitation. Abdicating control, he began a third invention; a second imposition.

Naturally his new self would be coloured by his past, his track record. He would not now be seen as runtish or insignificant; he would become a man of talent and substance, revered as a producer, celebrated as a story. He would be courted and flattered, he would make money and would influence, and he would still be a focus for gossip, emulation. What he wouldn't be though, was omnipotent. He wouldn't transcend all categories, and he would no longer dictate. When he made a record, it would belong less to him than to the artist or the company. It would still be a hit, no doubt, but it wouldn't be Phil Spector's.

In spite of this, or because of it, he still seemed the definitive rock'n'roll saga. No one else had so perfectly caught its potentials, and also its limitations. He'd been everything that was best – fast, funny and a bit heroic, full of style and marvellous follies; he'd also proved just how fast the medium went sour. It made for marvellous flashes, it never sustained: get into it two-handed, stampede right through it and then quit dead, without a backwards glance. Don't cruise and don't admire the view. Above all, don't ever stop to think.

The melancholy truth was that Spector understood this, had understood it from the start. Much of his fiercest contempt, in fact, was reserved for the men who hung about and got old. That was why he retired so fast in the first place, more or less, and that was what made his return so grey.

I packed away my white silk suit and prepared to go home. Angel went away, so did the man with the black moustache and, the day before my departure, the candelabra came crashing down in the lobby, to shatter in a thousand meaningless splinters.

I went to say goodbye. In his office Spector sat surrounded by numberless gold records and told me, for perhaps the third time, how he'd found the title for 'To Know Him Is To Love Him'. 'I took it,' he said, 'from the words on my tombstone.'

He was standing at the window, looking down into the Strip. For a few seconds he noticed nothing. Then he heard what it was he'd said and he turned round to face me, distinctly flustered. 'My father's grave I mean. My father,' he said, and shook his head, bothered. By the door I shook his hand and he shook mine. 'Weird. Very weird,' he said.

03
To Know Him Is To Love Him by Greg Shaw

The late Greg Shaw was one of the key figures in US fandom who became a major active player in the music business. His fanzine Who Put The Bomp *set standards that were often imitated but never bettered, and he devoted most of an issue (Spring '76) to girl group rock. This piece however comes from the excellent multi-part History Of Rock series (No 26 – The Spector Sound, 1982), and serves as a fine introductory piece to the early Spector history and his key hit period.*

So much has been written about Phil Spector, yet he still remains an enigma. The most famous record producer in the history of popular music, he advanced the quality and sophistication of pop to new levels in the early sixties, inspiring a whole generation of musicians, songwriters and recording engineers in both New York and Los Angeles. Not only was Spector a producer of genius, he also became one of the most dynamic of independent record company bosses, posing a genuine threat to the well-being of the major labels.

His private life was more mysterious but equally exciting. Nobody, not even Bob Dylan at his zenith, had his kind of style. Flamboyant in the extreme, he sported ruffled shirts, brocade waistcoats, pointed shoes, shades, and hair so long it flipped up at the shoulder – all in 1962! Manically intense, he was a blur of frenzied motion from 1960, when he arrived in New York as a young studio apprentice, through to 1966 when he mysteriously withdrew from the world of records.

Most of this is common knowledge, as is his eccentric lifestyle, the fortified mansion, the bodyguards, the guns and the paranoia, the darkened rooms and nocturnal prowlings, the pathological seclusiveness coupled with a paradoxical need to surround himself with an audience for his ranting and reminiscence.

The typical conclusion from this behaviour is that Spector is a desperately lonely, tragically romantic figure, forced to adopt the facade of an extroverted egomaniac, to reinvent his life on an epic scale. There may be truth in all this, but the real truth lies not in the gossip columns but in the music itself in the sheer excitement generated by Phil Spector's productions.

Bagels And Teddy Bears

Phil Spector was born in the Bronx, New York, on 26 December 1940 into a lower middle-class Jewish family. In 1953, following the death of Phil's father some four years earlier, Mrs Spector moved Phil and sister Shirley to Los Angeles, where they settled in the predominantly Jewish community around Fairfax Avenue, known locally as 'Bagel Junction'.

Phil enrolled at the local school, Fairfax High, where he became involved in various music-making activities. In his last two years at school he formed a vocal group (later to become the Teddy Bears) with two schoolmates, Marshall Leib and Annette Kleinbard. One of the songs Spector had written for the group was 'To Know Him Is To Love Him'; the title came from an inscription on his father's grave, 'To Have Known Him Was To Have Loved Him'. In contrast to his later productions, the song was slow and solemn, almost dirge-like – and yet, at the same time, soft and dreamy. It was not a great deal different from the sound that vocal groups like the Fleetwoods were making, but it did reveal a tender streak that Spector was never to lose.

In 1958 the Teddy Bears auditioned before Lou Bidell, the co-owner of Era Records, a small Los Angeles independent label. Bidell liked their sound and took them to the Gold Star Studios in Hollywood to make a demo.

In the studio, Spector played rhythm guitar and Leib played piano, with Annette Kleinbard on lead vocals. A series of overdubbed vocals were laid on the basic tracks before Sandy Nelson, a friend of Leib's, put down the drum track. Four numbers were recorded at that session and Bidell was sufficiently impressed to release the demo of 'To Know Him Is To Love Him' as an actual record. It was released in August 1958 on Era's subsidiary label, Dore, and following extended airplay on Hollywood's Radio KFWB the song became a local hit.

Having just graduated from Fairfax High, Spector worked for Bidell during the summer of 1958, packing records and doing the odd-jobs at Dore in order to learn the record business. When 'To Know Him Is To Love Him' went on to become a surprise national smash hit at the end of 1958 – holding the US Number 1 spot for three weeks in December – Spector knew he had made it, and thenceforth devoted all his time to promoting the Teddy Bears.

Dissatisfied with Dore, who refused to put money upfront to push the group, Spector moved the Teddy Bears over to Imperial. An album was prepared to follow up the success of the single and

Spector was installed as producer.

Even at this early stage, the teenage Spector was taking vast amounts of studio time in order to perfect the sound he desired – so much so that Imperial owner Lew Chudd brought in a house producer to make sure the album came out on time. Although the LP was not a great success when it did come out, it did provide Spector with sufficient technical know-how to follow through his own ideas. Furthermore, it confirmed him primarily as a producer rather than a performer.

Learning From The Best

While recording the Teddy Bears' album, Spector happened to meet Lester Sill, a Hollywood dealmaker and partner of Duane Eddy's producer, Lee Hazlewood. Eddy's records were noted for their echoey guitar sound, which Hazlewood had created in his small Phoenix studio. One of the most inventive of rock's early producers, Hazlewood took Spector to Phoenix with him and taught him how to experiment with echo, and how to get big sounds on three-track tape by a process of doubling-down or 'bouncing'. Sill, too, recognised Spector's talent and took him under his wing.

After learning all he could from Hazlewood, Spector asked to be sent to New York to understudy Jerry Leiber and Mike Stoller. These producer-songwriters had risen to fame with a succession of hits by the Coasters and had then progressed to work with other Atlantic artists, chiefly the Drifters.

Aged only 19, Spector arrived in New York in May 1960 and began work under Leiber and Stoller, at first playing guitar on Coasters and Drifters sessions and then moving on to production work of his own. The heavy string arrangements and the complex Latin American rhythms that were trademarks of Leiber and Stoller recordings in the early sixties had a marked effect on the impressionable Spector, and he was later to make great use of these techniques as part of his famed 'Wall of Sound'.

While in New York he gained something of a reputation as a songwriter, most notably as co-composer (with lyricist Jerry Leiber) of 'Spanish Harlem' – a hit for former Drifters' lead singer Ben E. King in 1961. Lyrics were Spector's weak point, but through his publishers he teamed up with various lyricists and was hired for production jobs that led to hits with Ray Peterson ('Corrine Corrina'), Curtis Lee ('Pretty Little Angel Eyes'), and Gene Pitney ('Every Breath I Take'), all in 1961. On these he was able to put his experience with

Leiber and Stoller to work. Pitney's record in particular presaged his later productions: daring, experimental, almost out of control. It was also one of the most expensive records ever made in New York up to that time, costing 14,000 dollars for a single session.

Leiber and Stoller also set Spector a good example with their expertise at hustling, working the publishers and record labels to get deals together, and all the rest that had to be done to be a successful independent operator in the early sixties. They also taught him the value of good songs. At the time, they had some of New York's best songwriters on tap, people like Jeff Barry and Ellie Greenwich. For the rest of his career, Spector would always come back to these same writers and publishers to be sure he had the best pop songs (or co-writers) for his productions.

Publisher Don Kirshner, who put together New York's greatest songwriting mill in the late fifties, was a genius at seeing the potential in songs and writers and exploiting that potential to the full. Spector idolised him. The youngster also looked up to some of the great label pioneers; these included George Goldner, who discovered Frankie Lymon and helped build the New York teen rock scene, and Archie Bleyer, whose Cadence Records (with quality acts like the Everly Brothers, the Chordettes and Andy Williams) similarly impressed Spector.

Philles Strikes Gold

In December 1960 Spector had made a trip back to the West Coast, where he resumed work for Lester Sill and produced the female vocal trio, the Paris Sisters – the first of Spector's girl groups. Like the Ronettes and the Crystals later on, the Paris Sisters proved ideal material for Spector: inexperienced and malleable, they could be manipulated by him as he chose. Spector produced five singles with this group, of which 'I Love How You Love Me' reached Number 5 in the US pop charts late in 1961.

Tired of being merely a producer working for others, Spector went into partnership with his old business mentor, Lester Sill, in November 1961 and formed the Philles (Phil-Les) record label. The new company established itself with 'There's No Other (Like My Baby)' and 'Uptown' by Spector's latest find, the Crystals.

In 1962 Spector bought Sill out and from then on Philles was under Spector's control alone. Demanding the best, Spector gathered around him some of the most talented musicians, arrangers and studio engineers then working on the West Coast. With this nucleus of talent he was ready to go out and conquer the pop charts.

Following on from the success of the Crystals, there came a run of major hits: 'He's A Rebel', 'Zip-A-Dee-Doo-Dah', 'He's Sure The Boy I Love', 'Why Do Lovers Break Each Other's Hearts', '(Today I Met) The Boy I'm Gonna Marry', 'Da Doo Ron Ron', 'Not Too Young To Get Married', 'Wait 'Til My Bobby Gets Home', 'Then He Kissed Me', 'Be My Baby', 'A Fine Fine Boy', 'Baby, I Love You', 'Walking In The Rain', 'You've Lost That Lovin' Feelin'' and 'Just Once In My Life'. There was also a wealth of lesser-known gems.

The artists credited on these discs included the Ronettes, the Righteous Brothers, the Crystals, Bob B. Soxx and the Blue Jeans, and Darlene Love. But the artists – even those comparatively well-known before they met Spector were secondary to what Spector did with them, and all these records may legitimately be referred to as 'Phil Spector records'. Talented as these artists were, their success came through their producer – as Spector proved later when he came out of retirement in 1969 and took an undistinguished Vegas lounge singer named Sonny Charles to cut the brilliant track, 'Black Pearl', Charles' first and only hit.

Little Symphonies For The Kids

Spector may have heard great orchestral movements in his head, but to get them on record he needed the right arranger. With typical luck, he came upon Jack Nitzsche. The arranger's job is to comprehend what the producer has in mind (no simple task with Spector) and translate that into detailed instructions for the various players of horns, strings and percussion instruments, as well as backing vocalists on the session – and with Spector's sessions, that could mean a small army.

Although Spector claimed he was quite capable of handling his own arrangements it is probable that he learned much from this association. Nitzsche's creative contribution, from the string lines on 'Baby, I Love You' (the Ronettes) or 'River Deep Mountain High' (Ike and Tina Turner) to the thundercracks in 'Walking In The Rain' (the Ronettes), was as crucial as that of the songwriters, engineers, players and every other quality ingredient that went into the final product.

Spector and Nitzsche consistently made what could be called two-minute symphonic operettas with bold, aggressive arrangements that made classical elements sound as powerful in the rock'n'roll idiom as the more traditional guitar (which, despite Spector's proficiency with the instrument, is rarely heard in a solo vein on his records). Once they began experimenting, the R&B flavour of the early records gave way to a new style – soaring wide, bursting the limits of standard pop. Along with Spector's production technique, Nitzsche's arrangements provided the desired effect. Spector said that he was 'writing little symphonies for the kids'.

Although an adequate songwriter, Spector preferred combining his melodic ideas with the finely honed skills of the best Brill Building writers. Don Kirshner provided most of the early songs, like Goffin and King's 'He Hit Me (And It Felt Like A Kiss)', and Mann and Weil's 'Uptown', 'He's Sure The Boy I Love' and later, 'Walking In The Rain', 'Lovin' Feelin'' and others. According to Mann, Spector was not above adding his name as co-author, although he soon began contributing so many ideas that the writers had little cause to object.

An All-Star Team

Working under virtual sweathouse conditions, chained to pianos cranking out teen fodder for the likes of Paul Petersen and James Darren, these gifted writers found Spector so refreshing that he often ended up with their best songs. Kirshner's writers were overworked, some of them producing over a hundred songs a year, but Spector refused to see himself as just another customer.

As always, the right person joined his all-star team. Ellie Greenwich was writing arguably the most realistic, passionate, good-humoured pop songs of the era, even before she met Spector. With him (and her co-writers Tony Powers and Jeff Barry) she wrote a succession of superb songs. Ellie's compositions worked so well because, like Phil, she seemed to believe in the myth she wrote about, the purity of the dreams in a young girl's heart, and the magic of rock'n'roll.

No great intellectual process went into the writing of these songs; rather, they emerged spontaneously from the well-tuned instincts of Spector and his co-writers. Ellie Greenwich tried explaining it: 'It was a hotchpotch... the three of us were spewing out ideas simultaneously. I'd be pounding on a piano and Jeff would be playing a tambourine and Phil would be strumming his guitar and the three of us singing away like maniacs at the top of our lungs... we'd find something that hit all of us at once more or less, because our minds were sort of on the same wavelength... and before you knew it, a song emerged.'

In 1964, Spector started writing many of his songs with the team of Pete Anders and Vinnie Poncia. Barry and Greenwich were devoting more of their time to the Red Bird label, but Spector still used them occasionally, as he did Mann and Weil, whose 'Lovin' Feelin'' was written late in 1964. Significantly, it was to Barry and Greenwich that he turned to for help for his ultimate creation, 'River Deep Mountain High'. It is clear that Spector took great care in his choice of writers so that the songs conveyed the same emotional impact he wanted the final product to possess.

Spector's talents as a musician and songwriter may often be overlooked, but the one thing universally acknowledged is his triumph in forging a totally new sound, something never before heard on record. Considering the limited equipment available to him, it was a superb achievement.

Some commentators consider the influence of the Gold Star Studios to have been vital. Larry Levine, his engineer at Gold Star, thinks not. 'If Phil hadn't gone to Gold Star, he would have gone to another studio and gotten a different but equally great sound.' Nevertheless, Gold Star was the one studio in the world where that sound could be made, because of its uniquely designed live echo chamber. The echo in the studio was so overpowering that it took Spector some time to adjust to it and it got the better of him on 'To Know Him Is To Love Him', his first Gold Star recording.

Hits, Flops And Faded Dreams

Judging from his records, the sound in Spector's head was a powerful surge of rhythm, as thick as ocean waves. He possessed an acute sense of balance and was able to blend many different elements into a unified sound without it all becoming murky. Yet it was far from clear; when the chords altered you just felt the change. He drew attention away from individual instruments by massing them together to build dense chord patterns. The only instrument that stood out was the drum kit, usually played by Hal Blaine or Earl Palmer. Its rolling sound was turned to thunder by Gold Star's echo chamber, and this gave the tracks a solid underpinning.

All these instruments, sometimes 40 or more, playing Nitzsche's arrangements over and over – he insisted upon doing hundreds of takes until his ears told him each detail was right – gave Spector the raw materials for his sound, but it was in the mixing that it really took shape. In today's studios, each musician can have a track of his own, and the whole thing can be mixed at leisure later on. But with three- or four-track equipment, it is necessary to keep 'bouncing down' several tracks onto one as the session proceeds, and to combine many instruments on each individual track.

Spector's approach was to perfect his rhythm track (drums, piano, bass, sax, guitars), dub it all down to one track, then add strings and vocals. Ordinarily this muddies the original 'bed track' out of all recognition, but through experimenting he devised ways to apply different forms of echo to each track as it went into the mix; and by using several different tape machines he constructed a sound that was both well-defined and 'big' at the same time.

Phil Spector had created Philles not merely to realise his musical dreams in the studio, but also to package and promote them in his own manner. Although there were, and had been, many successful independent record company bosses, Spector was particularly noteworthy in the way he challenged the established industry. Whereas most indies specialised in R&B, country and western and other regional or specialised areas, Spector moved into the majors' home ground: the pop market. And it was for this that he earned such enmity from his rivals.

Refusing to join forces with major labels in any way – as most independents were forced to – Spector handled his own pressing and distribution. Unlike so many indies who foundered in the shark-like world of the US music business, Spector succeeded because he was able to impress his regional distributors with his hit potential; they would pay him for his latest hit in order to receive stocks of the next.

If his success failed to endear him to others in the music business, then nor did his brash, almost megalomaniac style which alienated him from the conservative mainstream of the music industry.

After he had got bored with his girl groups, Spector found renewed vigour when he began work with the Righteous Brothers. His biggest success with the group – and undoubtedly one of his greatest productions was 'You've Lost That Lovin' Feelin'' which, in spite of its length (nearly four minutes) and its doom-laden tempo, proved a massive world-wide hit, topping both the US and UK charts in 1965.

Despite this triumph Spector had difficulty working with the Righteous Brothers, who proved far less malleable than the Crystals and the Ronettes ever had. Accordingly he looked around for something new to engage his talents and found it soon enough when he acted as musical supervisor on a Hollywood TV rock show that included Ike and Tina Turner.

Although successful on the R&B circuit, Ike and Tina Turner had never established themselves in the Hot Hundred. And when Spector offered them 20,000 dollars to sever their contract with Ray Charles' Tangerine label, Ike and Tina jumped at the chance. Once they were signed to Philles, Spector searched for a suitable song for them to record. He found it with the Barry-Greenwich composition 'River Deep Mountain High'. Staking everything on his magnificent, if controversial, recording of the song, Spector was profoundly shocked when the record flopped and the music business turned its back on him.

All Things Must Pass

The resentment the industry felt towards Spector by 1966 was sufficient for them to cold-shoulder his brash trumpetings for 'River Deep Mountain High'. The trade reviews were suddenly indifferent and the radio DJs followed suit, giving the record only occasional airplay. The blow to Spector's highly-strung pride was too much; his darling child had been rejected, and he retired from the music business overnight. Philles virtually came to a standstill; his most successful acts being palmed off to other producers. That spelt the end of the Phil Spector era.

After a period of retirement, Spector re-emerged in the late sixties and began production work with the Beatles – but they were then fast disintegrating. His best work was done with George Harrison (*All Things Must Pass*) and John Lennon (*Imagine*), but Spector was no longer a trendsetter: he was working with artists whose current reputations far exceeded his own and – perhaps more significantly – the rest of the world had caught up with him. The truth was that he was now only one of a number of very good producers.

During the seventies he worked with a variety of artists including Dion and Cher, but the magic had gone. Nevertheless, Spector had been at the top in the sixties and had given the word 'producer' a new meaning. He never saw his job as merely the accurate recording of someone else's music. Spector's own assessment of his work was typically grandiose: 'My records are built like a Wagner opera. They start simply and they end with dynamic force, meaning and purpose. It's in the mind, I dreamed it up. It's like art movies.'

When accused of upstaging his artists, Spector always countered by asking why nobody saw anything wrong with a film director receiving top billing in his films. He genuinely saw himself in the same terms as a filmmaker like Fellini, working in shades and textures of sound, consciously directing numerous elements toward the ultimate artistic vision that existed only in his imagination. Singers to him were like actors: he only needed them to read their lines while he worked his magic around them.

Spector's slogan hack in 1961 was 'Tomorrow's Sound Today' and he more than lived up to the title: his records continue to sound as exciting in the eighties as they did in the early sixties. Advancing technology has made many other records of the era seem quaint, but not Spector's. Made in primitive three-track studios, they still have the power to astound.

04
Phil Spector's Wall Of Sound by Rob Finnis

Written by long-standing Spector/girl group expert Rob Finnis, this piece appeared in the multi-part Radio One Story Of Pop *in part 14 (1973), and was one of the first pieces that ever attempted any analysis of Spector's sound and recording practices. Finnis was also responsible for the second UK Spector book,* The Phil Spector Story *published by Rock On in 1975, at a time when decent music book writing was in its infancy. The first Spector book had been Richard Williams'* Out Of His Head, *published the year before by Abacus at the princely sum of 65p.*

Much of Phil Spector's work until mid-1962 had been done in New York studios using session men who were not particularly well disposed to his unorthodox methods. Then, in July 1962, he turned up at the Gold Star Studios on the West Coast, with a hot new Gene Pitney song titled 'He's A Rebel'. Spector's top act, the Crystals, were reluctant to fly out to LA and lack of time forced him to record it in Hollywood with a session vocal group, the Blossoms, standing in for the real Crystals. On the session he also used a new arranger, Jack Nitzsche, and an engineer he had never met before, Larry Levine. The session went so well that Spector formed a working relationship with them that went on to produce nearly 20 consecutive hits, in a short space of time.

'I was looking for a sound,' said Spector in 1964, 'a sound so strong that if the material was not the greatest, the sound would carry the record. It was a case of augmenting, augmenting. It all fitted together like a jigsaw.'

Gold Star was renowned on the West Coast for its unique echo-chambers, which produced a very cavernous sound and created an audile impression of infinite space. This, too, would play an important part in Spector's sound.

'The moment you heard "He's A Rebel", you knew it would be a smash,' recalls Levine. 'Everyone else had been into rock & roll and they were using single instruments. When Phil came in, the set-up was two basses, two pianos, four acoustic guitars, a few horns and several percussionists, which became a trademark.'

'He's A Rebel' was only the prototype of what was later termed the 'Wall of Sound'. Although all the instruments moved in mesmerising unison with an underlying syncopation, the sound was not yet audibly extravagant or echoey. Although it was a #1 hit in America in October 1962, 'He's A Rebel' only hinted at Spector's new found potential.

About a month later, he took the Blossoms back into Gold Star and recorded a novel revival of the 30s classic, 'Zip-A-Dee-Doo-Dah'. The new record, based around a gigantic, clanking riff, had a sci-fi sound, which transcended the hackneyed arranging and recording techniques of its era. Although only a few people in the industry realised it, Spector had stepped into a world where there were no apparent limits to recording technology. He credited 'Zip-A-Dee' to the mythical Bob B. Soxx and the Blue Jeans, and saw it zoom into the US Top 10 in November 1962.

These successes encouraged Spector to make more records with artists who existed only on the label credits – a practice that was not so unusual in the States at that time. Session singers enable record producers to make commercial one-shot records, unhindered by temperamental or self-opinionated artists. Profits are also greater, since session singers are paid a standard fee – leaving the producer and music publisher to share any subsequent royalties. With this sort of incentive, Spector soon had a largish coterie of Hollywood vocalists on call for lead or background work, and greatly favoured Darlene Love of the Blossoms for the lead vocals on Crystals and Bob B. Soxx records.

From this time Spector began working very fast with Nitzsche and Levine in the studio, and three huge, near consecutive hits in the summer of 1963 – 'Da Doo Ron Ron', 'Then He Kissed Me' and 'Be My Baby' – demonstrated the variety in his early work. Sound-wise, all three were unrelated yet seemed to follow a certain stylistic progression. Although always fully aware of the lucrative commercial implications of his records, Spector was, as yet, relatively unconscious of his art. Levine: 'Phil was never hung up with the idea of a sound that he had until later when he got into the Righteous Brothers in 1964-65. Up until then, it was always what the song said, what the song needed.'

Square Foot Of Sound

'Da Doo Ron Ron' by the Crystals was the last Philles record to retain any semblance of presence or 'reality'. Each instrument and vocal part dovetailed into one another, and it sounded as if Spector had taken the individual sounds coming from the studio floor and compressed them into one tight, pounding square foot of sound.

After 'Da Doo Ron Ron', the echoes deepened, the backings became symphonic, and any presence felt on earlier records vanished forever; someone christened it Phil Spector's 'Wall of Sound'. This Wagnerian concept in pop music was first heard on 'Be My Baby' by the Ronettes, who were not session singers but an exotic looking trio of girls Phil had signed from another label.

'Be My Baby' was the gratifying culmination of Spector's intense courtship with the recording studio during the past year. It had everything: a huge rhythm track, strings, horns and a background chorus, yet nothing protruded from this massive backdrop; there were no weak links, no holes in the sound, and even the song itself was good. Spector had produced the biggest sound ever heard in pop – a giant roller-coaster ride with every musician in Hollywood.

Throughout 1963, exciting commercial sounds evolved everytime Spector and Levine blended Gold Star's unique echo with the arrangements Spector had sketched out with Jack Nitzsche. As Levine said:

'I had no idea what Phil was searching for, and it was a question of if he even knew until he heard it, because we almost never rolled tape on a session until we were two and a half hours into it. Sessions always ran overtime, we never finished on time. Most of the time was not in actual recording. Every time we'd get something, he'd have to listen and then he'd listen again until he heard something that said to him, "this is what I want to do, and this is the way I want to go". He had to listen always. I remember it was very tiring working with Phil. I could never just sit back and relax while Phil was listening because I always had to mix it as if it were a final record so that he could hear the perspective of what was happening, and it always meant being alert and I got very tired.'

Spector's use of horns contributed greatly to the blurred overall mass of his sound. Horns were arranged to play sustained chords in droning unison behind the rhythm section... subtly strengthening the chord sequence without actually being heard. 'All it would do was modulate the chords,' says Levine. 'You'd hear the chords changing, but there weren't instruments to say, "I'm changing", so it would be in the mind of the listener.'

No Split Tracks

Contrary to popular belief, Spector did not overdub en masse. The rhythm sections and horns were recorded simultaneously, and the vocals and any strings overdubbed later. 'And not only that,' as Levine said, 'but it was all done monaurally because he insisted that we didn't split tracks. He had a very definite feeling that he wanted to hear tomorrow what he accepted today. Even later, on "You've Lost That Lovin' Feelin'", the only things that were added afterwards were the voices and strings.'

In 1964, many previously unassailable American artists were eclipsed by the 'Liverpool Sound', and Spector himself suffered a setback when four Philles singles – two each by the Crystals and the Ronettes – were only moderate hits. Earlier that year, during a visit to Britain, he had confided: 'The English sound could dominate the US market. These group boys have a sexual animal-type appeal for the girls. A lot of people in the music business are going to get hurt, unless they've got something distinctive.'

Perhaps with this in mind, towards the end of 1964 Spector began a re-evaluation programme. He hired an ace promotion man, Danny Davis (Spector had previously run Philles single-handedly) and issued two trump cards – 'Walking In The Rain' by the Ronettes and 'You've Lost That Lovin' Feelin'' by the Righteous Brothers.

He had at last abandoned the churning, symphonic bubblegum sounds of 'Da Doo Ron Ron' and 'Be My Baby' in favour of a calmer, more subtle approach. 'Walking In The Rain' was a perfect evocation of its title; a slice of restrained atmospheric magic which drifted in and out ethereally, as if Spector had edited it from some concerto he'd secretly produced over the months. The thunder effects heard on the record were not simply stuck on at each end, but were cross-faded within the sound until they actually became part of it. 'Walking In The Rain' brought the Ronettes, by this time a spent force, back into the limelight in November 1964.

The Righteous Brothers, Bill Medley and Bobby Hatfield, were a minor-league, blue-eyed soul act until they obtained a residency on *Shindig*, an American TV pop show hosted by Jack Good in Hollywood. At this point Spector stepped in and signed the Brothers to Philles – knowing that any record he made with them would receive immediate national exposure on *Shindig*. He then asked Barry Mann and Cynthia Weil (who had recently written 'Walking In The Rain') to provide a suitable emotional ballad, and suggested something similar to the Four Tops' then current hit, 'Baby, I Need Your Loving'. The result was 'You've Lost That Lovin' Feelin'', which many consider to be not only Spector's finest production, but possibly the best pop record of all time.

The King Was Back

It conformed to the pattern of restraint established by its sister record, 'Walking In The Rain', but the sound was bigger, with added touches like bongos and a harpsichord echoing from the sonorous depths. At 3 mins, 50 secs, 'Lovin' Feelin'' did initially seem a little laboured, but Spector took risks over length and tempo – safe in the knowledge that the lingering melody would quickly sink into the mass consciousness through the Brother's TV plugs. Sure enough, it broke out across the country within a week of release, entered the Hot 100 at #77, and made steady progress every week. It reached #1 in January 1965, and went on to reap the ultimate rewards internationally. The king was back.

In January, 1966, Spector signed Ike and Tina Turner to Philles. Over the years they had done a round tour of small R&B labels and though very popular as a live revue, they were something of an anomaly on record. In his usual purposeful manner, Spector set about making a classic record – 'River Deep Mountain High'. If 'Be My Baby' belonged to 1963, and 'Lovin' Feelin'' to 1965, then 'River Deep' was 2001 – space-age celestial R&B recorded somewhere out in the galaxy. The powerful bass line was rubbery, like a squash ball hitting a wall, denting for a fraction of a second then leaping off at another angle. Rows of horns blared out little riffs mixed deep into the track to create blurring cross-currents of sound.

'River Deep' had been designed to bring Spector the sort of kudos 'Lovin' Feelin'' had brought him 18 months earlier. He saw it as the high point in his still impressive track record. By this time, however, Spector's relationship with the industry had reached a critical stage. Not even Danny Davis' sweet-talk could vindicate Phil's established reputation for outspokenness, and many resented him simply because he seemed to be able to do what he wanted... and get away with it. As a consequence, America's record industry decided to silently scuttle 'River Deep' – to settle a score no one was exactly sure of. In Britain, however, 'River Deep' spent nine weeks in the charts, reached #3, and became almost the record of 1966 – its American failure being a major mystery of the age. To Spector, the rebuttal was like failing a crucial exam after months of preparation and, crestfallen, he let his activities slide to a standstill. Within months he was unofficially retired, and nothing more was heard from him for two years. He remains one of the only record *producers* to have had a sound named after him – the Spector Sound.

05

Arrangements: $50 A Pop by Kingsley Abbott

It is impossible to look at the worth of Spector's work without taking account of Jack Nitzsche's arrangements for him. A great producer and writer in his own right during and after his work with Phil, his influence on the success of the Wall of Sound cannot be underestimated. For more details about him, as well as a very complete discography, you are directed to the Jack Nitzsche pages at www.spectropop.com. Ace Records have issued two volumes of material called The Jack Nitzsche Story, Hearing Is Believing 1962-1979 *(CDCHD 1030) and* Hard Workin' Man *(CDCHD 1130). Both are highly recommended.*

'The Wall of Sound was Spector's idea, but Jack was the architect.'
Denny Bruce, LA producer and one-time Nitzsche roommate

The history of artistic endeavour is littered with examples of grand ideas credited to those other than the real creators, and to some extent this is true of the relationship that Jack Nitzsche has to the Wall of Sound. He was the arranger who gave life to Spector's ever-growing dream of giving teenagers the symphonies he believed they deserved. It was Jack who worked out how the desired plan could be translated into workable charts for the musicians, and Jack who thought out how the instruments might blend to achieve the overtones and grandiose sounds that Phil needed to bring the Wall to reality. And it was Jack who during the sessions would talk to the musicians and tweak the charts if necessary to make it all work. Yet for all this, he was reportedly paid just $50 per song.

Jack Nitzsche was born on April 22nd, 1937, in Chicago, and raised on a farm in Michigan. Interested in music from an early age, he had aspirations to become a jazz saxophonist, but also played piano and clarinet. In Muskegon, Michigan, he played in a band whilst working at a steel foundry, before moving to Los Angeles around 1955. He had also begun to learn orchestration through a correspondence course, and it was through these developing skills that he landed his first LA music job. He met Sonny Bono who at that time was working as an A&R man at Speciality Records, and Sonny gave him work as a music copyist. Initially Jack worked on lead sheets for acts like Don and Dewey and Larry Williams, and he also came in contact with key figures like Lester Sill, Lou Adler, Nik Venet and the young Terry Melcher who he recorded as Terry Day. Jack and Sonny were later to co-write 'Needles And Pins' (though based upon a Jackie DeShannon riff), a key staging post for many, including the Searchers, the Ramones and Willy De Ville. Bono was well placed on the local LA recording scene, and was continually hustling around for hit records for himself or others, and through him Jack eventually got introduced to Phil Spector just as he was in the act of transferring his recording base from New York to LA. The first major hit they worked on together was 'He's A Rebel'. Jack seemed to know instinctively what Spector wanted to achieve, helped by the fact that he had a liking for Wagner and sought to arrange dramatic, atmospheric work.

'Phil had a feel for what kids wanted, and Jack understood him,' recalled famed session drummer Earl Palmer years later. 'There was a mutual respect there, and when it came to talking to the musicians, most of it was Jack. When it came to working "River Deep Mountain High", which was probably the most elaborate arrangement we ever did, it dawned on me how much control Jack had over the music.' Hal Blaine was the other key session drummer in LA, and he recalls the working relationships fondly: 'The mystique was something else. Brian Wilson came to see. Mick Jagger came. Everyone wanted to see how Phil was sprinkling fairy dust all over those records. It was a feather in everyone's caps to be part of the Wall of Sound.' Brian Wilson has long been associated with taking inspiration from Phil Spector, but although he was undoubtedly overawed by the tremendous power of the records, keen ears will soon discover that he may have taken more from Jack Nitzsche. Al Kooper puts it like this, 'Brian was initially very influenced by Phil. I don't think it got reversed. A lot of what Brian got from Phil was Jack Nitzsche orientated – i.e. the arrangements, and then he'd go to the same studio and used the same crew.' This is borne out by current Wilson sideman Darian Sahanaja who points specifically to a little known soundtrack *Village Of The Giants* that Jack scored in 1965, '(It was) maybe the first heavily orchestrated teen soundtrack. Like Brian Wilson, he could utilise instruments and voices that would complement each other, especially in the way he paired strings and percussion.'

Jack's most active period arranging for Spector was from autumn 1962 through to 1965, a period that took in all the main Crystals, Ronettes and Bob B. Soxx hits, and the famed Christmas album. In an interview with Ken Barnes for *Who Put The Bomp* magazine (Issue #16, winter '76/'77), Jack recalled how he came to work with Phil: 'Lester Sill and Lee Hazlewood were partners and I was working with them. Then Lee split from Sill and made a deal with me, and that was when Eden Records happened. I'd just do all the arranging, wouldn't have to pay for an office, and if a record was a hit I'd get so much percentage, but I wouldn't get paid for the arrangement, I'd just get the office. It was all right, I got to ride in Lee's Cadillac and all that. Then Lester got an office upstairs... 6515 Sunset, I think, the first record building in LA. One day Lester Sill called down – he and Lee were really enemies by now – and said that Phil Spector wanted to talk to me, and that was that. "He's A Rebel" was the first, written by Gene Pitney.' In 1988, in an interview for *Goldmine* with Harvey Kubernick, Jack expanded on the importance of that session, 'Phil played me the demo for "He's A Rebel". We went to a rehearsal with the Blossoms. I had been working with them for years. I didn't do the lead sheet for "He's A Rebel", just the arrangement. I put the band together for the session, a lot of the same guys I had been working with for years. Phil didn't know a lot of these people. He had been in New York 1960 – 1962. Leon Russell, Harold Battiste, Earl Palmer, Don Randi, Hal Blaine, Glen Campbell – a lot of the players came out of my phone book. Phil knew Barney Kessel. At one time he had taken guitar lessons from Barney, years before.'

The classy arrangement, though employing some of the trademark features of the Wall of Sound, does not give the real feel of the blockbusting full force that was to come, possibly due to the speed at which the session was put together (see elsewhere in this reader for the full story). Widely referred to as the Spector sound, Jack's arrangements have still never received the credit they deserve, and according to Barnes, Spector was himself instrumental in this. 'Spector never shared the honours, asserting that Nitzsche was merely a musical secretary, taking down Spector's ideas, but Nitzsche's track record as a producer/arranger apart from Phil demonstrates his mastery of that production style.' Certainly many of the ideas were Phil's, but Jack's role was to make them become reality, to translate them into workable charts for the musicians to follow; no mean feat with the numbers of musicians involved. Jack himself described it as if it were the simplest thing in the world, 'Four guitars play 8th notes; four pianos hit it when he says roll; the drum is on 2 and 4 on tom-toms, no snare, two sticks – heavy sticks – at least five percussionists.' Judging by the many examples of producers trying to emulate the sound both at the time and in subsequent years, it proved to be very far from simple.

As with many relationships, it seems that Jack provided Spector with more than his musical skills. Phil would sometimes insist Jack accompany him on plane flights, as his neuroses might be calmed by thinking he might not die alone! Phil would also call Jack up in the middle of the night and suggest a trip to an ice cream parlour, but despite seeming to be very much a junior partner in the relationship, Jack was generous in the *Goldmine* interview, 'Producers these days seem like PR people or business people. Maybe they like the records, but Phil loved the records. He was really the artist. He knew what he wanted from me and gave me a lot of input for the arrangements. We were friends and had a lot of ways to work together. It was easy and fun. My fee was $50 a song. I don't feel any bitterness about the money or payment whatsoever. The credits helped me secure employment for years. Phil knew what he wanted. He put my name on many of the singles as arranger. I loved it. What an education...'

One of the last, if not *the* last, songs that Jack and Phil collaborated on was Ike and Tina Turner's 'I'll Never Need More Than This', long a favourite of hardcore fans though less well known to the general public. Jack recalls, 'That was after "River Deep"... That was the last attempt, I think that was the last one that he and I ever did together... I think that song would be fun to do again. It's so good. I can see why it wasn't a hit, though – a little too "pop"-orientated, isn't it?'

Away from Spector, but overlapping the same period, Jack arranged and/or produced dozens of fine records, many of which are now compiled on the Ace CD dedicated to his work. Standout recordings for any fans of Nitzsche's style of spacious and cinematic arrangements include records he cut with the Cake ('Baby That's Me'), Karen Veros ('You Just Gotta Know My Mind' and 'Little Boy'), Hale & the Hushabyes ('Yes Sir, That's My Baby'), Lesley Gore ('What Am I Gonna Do With You (Hey Baby)'), and the seventies albums with Michelle Phillips and Mink De Ville. Many, many more examples could be cited. As well as these, he was always busy on a range of other issues through the sixties, including Bob Lind's wonderful 'Elusive Butterfly' worldwide hit. So busy was

Jack, that he didn't get the job for Spector's biggest record 'You've Lost That Lovin' Feelin'', the task falling to Gene Page.

The 70s and 80s saw him working on movie soundtracks, including *One Flew Over The Cuckoo's Nest* and *The Exorcist*, and gaining an Oscar for the hit song 'Up Where We Belong' from *An Officer And A Gentleman*. A surprise hit in 1963 with the instrumental 'Lonely Surfer' and his later 'St Giles Cripplegate' orchestral recording all add to the picture of an incredibly talented man. He also played with the Rolling Stones, through his association with Spector, and with Neil Young (circa *Harvest*) after his production of Young's soaring Buffalo Springfield masterpiece 'Expecting To Fly', and has a host of other credits too numerous for the remit of this book. For a fuller account and a full and extensive discography, go to the special Jack Nitzsche section of *www.spectropop.com*.

Jack died on August 25th, 2000 of cardiac arrest, following a bronchial infection. The latter years of his life had not always run smoothly, with incidents of drug problems, interpersonal problems and even some gun abuse. His funeral brought out many from the successful side of his life, the mourners including Jackie DeShannon, Nancy Sinatra, Carol Kaye, Earl Palmer, Don Randi, Gracia Nitzsche (his first wife who sang back-ups on many Spector records), Gerry Goffin, Jewel Akens, Denny Bruce, actors Sean Penn and Don Calfa, Sonny Bono's daughter Christine, fellow arranger HB Barnum and his son Jack Nitzsche Jnr. Neil Young provided red roses, Jimmy Bond conducted the service, and a nervous Phil Spector gave a eulogy for his friend, quoting from 'To Know Him Is To Love Him'. Jack was laid to rest at Hollywood Forever on the Santa Monica Blvd. Not too far from the site of Gold Star Studios where he and Phil made their particular little piece of musical history.

06

The Big Rumble: Constructing The Wall. An Interview With Phil Chapman by Kingsley Abbott

To help take us deeper into an understanding of exactly how Spector created his Wall of Sound, we turn to Phil Chapman, who after initial extensive work as a successful British studio engineer became the producer that most accept is the best able anywhere in the world at re-creating the Spector sound. This interview was conducted on Wednesday 29th October, 2003.

Could you describe what you see as the different stages of Spector's productions?
If you go back to 'To Know Him Is To Love Him', that has to have been mono, even though I've since listened to the session tapes and realised that the snare was overdubbed afterwards, which really took me by surprise. The actual track was just guitars and someone with a brush ticking the hi-hat. The snare was put on afterwards. So he had obviously had overdubbing... multi-tracking in mind even at that time. I think it was Les Paul and Mary Ford who were the people who were doing it at that stage, playing on top of themselves all the time. When he was working at Atlantic, those productions don't really give any indication of the sound that was to come. Certainly the Teddy Bears does, with that lilt and that dreamy echo... a mood to it.

Do you think that he was responsible for that mood, at that early stage?
I don't think Stan Ross would have put that much echo on without encouragement. He (Spector) would have asked for that amount of echo. Even as a teenager, he was the client. I listen to other records from that period of time, and presumably some of them would have been done at Gold Star, and they don't use that amount of echo... they're not that... dreamlike. The A-side that is – the other side 'Don't You Worry, My Little Pet' had normal amounts of echo – for that kind of record at the time. I was only about 7 or 8 at the time, and I wasn't analysing it but I remember thinking that there was that dreamy record with the girl singer, and I really liked that kind of thing. And then, he goes through the Atlantic period when he was producing in

the style of Leiber and Stoller, the Drifters sounding things. Then he started his own things, and I suppose the first touches of it must have been introducing the Latin percussion. The early Philles things, they're actually quite dry. They don't seem to have echo. I remember Spector being interviewed at his height about the echo he used, and he said, 'Actually people like Johnny Mann and Ray Connif use far more echo than I do'. If you listen to his early ones like 'Uptown', 'Da Doo Ron Ron' and 'Be My Baby', they actually haven't got much echo on at all. In fact I don't think Ronnie's got any echo on her voice at all on 'Be My Baby'. It's all done by the weight of the stuff in the background, just the sheer density of the instrumentation. Because of the recording conditions of the day, you wouldn't really have heard acoustic guitars being played in rhythm once other things like drums and percussion were over the top. You would have heard this drone in the background, but you wouldn't have realised they were acoustic guitars playing rhythm unless you actually heard them in isolation on their own. That kind of churning sound has always been the basis, the hidden element that no one's really been able to emulate.

Did he do that by having four or five guitarists playing in unison, or was he overdubbing a couple?
I always thought that possibly he added to them, but he developed and had more and more musicians. I remember a joke at the time that he had overbooked musicians and just didn't want to send them home, so he had too many people all going at once! If you listen to some of the session tapes that are doing the rounds, and hear the 'Baby, I Love You' sessions, the whole racket actually stops. It's interesting to hear it stop. And on 'River Deep Mountain High' you can hear the three piano players all playing the same thing, and you can hear them talking to each other about who's going to play what octave. Then you listen to the finished record, and you wouldn't think there are any pianos in there! It's just some kind of noise – something's there in the background, a wadge of... thing! It was just achieved by density, and that got misinterpreted as echo. You can quite clearly hear echo on the drums on 'River Deep', but, again, on 'Da Doo Ron Ron' there's no echo on the drums there, and that tom that's overdubbed on the chorus, that's bone dry. I think it was from 'Be My Baby' onwards that it started getting bigger – the pronounced rhythm and that huge crash on the offbeat that everybody copies. But the power was there from 'Da Doo Ron Ron', but it didn't go over the

top. Then there were a huge number of recordings in that '64 period, until he started to use things like harpsichords and combinations of instruments with 'Lovin' Feelin''. I think that *Pet Sounds* and 'God Only Knows' were all based on what Spector was doing, though at that time Spector wasn't having hits. Things like 'Born To Be Together' by the Ronettes – if you really listen to it, it's fantastic. It just sounds like nothing – very quiet... piano, harpsichord, tiny percussion... all providing this very quiet drone.

Can I take you back to 'Da Doo Ron Ron'. What would have been the steps towards recording that?
It would have been done all at once. It would have been bass, drums, acoustics, a couple of pianos and saxophones. That was basically the line-up of all the early stuff, like 'Why Don't They Let Us Fall In Love?', 'Be My Baby' – they've all got the same line-up.

How would he have used the tracks he had available to him at that point?
It would have been three-track, I'd imagine by then. This is what I'm predicting he did: he would probably have recorded the instruments on a three-track. He'd probably have kept the drums and bass separate from the guitars and pianos, and separate from the saxes. They would then mix that down from that three-track onto one track of another three-track. The remaining two tracks would have had the vocals – stacked the backing vocals on one, leaving one for the lead vocal. And then what he would have done, when he'd moved along the bus a bit, when he started to add strings on, he would have had to stack the lead and background vocals all onto one track. I think he was careful not to do too many generation jumps, because the tape would have got too hissy. You can quite clearly hear strings on several early things, Crystals and Ronettes' 'Be My Baby', – the session tapes give it away – the track is in one place, the vocals in another, and the strings are on the third track. The Christmas album is plastered in strings and extras, and that really was only three tracks. It's quite amusing, because at certain points in some of the earlier ones you can actually hear how the musicians are placed. You can hear certain parts stopping and something else starting. You can hear background vocals stopping to let something else have a space because they didn't have enough tracks! Another interesting effect you can notice is on the heavily layered backing vocals on 'Be My Baby' and 'Baby, I Love You'. Whenever Ronnie sings she's obviously singing through a compressor because

it's like a voice-over. The backing vocals just disappear. Sometimes you hear the end of the (backing) line, but the moment she sings they simply disappear. Technically it's all done by compression. I would have thought that experimentation started just after those really big hits. When he started introducing more exotic instruments.

So, what's normally called the 'Wall of Sound'... the big rumble... the Ronettes sound... was exactly what?
The drone all the way through is usually the acoustic guitars – they throw up so much... overtones... and he balanced them with the bass so it just became one solid rhythm track, and the keyboards too. All the string writing was blended in. Cellos and acoustics blend really well together, and all the lower string parts were blended right into the acoustic sound so it just became one powerful force.

Is that why he was always so particular about the mic placement? To get and to keep that balance right? The musicians tell stories of Spector yelling 'Don't touch the mic!' if they were moving away from their position for a break.
Mic placement would have been really really important. There were a lot of people in a small space. I think it would have been more to control the sound of the drums, rather than the other way round. The acoustics certainly wouldn't have been loud enough to bleed anywhere else. One thing musicians do, if they're sitting there with a mic at their side, and they want to go away, they just move the mic out of the way. The mics have to be where they are – just moving them a few inches will change the sound, so if you have your guitar sound or your bass sound, you don't want it to change. Especially with something as complicated as balance – it's a really fine balance to get it right. Any slight movements of the mic will change the balance. It would change the sound. For example, moving the bass mic might change the frequency of the bass, and if the part's been worked out to blend in and not to jump out, and you change the characteristic of the bass, you'll find it coming out where it shouldn't.

So to set up that balance in the first place, he would have started with the guitars, blending with the bass, layered other things on top of that, and perhaps ending with the drums?
The drums probably would have been around, but not concentrated on, because there is so much energy required for the drums, you

tend to leave the drums until last so people didn't waste themselves too much. So he would have spent a lot of time getting the internal balance of the acoustic rhythms and keyboards right, especially as they are carrying the chord sequence. He would have spent a lot of time making sure they were all playing the right inversions. For example, I had a lot of trouble when I was doing my Spector soundalikes, I'd get the guitars assembled and get a couple of people to play things but somehow it just didn't sound right, and then I'd just get them to change the inversions and play exactly the same chord sequence in a different way and all of a sudden it would sound really full. So if a musician came in and Jack (Nitzsche) had dotted the parts out, ten to one Phil might say 'Can you play that in a different shape?' He'd be changing the shapes of all the chords and get the piano players to play different parts of the keyboards just to get that denser section really solid.

That suggests quite a degree of musicology. Did he have that?
I think so. Again, I've heard the stuff that Jack Nitzsche did without Spector, and, whilst he does it OK, you can tell the difference. It's all to do with exactly what people play. I've listened to those session tapes and I've heard him stop the tape and ask the guy if he had a different kind of tambourine. Can you change the glockenspiel? Can you put a different type of beater on that vibe? Yeah, he knew all that kind of thing... he knew when the horns were in tune. He had an incredibly good ear.

Having perfected the 'rumble', he then moved onto bigger examples of that, like with the Crystals' 'I Wonder' when he puts even more on top with the strings.
That's just really a mixing thing. You couldn't actually do that. The dynamics simply weren't available. On the board, he must have really whacked up the strings to about 20, if not 25 db. No other way would it have soared through like that, but it sounds so natural you think he did. I love that section because you can hear the cellos coming up, with the presence of those top strings turned up so much for that melody line to come through. That's probably one of my all time favourite Spector recordings, but it wasn't done at Gold Star. It was done at the other place, Mirasound, and it hasn't got the rumble like it should have. It's got the roar, but not the rumble. The bass end is just not the same. There are all sorts of invisible components that

feed in, things that even he couldn't get when he wasn't in Gold Star. I didn't know then, I was too young, but I knew there was something very different about that record. When I first wrote to him, that one along with 'Home Of The Brave' was one of the things I asked him about. The Mirasound ones don't have that roundness that Gold Star ones had. That's a really important feature – because when you're building sounds up like that and using particular motion, and again it's a feature of the console – at that time all the recording consoles were what I call home-made as they were all designed and built by the studio owners. There was no such thing as a Neeve or an SSL or a standard console – everyone had their own. They really affected how things sounded. I always noticed that anything at Mirasound had a particularly harsh top end. You can hear it on the Raindrops, on Neil Diamond, and on the Shangri-Las, and you can certainly hear it on 'I Wonder' – a blistering top end that builds up. The sound of the EQ on the board itself was quite a factor. Gold Star just happened to have a particularly smooth round bass end. Even then on regular old Dansette-style players, I could tell that 'Then He Kissed Me' had a really subsonic kick drum sound. Something I'd never heard on any other record, and it came through, but you wouldn't have got that on 'I Wonder'. You get that sort of thud – every time the drum sound happens, the track moves out of the way, like the parting of the Red Sea, and that's really vicious compression.

By that stage we were at the end of '63, did he then move onto eight-track boards?
I would pinpoint eight-track as Ike And Tina Turner. I think the Righteous Brothers were three- or four-track. Because if you listen to it with the stereo, it always gives it away – you've got the track all on one lump on the left, them in the middle and the strings on the right. And that smacks of three-track to me, at the most four-track.

What differences would his eventual access to an eight-track board have made to his work? Would he have said 'Goody Goody, now we can do X, Y and Z', or would he have said 'We'll do it the same way, but we've got more space'?
I would have thought that it gave him a chance not to stack down things so quickly, and probably at the same time he would have thought that he could put even more on. He did get more adventurous with his orchestrations after that. He left more spaces... Maybe it

was coincidental with the technical advances, because immediately he started trying to be more dramatic. He'd been churning out pop records, and then he started to introduce a bit of drama to things, and that would have required stops and starts... for contrast. He liked surprise attacks... explosions, and then you'd get ambushed on the choruses! Even when I listen to 'River Deep Mountain High' I often argue with myself if it was multi-track or not, because you can hear, again on those session tapes, the whole band rehearsing all in one go. With Tina there as well. You can quite clearly hear, the percussion, all the guitars, all the pianos, bass, drums – all the usual stuff – all at once. When you hear any of the mixes of that, they are all on one side. They never split – they're all in one wedge, so it wouldn't surprise me if even 'River Deep' was only 4-track. Because all the backing vocals are wadged on another track. There's no concept of spreading things stereo, and again, the strings are on a fourth track. It feels as if he hadn't got past 4-track even then.

Why do you think he didn't go for more stereo work?
Listening now, I'm actually more interested in the stereo, but listening then there was something illusionary about having everything at point source. The 3D was actually all in your head – it was actually just a point source. Because there were so many instruments, he naturally placed things in a 3D perspective. It was quite a surprise to me that, when I became a recording engineer, and I was working on things, when I analysed things I realised that actually everything was upfront, there's nothing at the back. Everything with Spector is upfront. Some of it's got echo on it and some of it hasn't, but it's all got equal amounts of presence.

Would that have been dictated by the car radio or home player speaker sizes?
Again I think it was actually coincidence. That was the technology that was available. He liked records to sound powerful. From what I can remember, he didn't monitor quietly, he monitored unbelievably loudly from what I've read. At the time I would have thought that no one would have wanted to hear the strings in one side, and the rhythm section in the other. The whole thing was meant to be a blend. It would have sounded very unnatural. As he was doubling things, as he had so many instruments playing the same thing, he wouldn't have wanted to see between them. I do now, personally, but then he

wouldn't have wanted that. It was just an illusion of power. It's floor to ceiling frequency-wise, and front to back spatially, but that's been achieved by illusion. From the start, you could never recreate his sound live. It's impossible – it's like jamming everybody against the shop window. You just can't balance everything. You have natural separation in live work. With his recording it was like everybody was there, right in front of you. At the time the radio was mono, so he probably thought 'Why do them stereo, they won't get played that way.' Also it would have been an uncomfortable sound to have them in stereo. There was all the hype as well, because once people started telling him he had a wall of sound, he would have thought that it works best in mono. I think he just adopted a lot of things that were said about him. He just took them on. I actually like some of the later things in stereo. The Checkmates – he did that himself in stereo. I think the 'Back To Mono' thing came later, when the fandom started. The Wrecking Crew, the Wall of Sound – all of these things came after the actual events. It all started in the seventies when the archivists got stuck in.

Apart from stereo, do you hear any other differences between the Checkmates time (1969) and the sounds from a few years earlier?
Yes, definitely. The earlier times it was basically a rock & roll combo – bass, drums, saxes, guitars and keyboards. Then we move a little more exotic with things like 'The Best Part Of Breaking Up', which has a harmonica in the background and some extra percussion stuff, but by the time you get to 'You've Lost That Lovin' Feelin'' you've got harpsichords, and strings just doing sustains as opposed to lines – that was quite a big difference as the strings became part of the drone as well. The strings were just holding chords all the way through, like the Blossoms were just holding chords. He did start creating a different sound. In the early days, the backing vocals were just backing vocals, but then they too became part of the wall. As well as other backing vocals! I found it fascinating hearing backing vocals and other backing vocals providing another function altogether. That was the middle period, when guitar parts started getting doubled with glockenspiels. Anything that had to come out of the mix was doubled with something else. That's the period I really liked.

Certainly Brian Wilson did that unusual doubling with Pet Sounds...
I thought that Brian Wilson was actually more imaginative because

he used a bigger selection of instruments. You could hear what he had chosen to use. With Spector you were just nailed to the wall with the power! Wilson allowed the qualities of the individual instruments to come through. He used bass harmonica and bass clarinet, and you can hear them, and it's nice to hear them that way. And the way he used accordions – they were Spector techniques, but Spector kept them all crammed in. So that was the middle times, and then he got more interested in rhythm. You can quite clearly hear in the working out of 'River Deep Mountain High' that it is based on 'My World Is Empty Without You'. They tried to get that same double beat (sings the bass led intro), and later it got modified. I heard the original intro on the first few takes and it's exactly the same – the Motown thing that they were borrowing. He was stepping up the excitement level. He did it on 'River Deep' and did the same on the Checkmates Ltd. He paid a lot of attention to the rhythm section. I noticed different line-ups – by the time he got to Checkmates Ltd he was using flutes as lead lines and a different kind of drum sound, a different kind of bass sound – things had changed. I liked it – it still had the basic feel, and on the Ronettes' 'You Came, You Saw, You Conquered'. Then there was a little gap when he went missing. Looking back, the extreme one was Ike & Tina's 'I'll Never Need More Than This' – that was when he really went over the edge. I really liked that because that was how it was going; from then on something went wrong. There was a gap, and out comes the Checkmates and the Ronettes again on A&M – kind of OK, but not quite with the passion of what had gone before.

That brings us to the end of the sixties, and you started engineering and recording at the start of the seventies. How soon into your career did you start trying to incorporate Spector influences?
From day one!

How would you build a Spector-type track?
I'd start with rhythm guitars and keyboards. Nowadays you could do it with one guitar, but if I didn't have to do it that way I'd probably have three or four guitars. A couple of keyboards, or a couple of pianos would do. A couple of percussionists would do. Depending on whether or not I was going to use brass... because these days I wouldn't need to think that way, as I probably wouldn't do it all at once. You would do it in stages... layer it.

Would you use both acoustic and electric bass?
I wouldn't use acoustic bass these days, mainly because of the nature of the material. Early Spector productions occasionally had upright bass, but in general he used electric bass shadowed by keyboard. I'd be happy with electric, but if I was trying to do an absolute Spector clone, I might use acoustic – just to give it that rumble. Once I had got past that stage, I'd be layering the percussion on. Then when you listen to all that, because its all so compressed, and because there are so many churning things, they throw up overtones and melodies that come forward of their own accord. That's usually how you can get your string melodies, your obligatos, your counter melodies and things like that.

You follow what naturally comes out...
Yes, I did that a lot. I used to get quite hypnotised listening to bass, drums and rhythm acoustics because, if you had used the right compression and there was a lot of them and enough echo, things just turn themselves up at you from that combo. You can get lines from that to put over the top. Then probably put the vocal on after that, because Spector always managed to get the vocals to come through everything. That's a real art, that's very very difficult. He'd put the vocal on after the rhythm section, and then the other lines would be sculptured around the vocals. It was all very carefully arranged. The only crashes I have ever found were on the Christmas album – on 'Rudolph The Red Nosed Reindeer'. If you listen to the stereo carefully, the strings and the backing vocals are actually doing something similar but not identical. They're a semitone apart in places, which is a real clash, a surprise that he let that go through. Again, if you listen to the backing vocals on 'Be My Baby', they really are rough and shabby. But because they are in there as part of the wadge, you don't individually notice it being like that. Those were the two things that were surprises.

So, on your clone, you now have a rhythm track and a voice on... do you put the backgrounds on now? And then what would you do to it?
Yep. There's a formulaic standard for that type of record from that time: You'd set up your rhythm section and your intros to get your hook, you get your lead vocal over the verse, and usually if you've got a really interesting voice you'd let them sing the first verse unhindered. Then when the chorus comes you'd pile a few extra

things in – usually the strings – and the backing vocals. Then the backing vocals would probably ease out a bit on the second verse, and you'd have some counter line. It's usually a string line, but some kind of counter line to add to the interest. Spector's method was generally to pile more in, play the same thing so it just appeared to get heavier, but then even he relented to standard technique. '(I'm A) Woman In Love' has got a counter line in the second verse. And on Crystals' things like 'Little Boy', usually the strings are playing an answer line in the second verse that they weren't playing in the first verse. After the second verse, you'd usually wander off into an instrumental section or do a middle eight. They are usually quite interchangeable as well, because I remember 'Little Boy', 'I Wonder' and 'Gee The Moon Is Shining Bright' [Editor's note: the latter tune being aka Veronica's 'Why Don't They Let Us Fall In Love'] – different versions of those songs have different middle eights taken from each other. For example, 'I Wonder' by the Ronettes has a different middle eight to 'I Wonder' by the Crystals, and 'Little Boy' has a middle eight taken from one of the other songs. So... after coming out of the middle eight, you'd either have a stop of some description like on 'Be My Baby' where it goes Boom-ba-boom, or on 'I'll Never Need More Than This' where it simply stops... there's usually some sort of interruption at that point before the chorus comes charging back in and you go on until fade. That really was standard construction, though if I was doing a Spector record today, I wouldn't use that same construction, but I'd certainly do the rhythm section exactly as I've described it. You wouldn't get carried away by EQing things and adding echo, because he didn't have loads of echo on everything. He had loads of things all doing the same thing.

Where was the echo most effective though?
The voice and the drums. I would say that the use of echo on the keyboards and guitars was minimal, and I think that the bass on Spector records only had echo on them because they were in the same room with something else that had echo on it. I can't recreate it exactly myself because I'd be doing it at different times. With all the musicians together at one time, one thing affects another. There's no doubt that with the bass player in the room, with echo on the drums, that the echo would stray to the bass. Like you can't put echo on the snare without it appearing on the kick drum.

So, from your producer's perspective, could you pick three Spector productions, perhaps one from each of the early, middle and later periods, that you think he ought to be most satisfied with?

Dear oh dear... he's particularly proud of 'Zip-A-Dee-Doo-Dah' isn't he? I think the first of them would be 'Da Doo Ron Ron' because of the power sound in there, though I accept that it's all on one level. It's the first of the pulsating ones where things are in there and you don't quite know what's going on as they're all playing the same thing. 'You've Lost That Lovin' Feelin'' has to be the second, because it's his first really dramatic one, and for a later one... he'd probably like George Harrison because it's all so terribly compressed in! But personally, not being him, I wouldn't know what he found as an achievement. I've made records that people have really liked and analysed, and I've thought that I didn't have anything like what they think in mind when I made them! So, I've often thought that a lot of the magic is in the listener... all the records I've made that I know inside out don't hold any magic for me, but they do to people listening. So I'm very much in the case of the listener with Spector, and the ones that have impressed me the most were things like 'Then He Kissed Me' which was the first one that I could hear floor to ceiling with frequencies I had never heard before in any other kind of record. It was all in there defined, and the vocals sat in there with the full orchestra going on. Then something like 'Lovin' Feelin'' had the drama, but 'Hung On You' was probably the densest, clattering thing he had done, apart from 'I Wonder' which I really like. And there's 'Born To Be Together' which I thought was really adventurous. And then Ike & Tina...

I liked 'He's A Rebel', which was the first one that I heard that had a very different togetherness with the vocals and instrumentation... and with a very good B- side too!

Yes... that was with the very satisfying guitars too.

Let me throw you an odd one... Jerri Bo Keno?

When I heard 'Here It Comes' I was really disappointed. In fact, that was the one that I set about remaking for myself in Ronettes style. I have a backing track for it that I did in 'Baby, I Love You' style.

Why were you dissatisfied with it?

I didn't like the modern drum sound. I didn't like the change. I still don't really like it. It's got this thick kick drum, and the sound is all floating... it's not sunk down. There's a couple of things that he did around that time that I just didn't like because of that. Not like the old Spector at all to me. The drums were too... presencey. He was trying to do it all under different circumstances... things had moved on. Things had changed. I loved the scale of it, but I didn't like the fact that it was like a curtain hanging across the speakers, rather than all of it in the middle. The drum perspective wasn't what I was expecting. That's what it hinges around to me, and oddly enough, I thought the George Harrison stuff was really good. That related much more to the old stuff than the actual stuff he was doing *himself* at that time.

(We then moved to the studio where Phil plays the Ronettes-styled 'Here It Comes' re-creation and another Spector-styled track in preparation – both are dramatic, full and exciting.)

You asked me about the records that made the changes and transitions in Spector's sound. I had forgotten about 'Paradise'. [Editor's note: a Ronettes track that remained unissued until the Britain-only *Rare Masters Vol 1* rarities compilation in the seventies.] I ran the fan club when I was at school, and I kept writing to Phil Spector and finally got a letter back. We got sent an acetate of 'Paradise' in the mid- to late sixties, and of course I'd heard nothing like it. We were under the impression that it was going to be the next Ronettes release at that time, but when it didn't come out we thought – well, we've got some gold dust here! But we were really disappointed that no one was going to hear it. Then as soon as I got into the studio, I set about making my own version – I couldn't wait! It took about three years off and on. I kept adding bits and pieces. It's still never been sung... successfully! It was through doing my own version of 'Paradise' that I picked up the skill of really listening to what was going on in a record, and I've been able to use that for my own work. I could play it for you and split the whole thing down for you.

What was the tone of the letter that you got? Did it go into details?
No, not really, it was just a nice kind of 'thank you' letter, but another friend of mine, Robert, used to get telegrams all the time saying 'I'm just going into the studio' and things like that. Robert was a bit more

effusive with things he would say. I'd just write letters, but he would write reams, and he got some very nice telegrams back. We've still got them somewhere. When I ran the fan club, I printed up some photos four-up on one sheet, and he sent one of them back to me signed 'To the Genius behind Phil Spector'. It was worth keeping!

What do you consider your most successful Spectorisation record?
I wouldn't say I had really done that many. I tend to keep the recreations as a hobby. I did the Tracy Ullman things, but they were really more just sixties things, apart from 'Sunglasses' perhaps. If people wanted it, I'd throw it in. I did 'Marvellous Guy' by Girl Talk, and I've done some film things that are perhaps somewhat closer.

And his legacy?
Really, I think that whole power trip was something that only America could have come up with, and later when he fell into disrepute and music went a different way, they still took all his same principles. Those principles are still there in corporate rock, but they create the illusions that it's real. If you listen to those *big* rock records that started up in the eighties and went through the nineties, I mean, drummers don't have eighteen-foot arm-spans that can play continuously! Hi-hats don't sound very posh: they sound pretty awful when you're standing next to them! And vocalists can't sing at the top of their voice all the way through, or without taking a breath. The whole thing's a complete illusion. The fashion became that it must be real, but yet they couldn't do without the power. They took all of Spector's techniques, like Celine Dion and all those big corporate releases, and they were all based on his recording principles. I just tie it in with the psychology of wanting to be powerful. Why did he want to make such powerful records?

There was probably a personal thing about wanting to be noticed. It was his way to say 'Look at me, here I am'. Also if you look back at some of the music of, let's say, 1961, there was a need for a kick in the pants. He certainly provided that.
Yes, it's interesting to note that he eventually teamed up with the biggest name from the sixties: the Beatles.

(At this point, Phil's version of 'Paradise' is played. As with his version of 'Here It Comes' it is wonderfully rich and full, but I notice more of the low rumble present on this track.)

What is the difference between the two tracks? Why do I notice that rich bottom rumble more there on 'Paradise'?
The key. This one's in C, and it's quite rich. The choice of inversions on the guitars must have been right! There's not much reverb on those drums. They were tuned the old fashioned way. And you're right... the other one has got the guitars, but they didn't quite work in that inversion. And the bass on 'Here It Comes' is synth, and on this it's real bass. These take me a long time to do, and all sorts of things can happen along the way. Spector things were done really quickly – all in one session. You can hear the sound all in one go when you do it like that – everyone's there in front of you. There's a lot of hit and miss this way... and a lot of hoping you get there!

(We then play a Phil Chapman version of 'I Wish I Never Saw The Sunshine' with Katrina Leskanish of Katrina & The Waves singing lead.)

Finally, how would you sum up Phil Spector's contribution to production?
I would say that in his endeavours to create a powerful wall of sound, he elevated the process of production, recording and mixing into an art form. M C Escher achieved illusions with his eccentric graphics, Busby Berkeley achieved extravagant illusions in his escapist musicals, and Phil Spector achieved grand illusions on record.

As a PS to this interview, we add this thought of Phil Chapman's from a discussion thread on the Spectropop website:
'Larry Levine deserves more of a spotlight. He was a "natural" engineer, leaving the individual sounds as untouched as possible. Gold Star only had 12 microphone inputs, so everything hinged on the balance of instruments, and that's a whole art-form unto itself.'

07
Spector's Musicians by Kingsley Abbott

The Wall of Sound was more than Spector's vision: it was formed by him with the talents of many of Los Angeles' and New York's first and second call fine session players working within some very specific studios. Their involvement was an absolutely essential part of the whole...

The fine LP-sized booklet that accompanies the *Back To Mono* 4CD boxed set of Phil Spector's best issued work contains, near the end, a list of the musicians that worked with the producer. The extensive list, presumably assembled with regard to the American Federation of Musicians (AFM) recording contract sheets, contains 182 names of 'Musicians' and an additional 36 of 'Phil's Regulars', the latter being the hard core of subsequently well known names that formed 'The Wrecking Crew' – a term often attributed to drummer Hal Blaine who suggests that it was in use back in the sixties, but one that was not in general currency until later. Assuming the list is based on AFM records, it suggests that all the players whose names appear were likely to have been members of the federation, but a cursory glance shows this unlikely to have always been the case. It is also reasonably well accepted that the session players listed on such contracts did not always tell the whole story as to who was at the sessions. Whilst some care obviously had to be taken with the sheets as they included pay rates and social security numbers for pension links, it is also likely that mistakes and omissions could and did occur as sessions could vary or extend from their planned route. Such pre-planning was done by the session contractor who received double scale for their key role of finding and hiring the desired players and ensuring that they were all gathered at the appropriate place and time. For Spector's sessions this was a job often, though certainly not exclusively, undertaken by Hal Blaine.

The list of 182 musicians in the re-issue booklet includes some interesting names of people who joined the sessions on a variety of occasions: Brian Wilson on keyboards (from the 'Don't Hurt My Little Sister'/'Things are Changing' session), Mac Rebennack (aka Dr John), Harry Nilsson on keyboards, Sandy Nelson (an old friend from schooldays) on drums, Herb Alpert on horn, and even Lenny Bruce and Gold Star engineer Larry Levine on percussion. However it is 'Phil's Regulars' who have become known as the hardcore of his recording team, the players whose open-mindedness helped him create studio sounds more powerful than anything that had preceded them. In his book, *Hal Blaine and the Wrecking Crew*, the drummer explains the nature of the group:

'The band typically consisted of Carol Kaye and Ray Pohlman on Fender basses; Lyle Ritz and Jimmy Bond on upright basses; Tommy Tedesco, Barney Kessel, Howard Roberts, Glen Campbell and Bill Pitman on guitars; Don Randi, Leon Russell, Larry Knetchel, Michael Melvoin and Al Delory on pianos. There was also a host of percussionists, and at various times different piano players, guitarists, drummers and horn men... Steve Douglas was usually on sax along with Nino Tempo, Jay Migliori and Roy Caton on trumpet along with Ollie Mitchell and Tony Terran. Virgil Evans, Lou Blackburn and other horn men substituted from time to time.'

This list of names from Hal is not a definitive list of the key Spector players, although it does seem to come quite close. Guitarist Irv Rubins, whose name crops up on several album covers, is missing, and pianist Michael Melvoin's name does not appear anywhere in the *Wall Of Sound* booklet, though this may be due to other factors as his name is also missing from certain *Pet Sounds* credits that he is known to have played on. When quizzed as to the possibilities of session credits being inaccurate or incomplete, Hal Blaine has indicated that, though unlikely, it was possible. Carol Kaye, guitarist and electric bass player on the majority of Spector dates explains the choice of musicians:

'You have to understand, our bunch of "clique" musicians as we were then called, were all independent contractors. Everyone worked with everyone else; there was no "set rhythm section" at all with anyone. We worked for all the hit-making producers/record companies/artists then. It was our job to help everyone get hit records. There were about 45/50 of us out of a pool of around 350 steadily working studio musicians.'

The later term 'The Wrecking Crew' appears to have arisen as a reaction to this new and younger breed of casually dressed session musicians, and was applied by the decidedly not rock'n'roll older guard of West Coast players. It was Blaine and his friends who were rapidly becoming the first call musicians, and were playing on hit sessions for Elvis, Connie Francis and Jan & Dean. However, it was their work for Phil Spector from 1962 onwards that really brought them into the consciousness of those beyond the, at that point, nameless and faceless world of the LA session musicians. The *He's A Rebel* album credits drummer Hal Blaine, saxophonist Steve Douglas, and pianist Mike Spencer ('Spenser' in the *Wall Of Sound* booklet) as guest soloists, and thereafter, with albums like Bob B. Soxx & the Blue Jeans and the famed Christmas album, a fuller set of musicians are credited that include most of the players on Hal's list above. Whether or not this was indicative of the value placed upon them by Phil is open to conjecture, but it was certainly against the industry norm for the early sixties.

What then was their real value to Spector at the time of his crucial growth period of late '62 into '63? Did they become pliant tools in his hands, or was it by some twist of fate a perfect marriage of young musical minds? Or were they simply able to put up with his seemingly absurdist building of sounds in a way that more traditional players would not have tolerated? In truth it was probably all of that and more. Carol Kaye considers this:

'We didn't especially have any personal opinions on this line or that line per se... You couldn't afford to have "opinions" about anything – no time, you had to get everyone a hit, and whatever lines it took to do that were "good" for that particular tune. You kept your personal opinions, if you had any, to yourself.'

Listening to various Spector session tapes that have been in circulation for some years, it is evident that there was at least mutual musical respect. Spector appears to have had very sharp ears, and was able to spot and describe any errors he noticed, and to have been very adept at picking up on commercial hook sounds or instrumental blends. A long-standing example is Phil's identification of Billy Strange's leaking guitar sound on 'Zip-A-Dee-Doo-Dah' as being perfect for what he wanted. He was as aware of what the musicians were doing when they were off-task as when they were on. Hal Blaine recalls:

'Phil Spector is the only producer I've ever known who always had an extra 2-track recorder running constantly from the beginning of every session. Everything said or played went on tape, and it was quite a trick. Musicians often walk into the studio cold and start warming up in their own way before the tracking begins. They come up with strange riffs, and when asked what they played they never remember. Not so at Phil's sessions. He would ask, play back the lick, and say, "Remember that. I want it on the front of the bridge." Phil would pick out the nuggets he wanted and by playing them back, make them history.'

In the case of the 'Zip-A-Dee-Doo-Dah' guitar example however, it was a matter of Spector identifying miking differences. Gold Star engineer Larry Levine explains what happened:

'We had been working on it for around three hours, and he kept boosting the levels, till finally it reached the point where everything was pinning (to the indicator's extent). It was my first session with Phil; I really didn't have the nerve to say anything to him at first. Finally I couldn't take it anymore, so I just shut down all the mics at once! Phil accepted that graciously – he started screaming at me! I told him I had no option but to do that. So slowly I started bringing the mics back up one at a time, balancing them as I was going along. I got to the last microphone, which was Billy Strange's guitar, and Phil jumps up and says, "That's it – that's the sound – let's record!" I told him I didn't have the guitar mic up yet, but that's what he wanted. So we went with it. And that's the most incredible recording experience I've ever had.'

The musicians quickly became aware that the relative placing of mics and baffles were very much part of Phil's sound, and would frequently be warned about not moving them on the less-than-often numbers of breaks they were allowed.

'Take 5, but don't touch the mics!' is a yelled instruction that seems to have been burned into the memory of many of these musicians. Isolating individual instruments' sounds was particularly difficult bearing in mind the size of the room at Gold Star (approx 25' x 35' with approx 14' height). The Wall of Sound, though not only created at the famed Gold Star Studio (Mirasound in New York being used for some of the very full Crystals recordings like 'I Wonder'), was a result of combining Spector's primary aim of recording massed musicians playing all together at once in a room with strong echo chamber qualities. Spector was aware that the drum sounds especially could change his delicate balance through leakage, apparently most awkward with the acoustic guitars; a situation that could be exacerbated depending on the key the song was in. Levine remembers how they coped with this:

'If it was a song with a lot of open strings and the guitars were louder, there'd be a lot less drum leakage. But if they were using capos or playing a certain way that meant less volume, you'd have more drums. So it was always a matter of balancing these variables. Phil never liked the drum sound – it was the bane of his recording existence. And when you put it through the echo chamber, it all blended together anyway.'

In an interview with Mark Cunningham for his book *Good Vibrations – A History of Record Production*, Levine also recalled other characteristics of the Gold Star studio:

'A lot of the sound qualities of the studio area could be put down to the acrylic paint which coated the walls. It was a now-outlawed lead-based paint which made the sound bounce all around the room, giving it a really crisp feel. Because of the small dimensions of the studio, it was subject to resonance depending on which instruments were played in certain areas and also the keys in which the songs were played. It was normally the guitars which had the most effect, with open chords or strings obviously omitting a louder sound then when they were fretted chords or closed notes. So whenever an acoustic guitar played a closed string, we would have to open up the microphone a little more to get the desired level, but in turn that would let in a little spill from the drums.'

The Wrecking Crew quickly realised that these complicated tracks they were cutting with Spector were becoming big pop hits just at the time the pop market was exploding, so they were eager to go along with sessions that were substantially different to their usual three or four songs in three hours work. The Spector session tapes reveal several examples of idea swapping as the players became more aware of Spector's modus operandi. The vast majority of the musicians in this select group had some form of jazz or urban academic background, and had experience of a wide variety of work including Big Band Swing styles. They were confident, able and perhaps most importantly open-minded enough to cope with Spector's ideas. The exceptions to this were men like Glen Campbell, Leon Russell and Billy Strange who came from more rural roots, but the others quickly saw their worth and integrated them into the group. Carol Kaye remembers Glen Campbell specifically:

'Glen Campbell and I would duel on "Tico-Tico" and I'd always win the speed contest, but Glen finally beat me on one of his TV shows. He'd stand up and sing some dirty hillbilly songs once in a while, and even would jam a little jazz. Glen was great on those dates. He had a certain rock solo sound and feel that you could count on.'

As the initial years of the explosion and chart success of the Spector Wall of Sound as exemplified by the Crystals and early Ronettes records of '63/4 passed, the arrangements became more subtle and varied as Phil moved towards tracks like 'Walking In The Rain', 'You've Lost That Lovin' Feelin'' and eventually to 'River Deep Mountain High'. Carol explains some elements of the 'Lovin' Feelin'' session:

'We recorded that live (full band and singers) at Gold Star with lots of spectators and the Righteous Brothers being right there in the main part of the studio. Ray Pohlman played electric bass while I played my usual acoustic guitar (Epiphone Emperor), the guitar that Phil loved. With the echo loud and big in our earphones, we finally gelled with a groove, Earl Palmer on drums, and we knew immediately that this was a big hit. The Righteous Brothers could sing fine gospel style. A ton of slapback echo was put on my rhythm guitar which is a little known ingredient. It's very subtle on the track, but you hear me doubling with Ray on the bassline in the middle part.'

It is evident from some of the session tapes that Spector enjoyed an artistic and productive relationship with Carol, Hal and the other key players. His personal respect for them, and their ideas and abilities, is clear. They in their turn tip their hats to the man who elevated the position of record producer to heights that could scarcely be even guessed at a few years before. Carol Kaye probably talks for all of them as she sums him up:

'Spector had a golden touch with studio techniques, sounds and hit feelings; a true pioneer genius in studio innovations such as baffles, headphones, panning the sounds between tracks, producing ideas etc. Yes, he was a little wild back then, but don't believe his image in that movie – he never was that stiff nor weird looking. He was happy and loose on dates, wore some pretty wild outfits, and would kid constantly... but pretty good to work for, just long dates with only one song per 3-hour date, with the B-side hurriedly cut in the last five minutes or so (jamming was all it was). Jack Nitzsche did some memorable arrangements, some innovative stuff with Spector, but they still needed us to make it happen.'

Indeed they did.

08
A Producer's View Of The Wall Of Sound
by Tony Hatch

Tony Hatch is a hit producer of long standing who has had experience over a period of great expansion of studio techniques and hardware. He has written this assessment of Phil Spector's sixties work especially for this book.

Before the emergence of the Wall of Sound, Phil Spector's productions were great and I had much admiration for him as a record producer. There was, however, no magic ingredient or formula to his Wall of Sound. It was actually a 'cop-out' on his part although, I concede, a 'cop-out' that worked well for him and his artistes.

In the 60s, despite the fast development of multi-track recording, producers would have *all* the musicians and singers in the studio at the same time and the record was made virtually 'live', then mixed after the session. Rhythm section and percussion would be in one corner of the studio under a lower ceiling if possible, drums screened, live grand piano with the lid down as far as possible, guitar amps miked with low screen, no direct injection of instruments to the mixer, solo singer(s) and backing singers in separate vocal booths and strings, brass, woodwind etc, in the 'live' part of the studio as far away as you could get them from the rhythm section. To get a good 'clean' sound one tried to achieve maximum 'separation' meaning that a mic placed on one instrument or group of instruments would pick up as much as possible of the sound that mic was aimed at and as little as possible of the other instruments in the studio. In the first half hour of a session balance engineers would spend a great deal of time adjusting mics and screens in an attempt to achieve 'separation'.

It was always a compromise, however, and the biggest problems were encountered on heavy productions where loud, high frequency sounds such as the top kit of drums and, in particular, tambourines and other loud percussion instruments would be picked up on other mics in the studio. The worst problem of all was the string mics as they needed to be placed fairly high above the violins and violas to get the fullest sound of the string section and therefore picked up a lot of other transient sounds in the studio.

A big test was to have everyone playing but to open only the string mics. Inevitably one would hear the 'spill' of a snare drum, hi-hats, tambourine etc. This meant that in the mix, if you wanted to lift the strings, the drum and percussion sounds would change. I would go to great lengths to reduce this 'spillage' by moving screens, adjusting mics and asking the strings to play with as much weight as possible and asking the drums and percussion to play as lightly as possible but with energy of course – not an easy thing to do for drums and percussion. There would still be some 'spill' on to the string mics but one took that into account and would use it in conjunction with the actual sound.

It is my opinion, having worked in both LA and New York studios and in UK studios during the 60s that the acoustics of UK studios were far better than those in America. Custom built or custom adapted UK studios were generally 'drier' than American studios, which meant that the sound was soaked up more in the area it was made and didn't travel around the studio so easily. Almost all of my Petula Clark tracks (including 'Downtown') were recorded 'live' in the Pye No. 1 Studio, London. The exceptions were 'My Love' and several album tracks (cut in LA) and 'Colour My World' (recorded in New York).

Phil worked in America. It was harder to get good separation there and if one listens analytically to the Wall of Sound one recognises immediately the sound of drums and percussion being picked up on the string mics. Deciding not to fight it he adapted it, almost certainly adding more reverb to the strings and other instruments picking up the drums and percussion. He probably even added reverb to the drums and percussion.

Basically, the Wall of Sound is just inferior studio acoustics, microphone spillage and extra reverb. What every other producer was fighting against he turned into a best-selling sound.

Damn it! I wish I'd thought of it!

09
The View From The Control Room: An Interview
With Mark Wirtz by Kingsley Abbott

For another producer's eye view of Spector and matters arising, Mark Wirtz was an obvious choice. A successful producer in the sixties, Mark has recently re-joined the music business and has attracted much interest from the music press as evidenced by the recent major piece for Mojo *magazine. In this exclusive interview, conducted over lunch in Shepherd's Bush, London, in November 2003, he adds much to our knowledge of Spector's work alongside wider entertaining comment.*

What were the first records that really grabbed you in your youth?
'Rock Around The Clock' was the first one I was exposed to. Great – I loved it! Beyond that I would say 'Diana' by Paul Anka. That blew me away. Also Neil Sedaka's 'Oh Carol' and 'I Go Ape', Bobby Rydell, Ricky Nelson... and early Gene Pitney. Of course Spector produced some of the early Gene Pitney... that's going back a few years when I was aware of some of his productions like 'To Know Him Is To Love Him' without knowing his name.

Can you link those records in any way? What was catching your ear?
In those days I was not actually conscious of the sounds per se. I think I was more drawn into the performance and the material. I did not have any comprehension of the audio production at that stage. When I came to England in 1962, my infatuation with some of those artists continued, but that was the time when Spector was starting to come out with records by the Crystals – his more conspicuous records. That was when I started to become more aware of sounds. I have to say that my influences, with very very few exceptions, all came from America. Even though I was appreciative of many of the British artists, the real sound influences came from the American market.

What was the first record that you really recognised as a Spector record?
The Crystals' 'Then He Kissed Me' – I would say that was the first one that went Bam to me... 'He's A Rebel'... Yes, but it didn't have

the same impact as 'Then He Kissed Me' which I listened to over and over and over and over again! I couldn't get enough of it – I inhaled that thing! It went from there, all the way to 'River Deep Mountain High'. It became more interesting when I found out *how* Spector recorded them, and when I realised the significance of the Gold Star room. It is such a significant part of his recordings, because when you listen to the A&M recordings, even with Larry Levine (the Gold Star engineer) at the board, they still have that Spector sound and the spirit to them, but from an audio point of view it is different. And especially if you listen to Spector's work with George Harrison on *All things Must Pass*, I think he only got the remnants of the Spector sound. It was down to the studio. I'm aware of the technical specifics. As you know I have a number of Spectoresque productions that tried to go for that sound, but even with my different arrangements, I found that there were differences between different studios. In those studios in Bond Street, I got very close! But when I was at Abbey Road, the record that came out of it, Simon & Pi's 'Sha-La-La-Lee', has the Spector kind of flair to it but it isn't really that successful. More successful actually was Tony Summers' 'May Time Stand Still' which again very much has that kind of sound, but it misses and I know why – it was ultimately not possible to make a real Spector record at Abbey Road. I don't know about now, because the technology has changed. Back then it was impossible because of one very fundamental difference. Abbey Road always had their machines lined up for the CCIR curve – I don't want to get too technical, but the CCIR curve, as opposed to the American NAB curve, has a very different frequency spectrum to the NAB curve which was used in America for pop and rock. CCIR is actually the traditional and optimum classical curve. It has a very very high end and a very low end. NAB is narrower and has a more rich and thicker punch, and at its high end it's not all up in the air, but has a crisper top end. In those days when Spector and I worked, we did a lot of overdubbing, and going from generation to generation. Each time you do that there's a natural harmonic distortion that happens, and a natural compression that the magnetic tape does to itself. There is an uncontrollable compression process, which translates into slightly different sounds, and this was *extremely* important for Spector because it created increasing harmonics and drones that were not intended, and they were all part of it, and he recognised it. I have my own thought about originality: I believe that popular originality can be nothing but successfully failed emulation. In other words that, in the process of trying to copy something, there are accidents that make it come out different and original. And it works. [Editor's note: the famed 'far away' guitar sound on 'Zip-A-Dee-Doo-Dah' would be a prime example of this.] There's a feeling. Some people wouldn't know what to do with it. Some would not immediately identify with it, because it is alien. Like with a snake, that is alien to us: the more something is alien to us, the less we can comfortably interact with it. To me some of the most original music that's been made, by design or accident, has been in jazz. But how many people can actually relate to it? There is a cultural root to it that is either embraceable or that can be downright repelling.

What special elements at Gold Star do you therefore think were so important to Spector's sound?
First of all it was the room itself. The physical room itself had its own distinctive character. Listen closely to 'Rhythm Of The Rain' by the Cascades, a record that had nothing at all to do with Phil Spector apart from maybe Larry Levine, and you'll hear that it has absolutely and recognisably some of the same room characteristics. Phil, who was a competent musician, didn't overdub so much. He had wall-to-wall musicians there, and all the microphones were subject to leakage all the time. That leakage created a sort of, how can I put it, amalgamation. It all worked together because they couldn't physically separate them all from one another. Phil would go for three pianos with the sound going all round the room. One of the most fascinating things about analysing Spector records is how few gimmicks he used. Some of these things have virtually no contrived echo at all – it's just a natural resonance.

That's one of the things I find so interesting – there was echo on the drums, and maybe on the voice, but the rest was often quite dry.
Absolutely. In fact if you listen to some of the vocals, some of them are dry. Except they had just a little bit of compressed echo return. The voice is dry, but there is a little bit of delay or repeat that comes at you a little bit. It's like the difference between mixing the artist with echo, which became a very popular way of recording that I always hated, and having the artist right here with a level of phase around that gives a level of three-dimensionality. Interestingly to try to duplicate Spector's sound, you have to use contrived echo! You

have to use all sorts of contrived things to try to duplicate the natural acoustics of that Gold Star room.

How do natural acoustics arise and differ?
If you take any room in your own environment you'll find it has a certain resonance, determined by whether it has wallpaper or bare walls for example. That's why control rooms are so difficult to furbish and create a sound from the monitor speakers that is actually true. Each room has its resonance, so you need to listen to see if you are hearing echo or the natural room resonance. You see, we often mistakenly assume with artists, not just Phil Spector, that these people went in there planning to do this or that. We have the idea that Spector had a Wagnerian statement in mind – you know, let's shake the world – but things just emerged. It may not have been planned, it just emerged.

Did you ever visit Gold Star?
Oh absolutely. It was maybe twice the size of this room (we were in a wine bar approx 7m by 5m), or I may be wrong... it wasn't a whole lot bigger than this. Western was much bigger. There certainly wasn't much room to walk through. Incidentally, Sonny Bono, who worked for Spector pretty much as a gofer, cut records later at Gold Star that were almost identical to Spector's sound.

He would have been able to duplicate how the mics and the baffles were set up.
Yes, but that was Larry Levine. Believe me, Phil Spector was not very technologically minded. He owed a debt to Larry – Phil was the entrepreneur. He had a good basic musical ability, and he could play an instrument. He had a good sense of melody and all that, but he was a Barnam & Bailey. It was his spirit, his concepts – he got other people to come in. You know, Larry Levine was like a technical version of Hal Blaine on drums. And let's not forget Jack Nitzsche who was very very instrumental for what is commonly thought of as the Spector Sound. Without Jack's ideas it wouldn't have been the same.

Jack's ideas – any that you specifically mean?
Well, remember the earlier work with people like Gene Pitney. Trying to get that echo sound, using boom mikes rather than close ones. Listen to that and listen to the Jack work with Spector and

there's the answer. Take Pitney's 'Every Breath I Take' and put it next to one of the Crystals' records.

I'll tell you something else interesting about Spector's work. Phil Chapman – I don't know anyone else in the world who can actually emulate the Phil Spector sound like him. He has almost dedicated his life to re-making it! That's why I work with him, because of my own admiration for Phil. Phil Spector's records were sexy, but they didn't have much viscera – they didn't have much charm. With 'Lovin' Feelin'', had it not been for the inherent sensitivity in the Righteous Brothers' voices – a lot of emotion, a lot of heart – that record was rich but it would have lacked a little bit of heart. You see, I myself come from a psychologically curious point of view, rather than trying to be mechanically objective. My biggest interest is to look behind the things emotionally and ask 'What's the motivation?' What made him (Phil) want to do this? And then I ask how successful was he, and how much of a reflection of his actual inner self is that work? I don't so much care if he used 10 degrees of this and 20 degrees of that. Though when I first met him I asked him, 'Phil, what kind of compressors do you use?' And he said, 'I don't know, ask Larry.' Phil didn't care, and when you see Phil produce he may just be walking around saying, 'More echo, more echo, more echo!' He'd walk around, make his comments, get excited, get his gun out and shoot up the ceiling. But he has a wonderful talent to work with artists – he gets a performance out of artists that can be unique!

He certainly did with Tina Turner...
Yes, but that's like an actor doing thirty takes on a scene – it's part of the package. It's like you and I as writers, tearing the paper up thirty times and re-writing it. Truman Capote could take three or four days on one word! The same with my productions – I may take a little bit longer along the way, but in the end it is probably as quick as anybody. Following that train of thought, Spector and Larry had to start contriving, more or less copying themselves on what before had evolved naturally. At A&M they would have used different Scully tape machines that inherently had their own sound. Annoyingly to me at that time, Scully in those days had an automatic auto-limiting feature – whether you liked it or not it was going to limit itself. Which was okay for a lot of engineers and producers, but for me it handicapped the freedom of the sound. It maximised the signal, and you could go hotter than normal because of the dynamic range, but I

don't like a machine to tell me what I can or I can't do. By the way, when I recorded at Oriole Studios, they had the NAB curve, and so did Olympic – they were so much more American sounding. They sounded so much better than Abbey Road.

Abbey Road were much bigger rooms?
Well, let's see... Abbey Road 3 was a small room, Abbey Road 2 was fairly large, and Abbey Road 1 is huge. All of us hated working there – we made the best out of a bad situation, but we couldn't go anywhere else because our contracts said it had to be Abbey Road. So we started inventing all these things and ways to make it sound more interesting. You know, Paul and John used to walk into the studio with a stack of 45s like Fats Domino piano stuff and say they wanted that sound! I had all these ideas and visions, but we never got it. But it did come out as something original, like the successfully failed emulation again. We all tried to get the Motown drum sound for instance, and we came up with something that was actually nothing like it, but it started to become what is now famously the Abbey Road sound!

It's been written that Gold Star was specifically set up for a Rock'n'Roll sound, with the famed echo chamber.
Absolutely, but remember that as soon as you build or set up a room, whether you like it or not, you are going to have an audio characteristic in it. You don't decide it, it just is; but you can adjust it. You can change around the buffers, and use certain devices that will cause a difference in reflection. Screens or whatever. You could be in India or somewhere, and if they happened to have the right materials, you could re-create Abbey Road 2 in India! And now, you can even do it in your living room! You could have a cathedral, and locate exactly where you are in that cathedral with sound reflection. Remarkable!

Yes, and with some of those big sounds, you get a physical reaction in the pit of your stomach...
I agree. It's very sensual. Spector's records were very sensual. Imagine all those big sounds bouncing off and coming back with a delay, and then with more of a delay when they come back again... enormous! It gets me excited just to think about it! The sound waves become like laser beams, and you can almost touch them. But remember that some of the most significant things in any artistic

creation are in the form of an accident. The artist or producer has to be attuned or open-minded enough to recognise the power of what has happened. Even when I have my sort of architectural design with me in the studio, my ears are always open to hear something and say, 'Oh, hold it, I want it!' One of my recordings was my Spectoresque version of 'I Can Hear Music', the trumpeter actually fluffed one note, but the take was actually such a good take that I said, 'Fuck it, I'll take it!' And even today you can hear him go wrong, but I don't care. That's real life.

The imperfections make it, like the grain of sand that makes the oyster...
Yes – we get infatuated with and fall in love with the imperfections. With Spector, you don't get perfection, you don't get a technician, you don't get an engineer or a mechanic – you get a spirit. You get the entrepreneur. You get the gift of someone, who when he's in the right place, to walk into a room and change that room. Just by walking in. It's metaphysical. There's a vibe... an energy. It's coming from God knows where. If you want Spector... leave him alone. Let him do what he does best... let him be Spector. It is not just a little bit of Spector, which is what in the end Starsailor did. That's terrible. It's like if you get Picasso to do a portrait of you, you don't send him packing for doing three noses!

The Starsailor material was, to my ears, weaker in the first place.
It was a kind of almost nursery rhyme material that did intrigue him. I mean, if you look at the material for some of the Ronettes records it was just three or four notes, but what made the Starsailor thing fall apart was that it didn't go anywhere. It started, went on and ended somewhere along the line, and what should have been a very hypnotic, emotional, escalating bombardment experience turned into a boring record. It starts off great, and builds a little bit. But it builds sideways. It doesn't rise. It would have if they'd just let it be. The whole thing was explained to me when they credited him as 'Echo Boy' – that's not what Spector is about. It's like saying Chagall is just 'Blue Pastel'. They failed to really understand. If you admire someone from afar, who cares why you admire them. You just admire them. But the moment you enter into any kind of integration with that person, it stops. Like some other stars – Dolly Parton isn't just tits!

Which would you say were the key Spector moments of recorded sound?
'Lovin' Feelin'' and 'River Deep Mountain High'. Without a doubt.

Because they took the sound further?
I think it's humanity. Before he did them, he did the overall excitement. He got into new dramatic territory... with both records. There's an *emotional* power there that is extraordinary. The fact that 'River Deep Mountain High' comparatively bombed in America; I don't think it was the record. It was because by that time he was so hated. In the industry, when you're on the way up, everybody's nice and friendly, but the moment you reach the top... some of the same people that helped you up are going to try and shoot you down. The moment that happens, all your enemies are going to come out of the woodwork. I'm so glad to have this conversation... I can't have a conversation like this very often! Phil Spector, as much as he is historically known, loved and admired, leaving aside the recent happenings, there are very few people I've met who really understand how he is. He's a magician. But once we know how the trick is done, it's not magic anymore. His fellow musicians might know how the trick is done, but then they have to trade off their own awe of the magic.

From a producer's perspective, where do you think Phil Spector affected people most?
I think that everyone was affected by it, subconsciously or consciously. It wasn't just the people who tried to make Spector-type records. They absorbed all the elements, even in terms of songwriting. There were so many elements of Spector that were revolutionary and affected everything. Like how Edison invented the light bulb, and it had an effect on everything, Spector affected pop music. More so than some people realise. No one had such an impact on popular music.

Was it in terms of 'fullness' of sound, or combinations of instruments?
First of all I think that Phil broke barriers. In other words, he set an example of how you can dare to take risks and be non-conformist. Without that, I don't think that the Beatles would have been possible. I went totally against the grain and convention, because I thought this is what I feel and it's going to be great. That's what Phil did. He had this vision, and he said 'I believe in it.' He created a feeling

of strength and spirit. Across the board. Like how the electric guitar shaped the direction of the music industry.

Can you pinpoint any other producer's work that has taken any Spector moments or ideas further?
I think Burt Bacharach did. Bacharach had a unique way of structuring a melody, almost akin to jazz, but not quite. As a music producer, he made an across the board difference. There was that courage – he didn't give a shit if people believed it. If he liked it, that was enough. It would have been interesting to have Spector and Bacharach work together, but they never did. And of course, obviously the Beatles; but there it's difficult to bring it down to just one person. It certainly wasn't George Martin. George Martin was an incredible diplomat, and a guardian, but he certainly wasn't a Phil Spector. George was a wonderful comic producer of some wonderfully eccentric people, like Peter Sellers. In another life George Martin would have become a politician. He would have been very comfortable there, but he was not a Phil, or a Tony Hatch, or a Les Reed, or others I could mention. But perhaps no one else could have had the ability to deal with the mixture of power that came with the Beatles. A lot of people have tried to make records like Spector did, but they haven't been so successful, and in the end it's the entertainment business. You succeed the most when you reach the most amount of people. Especially if you've touched them… I was successful within my own terms with some records that maybe four or five people heard, but in the entertainment business they were failures. My circus didn't have enough people in it – my lions roared for nothing! I wanted my circus to have more people in it, but some folk can feel successful without needing the applause.

Spector needed the applause... wanted to be noticed...
Absolutely, and it hurt him deeply when the applause left off. You know, his work with the Beatles was no longer Spector as you remember him, but it was an avenue to getting a lot of applause, and once again having a validity and meaning. I don't think that John Lennon needed Phil Spector to produce him. I really don't – no way. However, Spector was part of it... When he made his legendary records which were frankly quite gimmick free, it is interesting that later, when he started working with the Beatles and Lennon especially, he now used the gimmick like the old Sun Studios of tape

delay repeat echo. It was then that he did become 'Echo Boy' in a sense, something he didn't do in his legendary time.

But that would probably have been Lennon's starting point – he used to bring the pile of old singles into the studio to try to get that sound...
Absolutely... and let's face it, the Beatles used all kinds of effects, but it was never to the point where the voice would distort. Back when Elvis and Johnny Cash were at Sun Studios that is all they had – they would have loved to have had a Chamber No. 2! I don't actually think that the work with Lennon was actually the most attractive. It's not something that I have been eager to duplicate on record, because I thought it was kind of 'boxy'. I honestly don't think that the work that Spector did with John Lennon was good because of any of the sound elements that Spector brought to them – I think it was in spite of them. I would have been very happy to hear 'Imagine' recorded the way George Martin and Geoff Emerick would have recorded it. It would have meant just as much to me. However, that was part of the moment, part of the record, and that is how we've learnt to love it and treasure it – now we wouldn't want to hear it any other way.

How do you rate the George Harrison work?
I think that collaboration was really good. It was a hybrid. I loved *All Things Must Pass*. It was just wonderful, and it really didn't matter that it wasn't like the original legendary Spector sound – it had a lot of echo on it, and that's about it. It didn't matter, because whatever happened, that's what happened at Abbey Road. Whatever happened at Gold Star with Larry Levine, that's what happened then... The George Harrison collaboration was more *musical* to my ears than even the Lennon collaboration. I think Lennon and Spector clicked because they were both rebels, and I think Spector liked having that little part of that success because it gave him contemporary validity and credibility, because unfortunately after Tina Turner... let's face it... 'Black Pearl' and the Dion thing... his hardcore fans were more into what he did in between than the general public. The moment he teamed up with the Beatles, or Lennon and Harrison specifically because McCartney and he never were big buddies, he was back. The fact that Alan Klein was involved certainly didn't help matters. Remember that Spector had his Alan Klein connection. What happens on the canvas is very much related to what happens away from the canvas! Linda's arrival in Paul's life re-shaped his music,

and now that Heather's there it's again changed quite a bit. To our benefit, because Paul's out there kicking arse again. I don't think that Linda was as much a catalyst of that as Heather is.

Have you heard the de-Spectorised Let It Be*?*
I resent it. Absolutely. I think it's a sacrilege. I think it's disgusting. If Paul McCartney would have done this on his own album I think it would be wonderful. For years he went on stage, and had all the orchestrations right there. After John and George had died, and no longer had a say in the matter… especially as those two had a close relationship (with Phil).

Apparently George agreed to it… it was already in process before he died…
Okay, so George agreed to it. But I think it's very much like putting the baby back in the womb. I'm not trying to be judgemental here... I'm opinionated... this is just my own opinion. There's got to be a point where you stop. We never reach the ultimate goal with our artwork – we never do – we always find things wrong with it. Next time I'd do this better or that… it's part of the process. You don't put the baby back in the womb and say let's see if we can re-build it... all of it or something. There must be a finality. When you're creating, there must come a time when you say enough... enough already! You've got to let go. It's my own opinion, but to me it offends my sensibilities.

It sounds like it had niggled away at Paul for years and years though…
The whole project was a mess from the very beginning. George Martin and Geoff Emerick started it and then they stepped aside. I was working with Geoff at the time, and he was unbearable on those days when he came back from working at Twickenham or wherever it was when they were trying to record some of those tracks. He was just a mess. He was so calm and mellow usually. In the end he just didn't want to do it anymore. I think Glyn Johns got involved, and it went from there. Remember, 'Let It Be' the single came out as a George Martin/Geoff Emerick single long before the album came out [Editor's note: actually two months, two days before. For a complete overview of the Spector/*Let It Be* story refer to *The Complete Beatles Chronicle* by Mark Lewisohn – Chancellor Press]. Basically the *Let It Be* album was a political contract thing. And I don't recall *Abbey Road* as being naked, and Paul did practically all

that end section... and *Ram* was very orchestrated as well. 'Long And Winding Road' was really the catalyst of this whole thing, because Paul was even happy about Phil Spector's airbrushing of the thing. It's all been bootlegged anyway – there have been naked *Let It Be* versions for years and years. I mean... is Leonardo da Vinci going to scratch some paint off the Mona Lisa because he thinks that the sketch underneath is better?? Oh please, where would it end?

You have been in the studio with Spector.
As a guest – I haven't worked with him. I was around for George Harrison's *All Things Must Pass* because I was working at EMI. I was there at A&M studios in Los Angeles when he was working on the Dion album, and he was also doing something with the girls – a fantastic record – Jerri Bo Keno maybe. Nino Tempo was the arranger – charming man by the way, charming and very talented – Nino was one of the people who made records like Spector. (We both then enthuse about Nino's 'Boy's Town' record.)

Paint me a picture of what it was like in the studio.
When I was there, he was not sitting next to Larry Levine. He was basically moving around, sort of pacing. There were times when he was totally oblivious to us. He was somewhere else. When I was there others were there too, not millions but some that you would recognise. You remember the *Munsters* TV show – the granddad – well he was there. I guess he was a big buddy of Phil's. Maybe a handful of people. When you thought that maybe he wasn't listening, he might suddenly explode into a negative reaction, or a positive one. Sometimes he would be very animated, sometimes withdrawn. There was not a defined work process there, because some of it was so random and some experimental. Some of it worked, some of it didn't work. For instance, there are two versions of 'Isn't It A Pity', because there's the George Martin version and the Phil Spector version. That I think illustrates how they were trying to feel their way. It was a selection process, so the whole of George's album wasn't masterminded as such by Spector per se, but was a collaboration of different elements. Mind you he did have Jim Gordon, an American drummer, there, and Sneaky Pete who did some wonderful slide things. George was infatuated with that sound. I think it was a very successful collaboration, but George was the source of it with all the ingredients, and Spector cooked them. Whereas, with his own things,

Spector was also the source. That's the difference. I don't know now what's going to happen. Maybe Spector's going to be put away and never make another record. I hope to God that doesn't happen. I hope that Phil, motivated by what happened with Starsailor, will say 'Damn it, I'm gonna show you guys...' and go out there under his *own* motivation and direction and give us another Spector record. It would be such a tragic thing if he were to exit with Starsailor. By the way I like that band very much. I think they're great; it was just not a very good match.

Comparing producers back in the sixties, we know Brian Wilson took a lot from Spector, but also over here there was Joe Meek... do you have any thoughts about those two?
I've always thought of Joe Meek as an original. He was very very dedicated to creating sounds, at times when Spector wasn't really involved yet. Joe was a real pioneer, technologically more so than Spector, or any of us! He altered the landscape in England for us. But I'm not sure why we are comparing Joe Meek with Spector...

Because there were a few tracks where he was very definitely having a go at copying the Spector sound, and also the way that he would put a really big sound behind certain girl singers like Glenda Collins.
Ah yes, I guess you're right then. Brian Wilson, by his own admission, was a great admirer of Spector. I don't think he intentionally *copied* him. I don't think I did intentionally... well, yes, every now and then I did. Contemporaries do have admirations for each other. You inspire one another – like Brian Wilson and the Beatles. I don't know if Spector was influenced at all by Joe Meek... I doubt he heard Joe's stuff.

'Telstar' crossed over to the States as a big hit, but virtually nothing else.
Joe Meek went for this very ethereal thing, whereas Spector went for something much more basic and gutsy; almost primal. Spector's music was very very primal, and impressionistic. And of course he had the Wagner thing. Spector was absolutely obsessed with Wagner. Brian was coming from the Four Freshmen! Brian used Phil's thinking, the space, but he didn't try to copy the Gold Star sound.

What do you mean by Phil's thinking of space?
Phil created a spatial thing in records that was revolutionary. By the placing of the instruments, the wall of sound had a dimension

to it that was vast. Wall-to-wall. I work in depth, but Phil had this huge sound that came out of a vast sphere. I go for a 3D perspective where I place things almost like on stage with some instruments behind others and I try to put the listener *amongst* it. Phil had more of a sound, and I don't want to call it two-dimensional because that would sound like a putdown, where the listener was *in front* of it all, at a distance, so that they were almost seeing it on a huge screen. Like a city panorama. The thing I have in common with Spector is that I like to have my artist in the living room. In other words he would have Ronnie Spector right out in front of the Wall of Sound, almost astride it.

It's like Christianity, which had an impact even to non-believers. Some of it seeped in. Now, I'm not saying that Phil was like Jesus, God forbid, but every now and then something comes along that has an impact, something that resonates forever.

Yes, he had impact in direct ways, and also in smaller almost subliminal ways, like the way Motown would aim to fill the gaps with percussion, and later with Curt Boettcher's productions with the Millennium.

Yes, with Motown they would put it on there and make it loud. That was breaking the rules (like Phil). Some of the stuff was technically so distorted, but people said 'if it sounds good, let's do it!' That got me so excited. The Motown bass was *so* revolutionary in terms of conventional bass playing structures. Paul McCartney carried that on a little bit, using different roots and chords. So did Brian Wilson. Even to non-musical people, there is an energy and excitement there that comes across, and you don't even know why. (There followed a discussion of the various ways that music works on and with the emotions, and how it can evoke chemical changes in the body.)

Phil Spector had found a way to present chaos in an absolutely seductive way. That's what his records are – chaos, but put in a frame in such a way that it is not repulsive to us, or even confusing – well maybe a little bit – it's like being on the freeway and seeing an auto accident. You don't want to watch, but you do because it is morbidly fascinating. We hate it, but we can't look away. In a positive way, Spector showed us and gave us this very very graphic potential portrait of fear and we're fascinated by it. We identify with it, and on the whole art succeeds when the beholder identifies with it. You feel safe with it. Remember that those (Spector) songs were very simple melodies, very simple messages, instant explanation, instant identification. No matter who they were, they were us, in that raw emotion. I don't think that Phil Spector himself was really aware, as most artists are, of what he was accomplishing. Like in war, when heroes don't realise they are heroes until afterwards when people tell them. When you are that compelled to do what you do, you don't have time to think about what you are achieving. You just go. Spector had this vision, but it was abstract to him still, and he went in there and just did it.

What would be the best thing for him to do now, if he was able to get into a studio with whatever musicians and singers he likes at his command? First of all, he'd have to find a team-mate, like a Larry Levine, who really understands him. He needs a cameraman who really understands him and can deal with Spector the person in a very emotional collaboration process. He has to then do what he's always done, because the temporary part of it will happen automatically – it will evolve. Frankly, you know who I think he should work with, the one person in the world? Phil Chapman. He could trust him. Artist-wise, there is a certain kind of artist that Spector responds to. Reflective. He could almost pick someone off the street; in fact I think it would be better. Spector would be the judge. He would hear something, and it wouldn't matter if they had never had a record deal or whatever, as long as they had that quality and that projection. There's no way that Spector would go wrong. He could be trusted 1000% to pick the right person. Because, frankly, in the end, Spector's the artist. It revolves around Spector, even though the artist has to be top class, as all the musicians. The absolutely key thing is that Spector is allowed to be Spector... This has been the underlying theme of this whole conversation – it's about Spector the spirit.

10
Phil Spector Soundalikes by Mick Patrick

Many producers, both in the sixties and over the years since them, have drawn from Spector's Wall of Sound. Varying from straight down the line re-creations to subtler variations of the themes, a great many of these records were wonderful in their own right. Mick Patrick, well known in collectors circles as a CD compiler of taste and expertise and the publisher of the famed Philately *and* That Will Never Happen Again *fanzines, has been responsible for the critically acclaimed Ace 2003 issue* Phil's Spectre – A Wall Of Soundalikes *(Ace CDCHD 978) which is likely to be an essential purchase for any readers of this book. For this piece Mick offers a further selection of soundalikes to whet our appetites, several of which appear on the second volume of* Phil's Spectre.

Reparata and the Delrons – 'I'm Nobody's Baby Now' (RCA 47-8820)
The lovely Reparata herself rates 1966's 'I'm Nobody's Baby Now' as the best record she and the Delrons ever made. Jeff Barry wrote the song, which sounds as if it might have been intended for the Shangri-Las, or even the Ronettes themselves. Indeed, the end result, with its huge production and anguished mid-song recitation, sounds like a mash-up of those two groups – a mix made in girl group heaven. Almost as good: Reparata and the Delrons' 'I Can Hear The Rain' (also RCA).

The Shangri-Las – 'Paradise' (Red Bird 10-068)
Talking of the Ronettes and the Shangri-Las in the same breath... Although the Ronettes' Spector-produced original of 'Paradise' remained officially unreleased until the 1970s, test pressings were in limited circulation. Chances are that one of those illicit white label discs found its way over to the offices of Red Bird Records in the Brill Building, as the Shangri-Las' 1966 version of the song seems to be a carbon copy. Also recommended: 'The Dum Dum Ditty' from *Shangri-Las '65!* LP (also Red Bird).

The Castells – 'I Do' (Warner Bros 5421)

Brian Wilson famously took his hero-worship of Phil Spector to the point of near-obsession, giving vent to his admiration with many of his non-Beach Boys productions, a prime example being 'I Do' by the Castells from 1964. Same backing track: the Beach Boys' version of 'I Do' (Capitol CD).

The Four Tops – 'Wonderful Baby' (Motown 1124)

The Four Tops' 'Wonderful Baby' can be found on the B-side of their 1968 hit 'If I Were A Carpenter' or on the previous year's *Reach Out* LP. Phil Spector, a fan of the group, was known to wax lyrical about Levi Stubbs' voice. Indeed, 'Baby I Need Your Lovin'' is said to have inspired 'You've Lost That Lovin' Feelin''. Here, with help from writer-producer Smokey Robinson and a barrage of castanets, the compliment is returned. Suggested further listening: Barbara McNair's Spectorian opus 'You're Gonna Love My Baby' (Motown).

The Knickerbockers – 'Wishful Thinking' (Challenge 59366)

Wrecking Crew member Leon Russell, who played keyboards on many Spector sessions, arranged the Knickerbockers' 'Wishful Thinking', a track found on their *Lies* LP of 1966 and subsequently released as a single. Their drummer, Jimmy Walker, supplied the Righteous Brothers-style lead vocals. Later, when Bill Medley went solo, it was Walker whom Bobby Hatfield enlisted to briefly reconstitute the Righteous Brothers. Not to be missed either: the Knickerbockers' 'Turn To Me' (also Challenge).

Johnny Caswell – 'My Girl' (Smash 1879)

It's ironic that one of the most blatant Ronettes soundalikes should be by a male performer. 'My Girl' by Johnny Caswell from 1964 was masterminded by Madara and White, the Philadelphia-based duo behind great records by the Pixies Three, the Secrets and many others. While Johnny Caswell's other records are good, they're all without Spector quotient. Another from the 'male Ronettes' genre: 'I Adore You' by Tommy Regan (World Artists).

Maureen Gray – 'Goodbye Baby' (Mercury 72227)

Maureen Gray once complained to me that Ronnie Ronette stole her style. Unlikely, sure, but Maureen had great pipes, and made plenty of good records to prove it. She was also the regular demo singer for John Madara and David White. On her 1964 single 'Goodbye Baby' (Mercury 72227), the pair used Darlene Love's 'Christmas (Baby Please Come Home)' as a template. If you like this, you'll also enjoy Joey Heatherton's 'Live And Learn' (Decca), another Spectoresque treasure from the same producers.

The Cinderellas – 'Baby, Baby (I Still Love You)' (Dimension 1026)

The Cinderellas were actually the Cookies, of 'Chains' fame. Russ Titelman, who co-wrote the group's 1964 single 'Baby, Baby (I Still Love You)' with Cynthia Weil and shared producer credit with that lady's husband Barry Mann, was a friend and colleague of Phil Spector from the Spectors 3 period. Also recommended: almost any other record from this era bearing Titelman's name, including this track's B-side 'Please Don't Wake Me'.

Roberta Day – 'Someday' (United Artists 792)

Real name Roberta Silvanoff, the jewel in the crown in the recording career of Roberta Day was 'Someday', released in 1964. Talk about little symphonies for the kids! The wonderful Spectoresque arrangement is courtesy of Alan Lorber. Recommended further listening: 'Your Baby Doesn't Love You Anymore' by Ruby and the Romantics (Kapp), also arranged by Alan Lorber.

The Girlfriends – 'My One And Only Jimmy Boy' (Colpix 712)

The Girlfriends' 'My One And Only Jimmy Boy' from 1963 was written and produced by David Gates, one of the most prolific Spector pretenders. The group comprised Gloria Goodson, Nanette Jackson and Carolyn Willis, three primo Los Angeles session singers. Further top-of-the-range Gates-produced Spector soundalikes include 'A Girl Never Knows' by Connie Stevens (Warner Brothers) and 'Be My Man' by Suzy Wallis (RCA).

The Righteous Brothers – 'Night Owl' (Moonglow MLP 1002)

'Night Owl' from the Righteous Brothers' 1964 LP *Some Blue Eyed Soul* illustrates that the duo had dabbled with the Spector sound before ever signing with his Philles label. On LP-only in the USA, the track was released as a 45 in the UK in the wake of 'You've Lost That Lovin' Feelin''. Same Bill Medley-produced backing track:

'Night Owl' by the Clouds (Medley).

Clydie King – 'The Thrill Is Gone' (Imperial 66109)

Jerry Riopelle, famed for producing Bonnie and the Treasures' 'Home Of The Brave' on the Philles satellite Phi-Dan, manned the controls on Clydie King's 1965 offering 'The Thrill Is Gone'. Clearly, Riopelle learned a lot working under the wing of Spector. Other recommended sides by Clydie King: 'If You Were A Man', 'Missin' My Baby', 'My Love Grows Deeper', 'He Always Comes Back To Me' and 'Soft And Gentle Ways' (all also on Imperial).

The Kit Kats – 'That's The Way' (Jamie 1321)

For those who like their Wall of Sound served with a little folk rock on the side, a la Sonny and Cher or the Turtles, few recordings fit the bill better than 'That's The Way' by Philadelphia's Kit Kats from 1966. This track was released on a single three times: collect the set, why not? Nearly as good: the Kit Kats' 'Let's Get Lost On A Country Road' (also Jamie).

The Bonnets – 'Ya Gotta Take A Chance' (Unical 3010)

The Beehive & Mascara award for most authentic Ronettes wannabes goes to 1963's 'Ya Gotta Take A Chance' by the hideously obscure Bonnets. A photo of this group has yet to surface, but what's the betting that they looked as much like Ronnie and the girls as they sounded? Among the other nominees: Spongy and the Dolls with 'It Looks Like Love' (Bridgeview).

Josephine Sunday – 'You Won't Even Know Her Name' (Tower 184)

Never mind soundalikes, if there were a prize for the best Ronnie Ronette lookalike, Josephine Sunday would be one of the favourites to win it. Alas, this writer can't provide a photo to prove it. Waddya know, she made a record that fits the bill too; 'You Won't Even Know Her Name', released in 1965. Likely runners-up: the Dolls, purveyors of 'And That Reminds Me' (Toy/Loma).

The Sweet Things – 'You're My Loving Baby' (Date 2-1504)

Previously known as Mira label recording act the Darlettes, this group were protégées of the great Van McCoy, producer of their 1965 release 'You're My Loving Baby'. If Phil Spector had produced the Royalettes, it might've sounded like this. Soon afterwards, lead singer Francine Hurd left the group to form a duo with Herb Fame. Their name? Peaches and Herb. Another Spectorised girl group record produced by Van McCoy: 'Gee What A Guy' by the modestly named Fantastic Vantastics (Tuff).

Big Dee Irwin and Little Eva – 'Swinging On A Star' (Dimension 1010)
Bob B. Soxx and the Blue Jeans' 'Zip-A-Dee Doo-Dah' was one of Spector's most imitated recordings, and 'Swinging On A Star' revamped by Big Dee Irwin and Little Eva in 1963 is one of the best-known examples. In a similar vein: 'How Much Is That Doggie In The Window' by Baby Jane and the Rockabyes (United Artists) and 'Peter Cottontail' by the Taffys (Pageant).

Kane and Abel – 'Break Down And Cry' (Destination 607)
1965's 'Break Down And Cry' by Kane and Abel sounds uncannily like the Righteous Brothers, yet was put together on a shoestring budget in a small Chicago studio. The vocalists, in reality Little Artie Herrera and his brother Big Al, later enjoyed some success as members of the Mob. Same backing-track, but different lyrics: Kane and Abel's 'He Will Break Your Heart' (Red Bird).

Alder Ray – ''Cause I Love Him' (Liberty 55715)
Is it Darlene Love or is it Memorex? No, it's Alder Ray of the Delicates with ''Cause I Love Him' from 1964. The track was produced by ex-Teddy Bear, Marshall Leib, proving once again that, frequently, the best Spector soundalikes were those created by his closest peers. Other recommended Darlene-alikes: the other side, 'A Little Love (Will Go A Long Way)', and Nikki Blu's '(Whoa, Whoa) I Love Him So' (Parkway).

Jerry Ganey – 'Who Am I' (Verve 10454)
Last, but certainly not least, another stupendous blue-eyed soul epic produced by Bill Medley, 'Who Am I' released in 1966 by Jerry Ganey, former member of the aforementioned Clouds. Take a bow also, arranger-conductor Bill Baker. Equally good, if not even better: the other side, 'Just A Fool'.

11
Quotes 1

These quotes, and those elsewhere, have been collected from a variety of sources...

What did I learn from watching Phil Spector? Well, I saw how when you combined instruments, like a piano and a guitar, you got a new sound. Phil also used echo, and since then I've always loved echo, to make the sounds 'swim'. Most of all, I understood the difference between writing a song and producing a record. To make a great record, it definitely helps to start with a great song, but as I saw and heard at those Gold Star sessions, a record has to be a total sound experience for the listener. So the idea became, for me at least, to try to make the listener feel the way I did when I first wrote the song. To do that, I realised I would have to produce our records... in the end, only you – the producer – can really know when it's right.
Brian Wilson

I learned a lot from Phil Spector. I was around him in the very early days when he was doing the Paris Sisters – I played guitar and sang on their records – but before that his group the Teddy Bears used to rehearse in my living room. I was then actually in another group that he put together, called the Spectors Three, and we made a couple of records, so I got to see firsthand how Phil did it on a small scale before the big stuff happened. When the big tome came around I went to some of those sessions and I played guitar on the Righteous Brothers' 'Hung On You'. I was also there when he was putting the choir on 'For Once In My Life', and he said, 'Go out and conduct the choir,' so I did – I didn't really know what I was doing but I waved my arms around!
Russ Titelman, songwriter/producer

I'll always make a good record, and it'll be better than all that shit out there today. 'Cause they really don't know how to record. They don't know anything about depth, about sound, about technique, about slowing down. One company does know something – that's Motown.

They know how to master a record. You put on a Motown record, and it jumps at you.
Phil Spector, 1969

There's the Phil Spector type (of producer), where the whole thing is conceived in his brain. Every atom, every little platelet is provisioned by him, including the role of the artist; that would be your songwriter/musician/engineer. [Describing three different types of producer, the others being one who aims to re-produce what they have heard in live performance, and one who sets out to serve the artist (including John Hammond and the Erteguns).]
Jerry Wexler, Atlantic Records

Phil is utterly peculiar – he always was – but as a producer he was inspired. In the room at Gold Star he'd have, like, four rhythm guitars, two basses, a drummer, two percussionists, a horn section, and two pianos, so the place was full of musicians just slamming away, and that sound of his was there in the room. It was incredible. And then he'd go and lay strings on, the voice and all that stuff, but the basic thing was all these guys in a room that wasn't too big, together with his use of echo. Being there I got to see his style and how he related to musicians. I'd see him work parts out, and I became so aware of how each musician, each component, fits together. At the time I was just a teenager, but I was a witness to how some great records were made… It certainly was an interesting way to start a career, hanging around with a guy like that!
Russ Titelman, songwriter/producer

I remember sitting in Studio A at United Recorders and watching Phil Spector producing Ike & Tina Turner's 'A Love Like Yours' and 'Save The Last Dance For Me'. Phil's usual engineer, Larry Levine, didn't know the room, and so they decided to get me in... I remember we took the echo send, delayed it through a tape machine, and then sent it to an acoustic chamber. So, it was tape delay, but not the kind of tape delay that you had on the teeny-bop records where you had the straight forward echo effect of the voice repeating and so on. In this case you had the live sound going to the chamber and you had delayed sound going to the chamber at the same time, and the result was that it repeated in the chamber so that when it came back it was just a big blur. I always said that it sounded like Philip recorded those

tracks in the bottom of an empty swimming pool! He'd have the band play the chart over and over and over again, like a tape loop. The minute they reached the end they'd play it again, and he would go out and change people's parts. It was a great lesson in that kind of hands-on production. It would sometimes only be zillionths of an inch of change to make the difference Phil wanted, but he knew when it all fell into place. The amazing thing about it was, when that happened, it did have an incredible sound, but I'm not sure that some of it wasn't just down to the musicians getting beat by playing it over and over again, so that the sound began to all melt together.
Bones Howe, West Coast engineer/producer

Phil had the magic wand and sprinkled fairy dust on us all.
Hal Blaine

Phil had a way of holding me back while the band rehearsed. I felt like a racehorse who wants to run as soon as the gate opens, and Phil, the jockey, would rein me in until we were coming round the clubhouse turn, heading for the final stretch. When the right take materialised, he would start his incredible gyrations in the booth, running from one side of the glass to the other, looking at key people during crucial moments like Leonard Bernstein conducting the New York Philharmonic.
Hal Blaine

He (Phil) would conduct with one hand asking for loudness, while the other hand was directed at another section calling for quiet. Then he would give me that magical look that meant only one thing – Go! And we would both go crazy, me doing fills that were total lunacy. I would do eighth-note and 16th-note fills during a shuffle, and vice versa. One particular lick that I came up with during these bursts of madness stuck and became a regular Spector trademark: quarter-note triplets played against what the band was doing. The record was never done until Phil cued me to do triplets.
Hal Blaine

Jack Nitzsche did some memorable arrangements, some innovative stuff with Phil Spector, but they still needed us to make it happen, and you still invented to pad out what was written in arrangements or substituted your lines for failed arranged lines, etc.
Carol Kaye

Phil Spector, like Brian Wilson, only did *one* song per 3-hour date (or longer). Phil would do a quickie run-though of a jammed blues for the B-side in 3 minutes.
Carol Kaye

What Phil was doing was unbelievable. If he'd stayed at Atlantic and made those records it would have been our greatest period... he's the only producer who could produce a hit record without having a hit artist. He could just get a session singer – any session singer – and have a hit. The production was everything.
Ahmet Ertegun, Atlantic Records owner

That gargantuan leakage, everything leaking out of everyone else's mic, was something we guarded against at Atlantic. To me it was like a muted roar. I didn't like it, and I still don't like it. But I recognised its incredible, incredible value. Phil was making hits.
Jerry Wexler, Atlantic Records

I've never written a song. I only write stories. I write productions. I'm sometimes compared to Phil Spector (in reference to the big sound) but there really is no comparison. We come from a different place and we end up somewhere else.
George 'Shadow' Morton, producer of the Shangri-Las

I'd (like to) do a Dylan opera with him. I'd produce him. You see, he's never been produced. He's always gone into the studio on the strength of his lyrics, and they have sold enough records to cover up everything – all the honesty of his records. But he's never really made a production.
Phil Spector, considering in 1969 who he would like to record

Part Two
Little Symphonies –
Big Hits And Great Singers

12
Phil Spector: The Pre-Philles Years
by Mike Callahan

This short piece comes from Goldmine *magazine of March 1980, and offers the first instalment of a useful overview to Spector's record activity. Subsequent sections of the whole piece appear later in this section.*

Let's get one thing cleared up right away. Phil Spector is no lover of stereo. In fact, he is quoted in Richard Williams' book *Out Of His Head* as saying, 'I don't believe in eight tracks and sixteen tracks... I like to record on one track in monaural. The biggest records I've ever made were all done on one track. To me, the cloudier and fuzzier a record is, the more honesty and guts it has.' Phil Spector is the kind of guy who appears on his albums wearing a button that says 'Back to MONO.'

Yet Phil Spector is no stranger to stereo, either. Many of his 'biggest records' have already turned up in true stereo on albums, and there is good reason to believe that many more were recorded in stereo but have not yet been released in that mode. This seeming inconsistency requires a little explanation.

Modern records are often recorded in pieces, with the instruments and vocals recorded at different times. With the use of 16- and 32-track recording equipment, there are enough tracks so that virtually every voice or instrument can be recorded on its own track. The final record that we hear is a mlxdown of all those tracks into just the two necessary for stereo. After reading the above quote from Spector, one gets the impression that his recording sessions featured all the instruments, strings, and voices together in the studio simultaneously for one mono 'take' after another. Actually, this was not the case. Most of the records were recorded in three separate parts: the instrumental rhythm track, the vocals, and the strings. The recorded evidence indicates that at least three tracks were used for these recordings, the typical Spector stereo song having the rhythm on one channel, the strings on the other, and the lead vocal in the middle. Back-up vocals sometimes replaced the strings on the channel opposite the rhythm.

In other words, Spector's records were recorded in such a way as to make a true stereo record possible.

But the unconventional thing about Spector's stereo records was that the entire rhythm track, including all guitars, pianos, drums, percussion and bass, was recorded on the same track, i.e., in mono. And for Spector's records, especially during the Philles period, the rhythm track was a big part of the recorded sound. Therefore, when Phil Spector talks about his records being done in monaural, he is talking about the rhythm track: no sixteen tracks, where individual instruments could stand out of 'the Wall of Sound' for Spector. Nevertheless, because the voices and strings were added later, the finished product could be mixed into true stereo.

Let's go back to examine some of Phil's first stereo efforts while he was still with his group the Teddy Bears (Spector, Annette Kleinbard, and Marshall Leib) in the late 1950s.

Spector's experience with stereo while a member of the Teddy Bears probably served to reinforce his monomania. The group's first recording session was for the newly-formed Dore label, and took place at Gold Star Studios in Los Angeles. At that time Gold Star did not yet have stereo recorders, and Phil went through several dozen mono-to-mono overdubs to arrive at the fuzzy but commercially successful sound of 'To Know Him Is To Love Him'. On the strength of that hit, the group was signed to the larger Imperial label for a follow-up.

The recording session for Imperial took place at Master Recorders, which in late 1958 *did* have stereo capabilities. The result of the session was the album *The Teddy Bears Sing* (Imperial LP 12010, one of the first stereo albums on that label). The sound quality of the album was excellent; gone was the recorded-in-a-garage fuzziness of 'To Know Him Is To Love Him'. But with the newfound clarity, a new problem arose, perhaps best stated by Rob Finnis in his book *The Phil Spector Story*: 'Annette sang lead on every track like a junior Debbie Reynolds while Phil and Marsh hummed and bleated in the background in typical 50s fashion, but the excellent recording quality revealed them as awkward amateurs, three kids who had got lucky through one song.'

If the mono version of the album revealed the group to be unpolished, the stereo version was far worse. By separating Annette's voice on the opposite channel from the boys' background, every flaw in her singing became painfully obvious. By comparing the earlier mono version of 'To Know Him Is To Love Him' with the stereo version of *The Teddy Bears Sing*, it's no wonder that Phil Spector preferred the mono fuzziness.

At least as a historical footnote, *The Teddy Bears Sing* in stereo is an interesting album worth hearing. All twelve tracks are in true stereo. Annette's lead, along with the drums, bass, and piano, are on one channel while the guitars and background voices are on the other channel. Stereo recordings from the 1950s often suffered from a peculiar problem known as 'the hole in the middle'. Separation of voices or instruments was so exaggerated that on listening to the record, it sounded like the group was split in half, with each subgroup playing at either end of a wide stage, with no one in the middle. This problem led to the development of the three-track recorder used in the early 60s where the lead singer's voice was usually placed in the middle for the listener. Spector, however, used an interesting and unusual solution to 'the hole in the middle' problem on the Teddy Bears' album. On one channel, Annette sounds as if she's standing directly in front of the microphone, but her voice is also heard on the other channel, along with a heavy dose of reverb. The same technique is used for the background voices (on the opposite channels). The overall effect is a pleasant distribution of voices and instruments in space with a very strong illusion of 'presence'. As we will see, Spector used this technique many times later.

The music itself on the album ranges from the Teddy Bears' follow-up ('Oh Why'/'I Don't Need You Anymore'; Imperial 5562) and two other Spector-penned songs to eight pop standards. Five of the twelve cuts, including the four Spector songs, eventually found their way to Imperial singles. Of the pop standards, 'Long Ago And Far Away' is particularly good, but was not included in the singles. As a 'junior Debbie Reynolds' on 'Tammy', Annette is not quite up to the job. There is also a version of 'Unchained Melody', which is quite mediocre and can't begin to compare with the Spectorian masterpiece with the Righteous Brothers a few years later. The album bombed, and out of the three singles released, only one even made *Billboard*'s Top 100, peaking out at an anemic #91. Spector finally gave up and disbanded the Teddy Bears in late 1959.

After the Teddy Bears' demise, Phil moved to New York and spent several years producing and 'supervising' records for a variety of artists. His early efforts included work with Leiber and Stoller at Atlantic Records, although he was not given producer's credit on any major hits. But during the early 60s, he did produce quite a few legitimate hits with Ray Peterson, Curtis Lee, Gene Pitney, the Paris Sisters and Connie Francis. Many of these records were recorded in stereo, but to my knowledge, only the Ray Peterson and Connie Francis material has been released in true stereo.

By this time, Spector was already tending to isolate the rhythm instruments on one channel with the back-up voices and strings on the other and the lead voice in the middle. 'Corrine Corrina' by Ray Peterson had this format. The metronome in the song sounds like a throwback to the Teddy Bears LP stereo technique. On one channel, the ticking sounds 'flat', as if the metronome was right in front of the mic, while on the other channel it is present with reverb. Peterson's 'I Could Have Loved You So Well' is an Orbison-like arrangement with stereo treatment similar to 'Corrine Corrina'. What sets these Spector stereo cuts apart form the later recordings is the clarity of sound and the excellent stereo separation. These Ray Peterson songs were recorded at Bell Studios in New York for release on the Dunes label. Twelve of Ray Peterson's Dunes cuts are available in stereo on the MGM album *The Very Best of Ray Peterson* (SE.4250).

Spector recorded Peterson's label-mate, Curtis Lee ('Pretty Little Angel Eyes'; 'Under The Moon Of Love'), at Mirasound Studios in New York. Gene Pitney's 'Every Breath I Take' and some of the early Crystals hits were also recorded there. Although it is possible that Mirasound had stereo equipment in mid-1961 (they certainly had stereo in 1964), none of the Mirasound masters have been released in stereo, to my knowledge.

The Paris Sisters, on the other hand, were recorded at Gold Star back in Los Angeles. By 1961, Gold Star had acquired a three-track stereo system, and Spector used this equipment to piece together the Paris Sisters' hits ('Be My Boy', 'I Love How You Love Me', 'He Knows I Love Him Too Much', and 'Let Me Be The One'). Unhappily, the stereo versions of the Paris Sisters' song, recorded for the Gregmark label, suffered from the lack of an album for a vehicle. (A later album on the Sidewalk label (T 5906) called *Golden Hits Of The Paris Sisters* features re-recorded versions of their first three chart singles.)

The Spectors Three was Phil's first attempt at recreating the Teddy Bears magic (1960)

Finally. Connie Francis 'Second Hand Love' is a thoroughly conventional record, with bass, drums, and guitar on one channel, strings, back-up voices, and piano on the other and Connie's voice in the middle. The song is available in stereo on several albums.

By the time Spector recorded Connie Francis, 1962, he was well into his work at his own Philles label. The stereo groundwork had been laid; Spector liked rhythm instruments on one channel, strings on the other, and the lead voice in the middle. He also liked echo/reverb techniques to fill up holes. Later in this volume, we will conclude the Phil Spector Stereo Story and discuss how these early techniques exploded into bigger-than-life stereo productions for Philles and later labels.

13
He's A Rebel by Mike Kelly

When the Crystals' recording of 'He's A Rebel' became a major hit and introduced elements of the Wall of Sound in 1962, those in the know realised that Phil was using singers other than the name group. Always an accepted industry practice, in Spector's case, however, it indicated much more in terms of how he saw his role. This piece, from Discoveries *magazine, July 1996, unravels the story of this breakthrough record.*

One of the biggest and longest-running disputes in the annals of early 60s rock and roll focuses on the song 'He's A Rebel', released by Vikki Carr on a 45 on the Liberty Records label in late 1962. And poor Vikki isn't even a rock and roll singer.

The Legend
A legend which most rock 'historians' promulgate goes something like this: one day in 1962, while he was temporarily employed as a producer by Liberty Records in California, the legendary Phil Spector heard the equally legendary Liberty producer Snuff Garrett playing a demonstration record in the company's offices. Over the years, Snuffy had produced hits by Bobby Vee, Johnny Burnette, Buddy Knox and many others. So it was natural that Spec would consider any demo that Snuff was considering working on to be potential hit material.

The tune in question was, of course, 'He's A Rebel', composed by

Gene Pitney, who wrote some of his own records ('[I Wanna] Love My Life Away', 1961) and an Imperial hit for Ricky Nelson ('Hello, Mary Lou', 1961). Pitney had also composed Bobby Vee's recent (1961) hit 45 'Rubber Ball', albeit under an assumed name. So both Snuff and Spec knew this song could have potential.

Snuff, according to the popular legend (and there are a lot of legends in this tangled tale), planned to have a young Liberty singer named Vikki Carr cut the song. Spector loved 'He's A Rebel', so he surreptitiously made a copy of the demo (in other words, stole it), then told Snuff that he was going on vacation.

Instead of vacationing, Spector went straight to a recording studio. He'd just had a hit record 'There's No Other (Like My Baby)' (1962) on Philles Records with his girl group, the Crystals. But the Crystals were back East, variably (depending on the version of the story you hear) on tour, uninterested in the song, unavailable, afraid to fly, or something. Or maybe Spector just wanted to cut the thing as fast as he could to beat Vikki Carr's version into the stores.

In any event, Phil hired legendary (although as yet unknown) studio singers 24-year-old Darlene Love (real name: Darlene Wright) and the Blossoms, gathered the usual LA session crew, and quickly cut a cover version of 'He's A Rebel' for release on Philles as by the Crystals.

Meanwhile, the *real* Crystals; who were on tour, started getting requests for their new hit, which of course they had never heard! So they bought a copy, learned the song, and started performing it on stage.

(A major variation of the legend says that Gene Pitney wrote the song for the Crystals and Crystals alone. He is supposed to have written the previous Crystals' Rebel-esque hit, 'Uptown', and wrote 'Rebel' specifically as a follow-up to that record! This version never mentions the Shirelles or Vikki Carr, let alone the Blossoms!)

So much for the legend. What happened to the two versions of the song?

The cover version, by the pseudo-Crystals, became a #1 record in most cities, and peaked at #2 on *Billboard*. Meanwhile, Snuff's original by Vikki Carr, recorded the same day with the same session musicians in the same building, stiffed.

From The Source...

What do the participants in this affair have to say about it? Vikki Carr herself told her story, in passing, to magazine writer Jack Dey for a *Discoveries* feature article on Carr in the June 1991 issue (page 30).

'When Phil Scaff (sic) left Liberty Records, he took certain material with him. And Snuff Garrett who at that time in the early 60s was the golden boy at Liberty Records, he had this song for me and they said this is going to be your first single. So, I was all excited about it; it was going to be really, really great. We finished recording it in Los Angeles and we took a little break. As we were walking out of the studio, we hear 'He's A Rebel' coming back at us from across the hall in another studio. Phil Spector had taken that material with him and he never even had the Crystals record it. He got some girls together. He does mention that, yeah, this is supposed to be Vikki Carr's first single. But in Australia they preferred my version to the Crystals' version.'

As exciting as that story reads, Snuffy himself (at the Gold Star Studios, August 13, 1992) tells a vastly different version of the events that unfolded.

'Phil Spector did not steal "He's A Rebel" from me and Vikki Carr. The music publisher, Aaron Schroeder, screwed us both. He gave it to me "exclusively," and he did the same for Spec. We cut it on the same night, he used Darlene (Love); I used Vikki Carr. I heard during our session that he was cutting it the same night across town. We used a lot of the same musicians.

'Then when Darlene's came out under the name the Crystals, "The Big Bad Liberty Records covered us." But it was not true. And Spec, not only that, cut a better record. The only saving grace of my version of "He's A Rebel" was that it was the first record with Vikki Carr, got her on the label. Spec's was better; I haven't heard Vikki's since we cut it!

'But Spec didn't intentionally go out to cut my throat, and I certainly didn't go out to cut Spec's throat. I don't give a hang what [they] say. As far as I am concerned, we both got screwed by the publisher. That's my version. And I am one of the only two who were there, so who you gonna believe?'

Well, someone else was there, Snuff: Vikki Carr.

Basically, Snuff's recollection and Vikki's recollection match. The main point of contention between the two is: was the song stolen by Spec and did he and Snuff feud about it? Snuff is adamant.

'Spec did not steal the song from me. Aaron Schroeder, the publisher, gave me an exclusive on it, and he also gave Spec an exclusive on it. Everybody is trying to make a thing out of it all. We just both got taken by the publisher. Vikki's was the big hit in my home, Dallas KOIF radio, and Australia, places like that. But Spec had the record [meaning Spector cut the definitive version].'

A side point: contrary to what Vikki Carr asserts, Carr's record, Liberty 45 #55493, apparently was not her first single. She had an earlier Liberty 45 (#55465) called 'I'll Walk The Rest Of The Way' b/w 'Beside A Bridge'. Not only that, but Liberty 45 #55490, 'Submarine Races' by Danny and Gwen, was also Vikki Carr. She was Gwen, named after producer Snuff Garrett's oldest daughter, then aged two. Danny was in reality Jerry Naylor of the Crickets.

Vikki's version of 'He's A Rebel', credited to 'Vikki Carr the Singing Strings of Ernie Freeman', is a fine record. 'The Singing Strings' refers to the name concocted for an LP Snuff planned to do with Ernie, his arranger, an idea that was later abandoned. These violins, while not part of a wall of sound, are still powerfully evocative. Vikki's voice overdubs very well, and she also seems to be singing all the background parts. Sure, after hearing the Spector version for 30 years, Vikki's seems a pale copy. But, taken on its own, it is a great record that was not a copy and deserved to be a hit. Were the kids in Dallas idiots or something for making it a big hit there? No. They were just expressing their appreciation for a record produced more in the style of Gene McDaniels (whose records like 'Chip Chip' were produced by Snuff) than in the style of Neil Sedaka (whose records such as 'Stairway To Heaven' and 'Sweet Little You' were near-wall-of-sound recordings).

The best way to listen to Vikki Carr's version is at very high volume. This adds power to the recording and simulates the Wall of Sound, which is, after all, the way we expect to hear the song.

(For a truly inferior version of 'Rebel', try the Orlons' LP *All The Hits*, Cameo 1033. I love the Orlons, but they just were not given the resources to do the song justice. And for a late 60s rendition, try on the Goodies' cut from their LP *Candy Coated Goodies*, Hip Records 7002. Their hit was 'Condition Red', a great Shangri-Las-type tune; and their 'Rebel' is a bouncy, piano-string-horns production which bears little resemblance to the 1962 records. Finally, the Crystals' own version of 'Rebel' can be heard on several releases by Key Seven Music, including a 1982 LP *60s Dance Party* and a 1984 Radio Shack cassette *Oldies' But 80s* – although who can say whom is actually singing on this recording!)

Despite the differences, Vikki's record has all of the same basic elements as the better-known Spector version of 'He's A Rebel':

heavy drums, duelling on the lead voice, instrumental break, and a fade-out full of 'No No No.' That being stated, it should be stressed that these elements are mixed quite differently on the two versions. The drums on the Liberty version have a distinct military-marching flavour, tying in to the 'Rebel' or Confederate army theme. The break is only half as long. And the fade-out is more tame than Darlene Love's gospel-flavoured vocals on Phil's.

But the main difference is the clarity of the Liberty version. Ernie Freeman's 'Singing Strings' are clearly violins. In Spec's 'Wall of Sound' recording, as his technique of stacking tracks has been dubbed, the mix disguises the violins. Vikki delivers the song with a rock and roll style never heard elsewhere by her, least of all on the flip side of her 45. She was really a pure pop singer.

The Plot Thickens...

Vikki Carr's Liberty 45 has long been a rare collectors' item. But in 1992, it was included in an EMI CD compilation *The Best of Vikki Carr*. This album is the first stereo release of Vikki's version, and is followed by another great girl rocker, 'I Got My Eye On You', of unknown authorship. Wait 'til you hear what Joe Laredo's liner notes for this CD say about 'Rebel':

'Unfortunately for Vikki, Phil Spector picked up on the song during a visit with Garrett. He procured a demo from Pitney and rushed into the studio to record it...'

So now, instead of stealing the demo from Snuffy, or getting the song from the publisher as an exclusive, maybe Spector got the demo from Gene Pitney himself right in front of Snuffy?

Besides Snuff and Carr, there were other people there, as well. The recording engineer, the Blossoms; all kinds of people.

The Blossoms are no longer active – Darlene is now famous, Gloria Jones has passed away and Fanita James is retired. (Bobby Sheen, a sort of 'honorary' Blossom, also sang on 'He's A Rebel', but is never mentioned in any version of the legends.)

I asked Fanita James, Blossoms' founding member, if she remembered the 'He's A Rebel' session. Since Fanita was a singer on the 'Crystals' version of 'He's A Rebel', I thought that perhaps she could shed some light on the controversy. Did Phil steal that song from Snuff as most people claim and use the Blossoms instead of the Crystals in order to steal a march on Spec; or did Spec think he had a valid exclusive on the song like Snuff did?

'The only thing I ever heard about "He's A Rebel" was that Phil Spector was mad at the Crystals. It was his song, but he was angry with the Crystals about something, so he refused to fly them out from New York. He just got us to do it here. I always thought that Phil had the song as an exclusive. I never knew any different. I think I would have heard some kind of scuttlebutt.'

Mad at the Crystals? That is a new twist on the 'legend!' Another unknown fact was contributed by Fanita.

It Was Everybody's Party

'The follow-up to "He's A Rebel" was supposed to be "It's My Party". Darlene sang lead; it was to be released under the Blossoms name. We learned it and we were doing it slow – we would drag it. But Phil never put it out! Then here comes Lesley [Gore] and, boy, was that a big record! Isn't that something!'

Lesley Gore herself, who did have the #1 hit in the summer of 1963 with 'It's My Party', pretty much confirmed Fanita's story when she appeared on *Sally Jesse Raphael* August 4th, 1993. Except, where Spector told the Blossoms that their 'It's My Party' would be released under the name the Blossoms, it appears that Phil was in reality planning to use the Crystal's name on a Blossoms' track yet again! Here is Lesley on *Sally*, telling about the day she recorded 'It's My Party' with her producer, Quincy Jones:

'We recorded "It's My Party" on March 30, 1963. That night, Quincy Jones was at Carnegie Hall to see one of his artists on Mercury. That very evening, Phil Spector arrived, got out of his limo, ran up the steps, and he told Quincy that he was recording one of the best songs he ever heard with a group called the Crystals. And Quincy said, "Well, what's the name of the song?" And Phil said, "The name of the song is 'It's My Party.'"

'We realised at that time that the publisher had sort of double-dealt us both. Quincy got an exclusive for me, and someone gave Phil an exclusive for the Crystals.

'Quincy, the very next morning, went into the studio... and recorded 100 acetates, sent them out to disc jockeys... and I heard it on the radio the very first time April 6, one week after I recorded it!'

An 'exclusive!' Apparently once again, the publisher scammed the producers, and Spector was scamming the Blossoms!

Legend (there's that word again) has it that the Ronettes version of 'Chapel Of Love' was recorded well before the Dixie Cups #1 hit, but was held back by Spector and never got released. Well, I guess 'It's My Party' was the same kind of deal. People in the record biz are so often at the mercy of others. Like Snuff Garrett being at the mercy of the publisher of 'Rebel'.

When publisher Aaron Schroeder pulled this trick with 'Rebel' on Snuff, it was the last straw. The previous year, Aaron had pulled another stunt, when he brought 'Rubber Ball' to Snuff. 'Bobby Vee recorded the song and had one of his best records ever with it in 1961. It turned out so well that Snuff wanted to meet the songwriter, Anna Orlowski. Snuff thought, "My God! A secret writer! But who in heck is Anna Orlowski and when can I meet her?" Aaron kept side-stepping me and everything. It was a long time before we found out that it was Gene Pitney who wrote "Rubber Ball".'

Pitney was a BMI composer. Since he had an advance from ASCAP for 'Rubber Ball', he had to go through with the song, but used his mother's maiden name.

Aaron Schroeder got half writer's credit for 'Rubber Ball'. That could be another case of someone taking credit for a record that really was written independent of that individual. But since Aaron wrote the Elvis Presley hits 'I Got Stung', 'I Was The One', 'Big Hunk Of Love', 'Stuck On You', 'It's Now Or Never', 'Anyway You Want Me', and 'Good Luck Charm', I guess it is safe to assume that he and Gene Pitney really did collaborate on 'Rubber Ball'.

The Root Of Rebel – More Theories Than JFK's Assassination

But back to the 'Rebel'. Was it really true that either Spector or Garrett had an 'exclusive' on that one? Not according to Bruce Pollock, author of *When Rock Was Young* (Holt Reinhart Winston, 1981).

'Once Florence Greenburg advised the Shirelles against recording the song "He's A Rebel", claiming they'd get in trouble with it if they tried to sing it in the South. So they passed it on to the Crystals, who didn't have any trouble at all making it a Number 1 song.'

The Shirelles passed the song on to the Crystals? I thought that Spector either got it from the publisher or stole it from Liberty! An account similar to Pollock's was published in the liner notes written by Anna Hunt Graves for a 1995 CD called *My Boyfriend's Back!*:

'...The Shirelles were offered singer Gene Pitney's composition, "He's A Rebel" (which the Crystals would later record and make into a number one hit), but Greenburg rejected the song, thinking it might be controversial in the South.' This story has as many permutations as the JFK assassination! Wait. There's more!

Bruce McColm and Roy Payne, authors of *Where Have They Gone?* (Tempo Books, 1979) have another version of who-recorded-'He's A Rebel' to report. Was it the Crystals or the Blossoms? They quote Dolores 'Dee Dee' Kinniebrew as follows about Darlene Love's singing on a Crystals' record:

'Murray the K started all of that (about the Blossoms). I didn't even meet Darlene Love until 1964 when they were taking the photo for the Christmas album. Murray the K was putting on some Christmas show and there was some kind of blow-up between him and Phil. Phil never booked or managed us, but apparently Murray the K wanted him to get us on his show. I never found out exactly, though, what it was all about. Phil must have said no or whatever and they had a hassle. At that time Darlene Love was with the Blue Jeans and Murray the K wanted them to sing "He's A Rebel" on the show. But they didn't do it.' Well, maybe the Shirelles did turn down 'Rebel', but no one takes Dee Dee's claim seriously any more.

Rock historian Alan Betrock wrote a seminal book *Girl Groups – the Story of a Sound* (Delilah, New York) in 1982. In this book, he repeats the tale of Phil Spector's stealing 'He's A Rebel' from Snuff. He states that Phil pretended to go on vacation from Liberty when he really used the time to record 'He's A Rebel', and that Snuff was 'putting the final touches on his version for Liberty when Spector arrived at Gold Star' (page 35). He further faults Liberty for not promoting Vikki Carr's version very well. He says that Liberty president Al Bennett, A&R head Snuff, and promotion head Bob Skaff were in Chicago celebrating the opening of a new Liberty branch office. 'While they partied, Spector tended to business, and the next week the Crystals' "He's A Rebel" appeared [on the charts]'.

A similar account was offered by authors Bob Shannon and John Javna in their impressive rock reference book, *Behind The Hits*. In part, they state that Spector was still working for Liberty when he got hold of 'He's A Rebel', and 'had to get out of his contract with Liberty right away so he could use the song first'. The authors quote writer Gene Pitney as saying that Spector 'said he was ill and moving to Spain, so Liberty finally released him from his production demands.'

In July of 1991, on reading Betrock's and Shannon/Javna's accounts of the recordings of 'He's A Rebel', Snuff Garrett bristled.

'Both of them are full of shit. Here is what annoys me about this stuff. Thirty years later, guys who weren't even there write about this stuff. They have no idea what they are talking about.

'Spec may have known [that "He's A Rebel" was being recorded by both of us]. I sure didn't know. But Spec's leaving Liberty had nothing to do with "He's A Rebel". It's a great story, but it doesn't have anything to do with reality. That went on weeks and weeks before that and had nothing at all to do with it. Spec was already long gone from Liberty when "He's A Rebel" came about. What is funny is, when the record came out, Spec cut a far better record than I did, it is just as simple as that. It doesn't take a rocket scientist to figure that out.

'What they [Philles Records] did with the record, Lester Sill's son went on the road that night after they cut it, and went out and yelled that they had been covered by Liberty. He said that their little company had been covered by Liberty. It wasn't true, but it worked. I would have done the same thing. That was the record biz. That was also probably the last time that Spec flew, because he hated to fly.'

Did Snuff Garrett and Phil Spector remain post 'Rebel' friends?

'I never had a bad word with Spec in my life, or him with me. Hey, I was the one who got him the job at Liberty. Everyone was down on me because Spec was a pain in the neck in the New York office.'

And why did Spector really leave Liberty?

'I have no earthly idea. It was Spec's wish to leave.'

Some sources claim that Phil Spector took a position at Liberty only to hide out from his partners at Philles Records and to stall for time in his other business affairs.

'Well, that sounds good today, too. But I was head of A&R at Liberty, a small label that had become a major, and I was also producing and had a lot of good results. So I was in New York in a suite we kept at the Hampshire House and talked to Spec. We had been talking for two or three days, and he wanted to come to Liberty. I thought that would be great. With me on the West Coast and him on the East Coast, I thought we could really lock up some things. I had total respect for Phil Spector. Period. But I had a hell of a fight at Liberty when I hired him. It doesn't sound like a lot of money today, but at that time $25,000 plus royalties was a big salary.'

Did Spector produce any hits while he was at Liberty?

'No, no he didn't. He recorded Bobby Sheen, then took Bobby with him for Bob B. Soxx and the Blue Jeans. But saying Spec had a master plan [to hide out at Liberty and not try to make hits for Liberty] was not true. He would not have signed Bobby Sheen to

Liberty if he didn't have intentions of doing things at Liberty.

'I hired Spec in good faith, I picked him out of a lot of good people, but he just didn't fit into the corporate kind of thing. Neither did I, actually.'

Was Snuff in Chicago not tending to business with 'He's A Rebel' while Spec was on the ball? To that, Snuff says, 'Hell, sure I was in Chicago, but we had other records to promote besides that one "He's A Rebel". But as soon as I heard Spec's, I told everyone his was a better record.

'But I was shocked when I found out I didn't have an exclusive on that song. I think it was (session guitarist) Tommy Tedesco who came over from Spec's session and told me about it. He came in and saw the lead sheet and said, "Hey, I just cut this with Spec over at Gold Star." That was the first I knew about it. That did not make me happy at the time, I can tell you that. But I took it that I was screwed by the publisher, not by Spec.'

All Part Of The Record Biz

As mentioned earlier, besides the singers, including Vikki and Fanita, someone else who was at the 'Rebel' sessions was a recording engineer. Bones Howe, who worked around all of the studios of LA, happened to be at Gold Star the night 'He's A Rebel' was being recorded. Bones' account of the evening's events tends to confirm Snuffy's, although Bones was not actually involved in the 'He's A Rebel' affair.

'I was there though. I saw them recording the Vikki Carr version in studio B the same night that Phil was mixing the Crystals version in Studio E or C. He was mixing down in one studio and they were cutting Vikki in another. It was a real cover battle.'

Does that mean that Bones thinks that Spector stole the song from Snuffy?

'No no no. The story as I understood it was that Phil had the song first. In those days the song was the thing, and there were battles over songs. And publishers would double deal songs sometimes. Maybe Snuff had it first and then Aaron Schroeder felt that Vikki Carr might not have a hit, so he was buying himself some insurance with Spector. And if so, he was right, wasn't he!' Because Spector's version was the one that hit!

'Schroeder may have been right, but what he did was not right, and Snuff really never forgave the publisher's double dealing.'

Bones was right on that point. Snuff never did forgive:

'To my knowledge, I never recorded another Aaron Schroeder song after that "He's A Rebel" incident. When he did that to me that time, that was the end. Well, I did cut one more, years and years later. I saw him in New York and he gave me a song. So I got him, I told him that I had this hot new star on television and radio, some bull like that. I held on to the song. It was "This Diamond Ring" that I cut with Gary Lewis.'

Although Phil Spector and Snuff never did feud, Spec's stay at Liberty was brief nonetheless. Si Waronker was the founder and owner of Liberty. He was the one who hired Snuff Garrett before he had ever done anything besides be a DJ. Si agrees that Spec really didn't fit in at the company.

'Phil Spector and Snuffy were great friends. I was never that friendly with Phil. Phil signed with the company. And he wanted to take charge of the New York division – this was after we had become a little more successful. Snuffy had come up with this idea that he wanted to have strings with his rock music. Which I thought was great! The more [strings], the merrier! C'mon! And Snuffy got very hot.

'So when Phil came along a few years later, it was very interesting, because he had one god that he looked at musically as his king or god, and that was Richard Wagner, the great composer! Listen carefully to all of Phil Spector's records, and it was the "Ride Of The Valkyries" in there. And he was the one that filled up the studio with musicians, and I guess he got famous with this approach.

'But Phil was under contract with Liberty for not long, just a few months. We could never stay together. He could never see his way to stay with us, nor could we keep him, simply because this guy was too rough to deal with!' [Laughs.]

Be that as it may, thanks perhaps to Spector's competition on 'He's A Rebel', Vikki Carr would have to wait a few years to have a big hit. As good as the Liberty/Snuff Garrett sound was, it was no guarantee of a hit.

'Liberty didn't want Spec, but I fought my ass off to get Spec on Liberty because I thought that Spec was the most talented person out there, I thought he was a genius. We were good friends and I respected him a lot. He got in, but then everything went wrong. Spec is his own kind of cat, we all are, I have nothing but the greatest respect for Spec, always have. But he was not into being a big corporation team player. Neither was I, but he couldn't handle it at all. Spec and I got along great, it was all the other meetings and things. He just sat there and stared at them and thought they were squirrely and so did I.'

Probably no one at Liberty, except Snuff, liked Spec after the 'He's A Rebel' debacle. Getting Snuffy's story provides real insight into the legend.

And Now A Word From Gene Pitney

It would be great to talk to Phil Spector and get his spin on this song, too. Failing that, Gene Pitney was contacted on July 11, 1995, to see what he might say.

When was 'He's A Rebel' written; and was it intended as a follow-up to the Crystals' 'Uptown'?

'I wrote "He's A Rebel" about six months before it was recorded. It was an "Uptown" follow up, and actually, it is the only thing I ever wrote that was intended for someone in particular.'

Does Pitney know how Spector got the song? Did Phil 'steal it' from Snuffy or his office at Liberty?

'Phil Spector came into New York, he heard the demo, and you could tell he liked it because his eyes lit up. He was a guy who knew what he was looking for. But I did not know at the time that he intended it to be the record to start his label with. He went back (to LA), and I didn't know until later about the fight that went on between the production teams, because of Phil's being signed as a producer for Liberty Records at the time he got the song "He's A Rebel". Phil knew that he wanted it for his own record label (not for Liberty). So, Phil got out from under his Liberty contract to do his own production. But Snuff Garrett, the producer for Liberty, also had the song. It had been given to Snuff by Aaron Schroeder, the publisher I wrote for. To get away from Liberty, Spector told Liberty that he was burned out, was moving to Spain, and was leaving the record business. He even went so far as to take a course from Berlitz in Spanish. [Big laugh!] I mean, this was how Phil did things. Liberty believed that he was doing this, and that was how he wriggled out of his production contract before they found him right under their noses at Gold Star recording that song!'

So Gene agrees that both versions were recorded at the same time, that neither was a 'cover version'?

'There came a time when I was told that there was a guitar player in Gold Star Studios who came into the Snuff Garrett session, sat down to play his part, looked at his music, saw that "He's A Rebel" was the title and said, "I just played this over in Studio C!"

'That was when I found out that there was a battle going on! I am not sure what part of the song Phil recorded there, the vocals or just the instrumentals. And then it became a battle of putting the record out and seeing which label could do the best job. And I think that Phil just had the upper hand by having the better record.'

But there is so much talk about Aaron Schroeder offering the song as an exclusive to both Snuffy and Spec, plus the story of the Shirelles' turning it down. How could all that be possible, if Pitney wrote the song for the Crystals as a follow-up?

'My personal intention, the reason I wrote it, was for the Crystals to do it. But as far as an aggressive publisher like Aaron goes, I would not have any control over that whatsoever. Aaron Schroeder would have offered an exclusive to everybody [laughs], anybody who would have recorded it. There were a lot of times when I didn't agree with what he did, but as an aggressive publisher, he was the best you could have if you had a song that you wanted to get out there in front of somebody.'

The two versions sound so different from each other because the producers were from different backgrounds. Which one was closer to the demo recording?

'The demo was identical to Phil's version. He copied it exactly.'

Did the demo have the marching drums like a confederate army snare drum that is on Vikki Carr's version?

'No, no, no, no never. No, Phil's was virtually the same as what we had done in the studio. Pretty close, other than adding the sound that he had. Not the Wall of Sound, but close, compared to what we had on the demo. We had only four pieces doing the demo, guitar, drums, and bass. And it was just me singing, and I overdubbed myself on the end singing where it gets faster, "He's a rebel, no no no."'

A few months ago, Varese Sarabande released a CD entitled *Gene Pitney More Greatest Hits* (VSD-5569) that Gene was involved in compiling. The 'Rebel' demo would have been perfect for the Sarabande CD, featuring as it did lesser hits, LP cuts, and unreleased tracks.

'I don't know if Sarabande had access to the demo. It might be out there, I am not sure. That demo is one of the few things that I have never ever heard again since 1962. I don't even have it here myself. I don't know why that one has vanished. A lot of the demos still exist, but I have not heard that one for a long, long time.'

In total, Gene Pitney's version of the legend agrees more with Snuff Garrett's than with most writers. Yet, except for the fact that he did indeed write it for the Crystals and that Aaron Schroeder made a habit of offering simultaneous exclusives, the rest of Pitney's information is admittedly second-hand.

In the end, just what do we know? We know both Spector and Snuffy cut the song almost the same moment, in the same building, with many of the same musicians. We know that Snuff used Vikki Carr on lead, and that Darlene Love was indisputably the lead on Spector's version. (Just compare true Crystals' voices on records like 'There's No Other (Like My Baby)' or 'Uptown' to 'Rebel' if you doubt that.) We know that the song was written as an 'Uptown' follow-up. We know the 'big bad Liberty' did not 'cover' Philles. And we know Spector's version is the classic hit. Beyond that, it just depends on whose story you like best.

I'm just glad Gene Pitney wrote the darn thing!

14
19 + 1 Choices by Dave Marsh

Dave Marsh's acclaimed 1989 book The Heart Of Rock & Soul *details his ordered choice of the 1001 greatest singles ever made, and Spector recordings are well represented; so well in fact we can make up a top 20 of Marsh's choices and his comments. Well, we can with 19 records that do appear and one expected one that doesn't. The preceding numbers refer to the record's position in his top 1001.*

5: 'You've Lost That Lovin' Feelin'' – The Righteous Brothers
Produced by Phil Spector; written by Barry Mann, Cynthia Weil, and Phil Spector
(Philles 124 1964) Billboard: #1 (2 weeks)

The radio on my boyhood dresser was an old tabletop model with tubes. The top was cracked and at high volume, the busted brown plastic made it screech. My father got it when my great-aunt died but it looked the kind of thing you'd pick up at a junkyard. It was the greatest treasure he ever gave me.

One night, just before Christmas 1964, a strange noise began to emerge from the ancient box. A doleful male voice sang notes so draggy that it seemed someone down at the station must have slowed the turntable with his finger. Annoyed, I switched the radio off.

And right back on again. Already warm, the unreliable old tubes responded immediately, for once. In those brief seconds the record had transformed itself. A wall of sound – drums, tambourines, pianos, full female chorus, maracas, who knew what else – was carrying an uncountable number of male voices into the pits of hell.

At first they seemed content to ride the melody together, so much so that by the end of the first verse they reminded me of Little Anthony and the Imperials, although nothing Anthony and the boys had ever done was half this weird. The second verse began lugubriously again, strings swirling up out of the mix, as the harmonies built back up. I was hooked.

Then came the bridge. Now the voices were distinctly a pair, one mordantly growling, the other so high it was almost falsetto. No longer did they work in tandem. Now, even though they were ostensibly singing alternate lines to the same lover, they were also battling between themselves. The lower voice sang four sharp

'Don'ts' and then – I never did figure out another way to describe it – they just started to wig out. 'Baby!' sang one. 'Baby!' responded the other. 'Baby!' 'Baby!' Then 'I'm beggin' you please... I need your love' and finally 'Bring it on back,' they screamed at one another, relentlessly, as if trapped in a nightmare of what would happen if they didn't or couldn't.

'Bring back that lovin' feelin', whoah, that lovin' feelin',' they sang and the rhythm broke back down again. As they faded away, it felt shattered and pieced back together.

The deejay told me that this was the Righteous Brothers, who I already knew from TV's *Shindig*. They were a Mutt and Jeff act. Sombre-voiced Bill Medley stood way over six feet, dark and halfways handsome; tenor Bobby Hatfield was blond, five five or so and greaser cute. They were good but there was nothing in 'Little Latin Lupe Lu' that suggested they had anything like 'Lovin' Feelin'' in them.

Naturally, I bought the record, surprised at its red and yellow Philles label: producer/impresario Phil Spector made girl group records with the Crystals and the Ronettes. But then again, finding 'Lovin' Feelin'' among them made a kind of sense, for a couple of Spector's girl group hits approached this single's orchestrated grandiosity.

About Spector I knew only that he'd once told a TV interviewer that he was the first teen genius millionaire, or something equally astute and captivating, and that he'd been responsible for the *T.A.M.I. Show*, the only decent representation of rock and roll music ever to appear at a drive-in.

So I sat and stared at the label and being in another line of work at the time – eighth grade – came to no unnecessary conclusions. I loved the record (wore out one copy, picked up another used), harboured a half-secret devotion to the Righteous Brothers no matter what they did well into adulthood, moved on to other things but still turned 'Lovin' Feelin'' way up whenever it came across the radio.

In the spring of 1987, staying at a hotel in downtown Chicago, I strapped on headphones and went for a run. There was a parade on Michigan Avenue, and I dodged in and out among the crowd until I got down by the lake, where there was almost nobody. I'd been on the road a couple of weeks, and felt homesick, a little afraid, frightfully lonely.

The tape I listened to was composed of random favourites, deliberately jumbled so I couldn't remember what came next. Somewhere over by the lake, 'Lovin' Feelin'' came on. I jammed the volume all the way up and the clash of those voices came through again. When they started begging and pleading – 'Baby, baby, I'd get down on my knees for you,' sang Medley, 'If you would only love me like you used to do,' responded Hatfield – tears sprang from my eyes. In the centre of the continent, at the heart of a population of six million, I was suddenly, unmistakably, nerve-tinglingly abandoned and alone.

God knows what passersby thought. But with the title – 'You've Lost That Lovin' Feelin'' – echoing in my ears I understood at last: we worship the thing we fear.

20: 'Be My Baby' – The Ronettes
Produced by Phil Spector; written by Phil Spector, Ellie Greenwich, and Jeff Barry
(Philles 116 1963) Billboard: #2

21: 'Da Doo Ron Ron' – The Crystals
Produced by Phil Spector; written by Phil Spector, Ellie Greenwich, and Jeff Barry
(Philles 112 1963) Billboard: #3

22: 'Christmas (Baby Please Come Home)' – Darlene Love
Produced by Phil Spector; written by Phil Spector, Ellie Greenwich, and Jeff Barry
(Philles 119 1963) Did not make pop charts

To hear folks talk, Phil Spector made music out of a solitary vision. But the evidence of his greatest hits insists that he was heavily dependent on a variety of assistance. Which makes sense: record making is fundamentally collaborative.

Spector associates like engineer Larry Levine, arranger Jack Nitzsche, and husband-wife songwriters Jeff Barry and Ellie Greenwich were simply indispensable to his teen-art concoctions. Besides them, every Spector track featured a dozen or more musicians. The constant standouts were drummer Hal Blaine, one of the most inventive and prolific in rock history, and saxophonist Steve Douglas. Finally, there were vast differences among Spector's complement of singers. An important part of Spector's genius stemmed from his ability to recruit, organise, and provide leadership within such a musical community.

Darlene Love (who also recorded for Spector with the Crystals and Bob B. Soxx and the Blue Jeans) ranks just beneath Aretha Franklin among female rock singers, and 'Christmas' is her greatest record, though it was never a hit. (The track probably achieved its greatest notice in the mid-eighties, when it was used over the opening credits of Joe Dante's film, *Gremlin*.) Spector's Wall of Sound, with its continuously thundering horns and strings, never seemed more massive than it does here. But all that only punctuates Love's hysterical blend of loneliness and lust. In the end, when the mix brings up the piano and the chorus to challenge her, the best the Wall's entire weight can achieve is a draw.

The Crystals' official lead singer La La Brooks was much closer to the anonymous end of the Spector spectrum, and on 'Da Doo Ron Ron', the result is a much more balanced record. Basing the song in nonsense syllables can't disguise what it really is: teen desire incarnate. The battering Blaine gives his drum kit (if anything *he's* the star of this show), the droning background '000', the sassy handclaps, and Steve Douglas's raging hormonal sax riff add up to more of the same. When Blaine hits his tom-toms after each line of the chorus, the effect is like moving up into overdrive – the song smoothly surges forward.

'Be My Baby' is another story. Ronnie Spector's Brooklyn accent renders her pitch always uncertain, her intonation cracks on 'had' in the song's second line, and emotionally, she seems more dutiful than inspired. It doesn't matter. Phil Spector was in love with her (they eventually married), and he built a rock and roll cathedral around what little her voice had to offer. Blaine's intro is one of rock's grand statements, setting a tone of importance that Ronnie's entrance immediately cuts down to size. At the chorus, the Ronettes rise behind Ronnie, tripling her strength, and they stay with her, crooning open-throated vowels. Then there's the bridge, with its ranks of cellos, a mountainous mock-symphony that lasts for the rest of the record. Against all odds, Spector made an initially shaky proposition into what may be his greatest monument.

59: 'Then He Kissed Me' – The Crystals

Produced by Phil Spector; written by Phil Spector, Ellie Greenwich, and Jeff Barry (Philles 115 1963) Billboard: #6

As a kid, the way people moved in movies like *West Side Story* struck me as weird. The real teenagers who strolled the blocks near my house moved so much more fluidly and elegantly. The tableaus they set up were finer poses and better thought-out. Where Jerome Robbins made you understand something about the possibilities of human muscles, those kids back in the neighbourhood made you understand everything about passion and hope.

'Then He Kissed Me' captures what they looked like in its opening lines, sung at a stately cadence:

Well, he walked up to me and he asked me if I wanted to dance,
He looked kinda nice and so I said I might take a chance.

Hearing the Crystals sing those words, you can feel not only the size of the event, but exactly how he moved, slinking his way across the floor, stopping, turning, proposing as elegantly as any cadet, and envision just how she responded, with a mixture of delicacy and suppressed eagerness, each holding back smiles of relief, both hearts jangling like the busy castanets and triangles in the record's background.

Phil Spector sets the song as if it were a jewel, with the gorgeous melody established on guitar and carried away with tympani and strings and an orchestral bridge that tangibly evokes that first dance. It's no wonder that neither Brian Wilson nor Bruce Springsteen could resist covering the song, and it's no wonder that they could never match the original.

Never, because no man could make a mere kiss so meaningful. When she sings, 'He kissed me in a way that I've never been kissed before/He kissed me in a way that I wanna be kissed for evermore,' what you want to know, first time through, is how. But after a while, you realise that the real question may be where. There's a taboo being broken here, and it's far more meaningful than the line crossed by the Crystals' overrated 'He Hit Me (And It Felt Like A Kiss)'. As in Aretha Franklin's 'A Natural Woman', the real dimensions of female sexuality remain unspoken, but they're hidden only if you refuse to pay attention.

And that's probably why they had to get married in the last verse.

97: 'A Fine Fine Boy' – Darlene Love

Produced by Phil Spector; written by Phil Spector, Ellie Greenwich, and Jeff Barry (Philles 117 1963) Billboard: #53

You call the way Love sings testifying. It's a good thing Hal Blaine and Phil Spector are here, too, because they're about the only people in pop who could find a way to keep up with her. For that matter, when she lets loose with a 'Yeah' or charges back in after the sax break, everybody gets left in the dust.

By the way, who says that rock and roll objectifies only women?

195: 'Today I Met The Boy I'm Gonna Marry' – Darlene Love

Produced by Phil Spector; written by Phil Spector, Ellie Greenwich, and Tony Powers

(Philles 111 1963) Billboard: #39

Alone in her room in the early autumn evening, a young woman pushes aside her homework and tells herself what sounds like the truth about the magic she believes she's found. Now that rock and roll has been taken over by those of us who didn't get married straight out of high school, it's hard to remember how plausible the little lies she tells herself must have sounded. But Phil Spector understood. You can tell by the glockenspiel, which tinkles away against that gorgeous melody like it's sprinkling fairy dust.

248: 'He's A Rebel' – The Crystals
Produced by Phil Spector; written by Gene Pitney
(Philles 106 1962) Billboard: #1 (2 weeks)

249: 'He's Sure The Boy I Love' – The Crystals
Produced by Phil Spector; written by Barry Mann and Cynthia Weil
(Philles 109 1962) Billboard: #11

'I imagined a sound – a sound so strong that if the material wasn't the greatest, the sound would carry the record.'

So spoke Phil Spector in 1964, as a way of explaining the unprecedented music he'd been making for the past two years. But his own description didn't really go quite far enough for the sound that he imagined – product that it was not of his efforts only but of the industry of dozens of women and men – had a potency so great that he could change seemingly crucial parts without risk of detection or any decrease in either the quality of the music or the quality of the attraction.

Although Spector was never simply an apprentice or journeyman, he wasn't much more than that before he made these two hits. After understudying with Jerry Leiber and Mike Stoller, he made a variety of independent label productions, then moved to New York City and took a job at Liberty Records, where he worked under the label's Los Angeles-based A&R chief, the producer/engineer Snuff Garrett.

Nineteen-sixty-two was still the heyday of the Brill Building, the New York office building with its music publisher-operated songwriting factories that had so much control over the pre-Beatles record industry, and Spector, who knew what he wanted but couldn't create it from scratch, haunted the offices of the best publishers in both New York and LA. Lester Sill, one of the best music publishers in Hollywood, agreed to become his partner in a new venture, Philles Records (for Phil/Les, see?). But Spector still did outside projects, and his Liberty contract hadn't yet expired.

Still in New York, Phil went to visit another of his publishing cronies, Aaron Schroeder, who played him a new song by Schroeder protégé Gene Pitney (for whom Spector had already produced 'Every Breath I Take'). 'He's A Rebel' clearly was a smash for somebody, and Snuff Garrett planned to make that someone Liberty's ingenue, Vikki Carr. Spector couldn't wait; this was a song he *understood*. He believed that he could not only make the song a hit, he believed he could make a greater record with it than anybody else – including his boss.

He hopped a flight to LA and cut the song with the stellar session line-up pieced together by saxman Steve Douglas, the band that included Hal Blaine on drums with engineer Larry Levine rolling the tape and setting the echo. The track was meant for the Crystals, with whom Philles had already scored on 'There's No Other (Like My Baby)' and 'Uptown'. But the Crystals were teenagers, still in school, and they didn't want to leave home. So Spector winged it: he got Sill to hire the Blossoms, led by Darlene Love, who were the top girl group on the LA session scene. For triple scale. No royalties.

Ironically, Pitney had written 'Rebel' thinking about the Crystals – the real ones, not the Hollywood stand-ins – and 'Uptown'. But Darlene Love, one of the two or three greatest female singers in rock history, missed not a nuance of Pitney's lustful saga. She slurs the run-on lyrics – 'If they don't like him that way, they won't like me after today' sung as one gaspless line – in a husky voice that suggests that however hard he may be on the outside, she knows just the spots where he can be made to melt. Though the sax solo and handclaps date it, Larry Knechtel's piano, Love's bold shout, and Blaine's crushing drum attack mark 'He's A Rebel' as an ultramodern example of studio rock and roll, the equal of what the Motown staff and George Martin and the Beatles began to create that year, and the model for an enormous amount of what came later.

The phantom Crystals were even better than the real thing, and Spector cut 'He's Sure the Boy I Love', the group's next hit, with them, too. Opening with a Love soliloquy on her dream of a perfect boyfriend, each line set off with booming sax riffs, the disc explodes into life as a percussion extravaganza with drum, bass, and sleigh bells. 'He doesn't hang diamonds 'round my neck,' Love cries and then 'whoa, whoa,' as it could never possibly make any difference, as if this guy, unemployed and without prospects or qualifications ('cept for *her*) is a prize everybody in her right mind ought to envy.

If 'Uptown' had been Spector's tribute to the everyday heroes of his working-class origins, he made 'He's Sure the Boy I Love' something better – their exalted revenge, a tribute to what money can never buy.

317: 'There's No Other (Like My Baby)' – The Crystals
Produced by Phil Spector; written by L. Bates and Phil Spector
(Philles 100 1961) Billboard: #20

I think the part where they're walking down the street and he promises to marry her is just as corny as you do. But the way Barbara Alston sings it, there's another story being told here. It's about the importance of feeling psychically unique, especially for folks who are usually lost in the crowd. This was the first hit for the Crystals, and the first for Phil Spector at his own label, and it established a mood (elegiac in regard to teen love) and a theme (that drive to stand out somehow, no matter how the world tried to shape you). Other people made love songs as a matter of pleasure and preference; Spector's are about the crying need for romance in lives too barren to be supportable otherwise.

347: 'Walk On By' – Dionne Warwick
Written and produced by Burt Bacharach and Hal David
(Scepter 1274 1964) Billboard: #6 [Editor's note: not a PS production]

348: 'Do I Love You?' – The Ronettes
Produced by Phil Spector; written by Phil Spector, Vinnie Poncia, and Peter Andreoli
(Philles 121 1964) Billboard: #34

In the spring of 1964, I bought these two singles. They weren't the first records I'd ever owned, but they felt like it.

It's hard to remember why, exactly. Maybe it was just that I spent my own money on them. Whatever, the real root of the story is what they sounded like, and what those sounds represented. They were a kind of music that seemed a secret, a kind of sound that it was somehow wrong to like too much or to take as seriously as whatever British stuff was in the air at the moment. In fact, at home that night, (the memory remains distinct) when 'Don't Let The Sun Catch You Crying' came on the radio, it already seemed to me that if I'd only bought a Gerry and the Pacemakers single, life would have been easier and more normal.

Maybe it would have been. Or maybe there's somebody out there who's hip enough at fourteen to like what they like and not worry about what's cool, to understand that being able to hear the voices of black women speaking to you on the most personal terms is not only nothing to be ashamed of, but something that will absolutely change and enrich your life. But I wasn't that kid.

And maybe I wasn't even that smart. Because, come to think of it, what I hear in these records (which strike me now as pretty sophisticated choices for a teenager to make at a time when the airwaves were flooded with 'Love Me Do', 'A World Without Love', and 'My Guy') isn't even the singing. It's the prettiness of the music, the lushness of the Ronettes' strings and tympani and Dionne's strings and Latin percussion and the little trumpet introjections, and the idea that 'pretty' pop songs didn't all have to be as drab and predictable as a Muzak rendition of 'Autumn Leaves', the childhood memory of which is as scarring as this one is uplifting.

Of the two records, the one that stays with me best is 'Walk On By'. Ronnie Spector's singing just doesn't wear as well, even with Phil surrounding her with another 'Be My Baby'-style cathedral of sound.

On the other hand, Dionne Warwick remains a formidable pop singer even as we enter the 1990s, yet 'Walk On By' might still be the best record she ever made. Certainly it's the closest to straight R&B, thanks to the unending scratch guitar accompaniment and the girls in the background chanting 'Don't Stop'.

Listening twenty-five years later, what these records have in common seems obvious. 'Do I Love You' and 'Walk On By' bracket romance; the Ronettes sing about their fantasy of how great it's going to be, Warwick confesses what a misery it's been. The link is that they're both about secrets, about confessing in utterly public terms the things that you can barely stand to admit to yourself: how deeply you need to be loved, how painful it is to feel that you aren't, the grief and struggle it takes just to say these things out loud. Hearing them now, back to back, doesn't make me feel like such a dumb kid after all. At the very least, I heard what I needed and brought it back home.

361: 'Black Pearl' – Sonny Charles and the Checkmates Ltd
Produced by Phil Spector; written by Phil Spector, Irwin Levine, and Toni Wine (A&M 1053 1969) Billboard: #13

'Black Pearl', not the wildly overrated 'River Deep Mountain High', is Phil Spector's last great record. And leave it to Spector to use as his vehicle a multiracial lounge act, who would never make another truly memorable record, singing a song that expropriates black power rhetoric (the singer's lover must work as a servant) to celebrate transcendent romance (he vows to place her on a pedestal). Hardly anyone else would have thought of it, few would have had the nerve to try to pull it off, and only Spector could have converted the damn thing into music that's touching, even exciting.

502: 'Pretty Little Angel Eyes' – Curtis Lee
Produced by Phil Spector; written by Curtis Lee and Tommy Boyce
(Dunes 2007 1961) Billboard: #7

The first really crazed record Phil Spector ever made, and still one of the most powerful. Lee (who actually got his start by phoning the staff of *Dig*, an LA teen magazine, and singing to them over the phone – they brought him to Hollywood from his home in Yuma, Arizona) wasn't going anywhere before he ran into Spector with his finger cymbals ringing like a cash register, and he wasn't going anywhere after the wild sax solo, but while he and that deep bass careened along, he was one of the greatest rock and roll singers in the world.

637: 'Karma Chameleon' – Culture Club
Produced by Steve Levine; written by George O'Dowd [Boy George], Jon Moss, Roy Hay, Mikey Craig and Phil Pickett
(Epic 04221 1983) Billboard: #1 (3 weeks) [Editor's note: not a PS production]

638: 'Instant Karma (We All Shine on)' – John Lennon
Produced by Phil Spector; written by John Lennon
(Apple 18181 1970) Billboard: #3

In rock mythology, the big distinction is made between the sixties and the seventies, but as Lennon's record (a sixties swan song) and Boy George's demonstrate, the sixties and the eighties contrast more starkly. Both records toy with the idea of 'karma' as a symbol of cosmic comeuppance for the star-struck, but while it's interesting that pop stars of such different generations, with the careers of their peers splayed out before them like so many used-up Corn Kings, return to a concept steeped in rebirth, there the resemblance ends.

Over the clunkiest track Phil Spector ever produced, Lennon does his best to level himself, not in order to obliterate his own superstardom but as a means to (at least theoretically) elevate everybody else. By 'instant karma' he seems to mean immediate consequences. Having just emerged from the cocoon of the Beatles, he spoke with tremendous authority about the havoc wreaked by trying to keep your head in the valet-attended clouds. Whether he's identified a universally applicable cosmic revenge principle is harder to say.

Where Boy George and Culture Club come from, authority means nothing. In their version of pop culture, authority is powerless and it's around that conundrum that they base their song. 'Lovin' would be easy if your colours were like my dreams,' declares George, over the slickest soul track his group ever made. For him, consequences can be avoided by becoming a changeling who eschews anything resembling permanent allegiance. Permanence itself may be the problem: 'I'm a man without conviction,' George says and then without a wink, 'I'm a man who doesn't know / How to sell a contradiction.' But of course, that's all he's ever sold.

Boy George sings as if in toying with the idea of a love that might last, a future that might actually come to exist, he's found the greatest sorrow of his life. And the harmonica backs him up. Lennon, for all his espousals of faith, struggles to keep up with the inexorable cadences of guitar and drum. Neither, in the end, mastered fate at all.

764: 'Just Once In My Life' – The Righteous Brothers
Produced by Phil Spector; written by Gerry Goffin and Carole King
(Philles 127 1965) Billboard: #1

Every record that Phil Spector made with the Righteous Brothers was a paranoiac symphony, and 'Just Once In My Life', with its looming tympani and nerve-wracked strings, may be the most paranoid of all ('Lovin' Feelin'' is just the most symphonic). Bill Medley sings it virtually solo, until he's joined by Bobby Hatfield for the lines that demarcate the real spiritual thicket in which they're trapped: 'I can't give you the world but I will crawl for you girl,' Medley declares. 'I will crawl,' and then, joined by Hatfield, 'Every day, I will crawl.'

784: 'Happy Xmas (War Is Over)' – John Lennon and Yoko Ono
Produced by John and Yoko and Phil Spector; written by John Lennon and Yoko Ono
(Apple 1842 1971) Did not make pop chart

John Lennon was always rock's most Dickensian character, and here, he emulates *A Christmas Carol* to a tee, stopping just short of pronouncing 'God bless us, every one!' Well, Christmas is the season of sentimentality and if there were greater sentimentalists in rock history than Lennon (at least in one of his guises) and Phil

Spector, I've never heard of them. Let's remember, then, that Dickens is remembered in part because of, not despite, his warm and open emotionalism and that *A Christmas Carol* is the best-loved of all his stories not only because it fits the season's hopes, but because, like the best records of the Beatles and Phil Spector, the love it inspires is equal to the love it creates.

786: 'Baby, I Love You' – The Ronettes

Produced by Phil Spector; written by Phil Spector, Ellie Greenwich, and Jeff Barry
(Philles 118 1963) Billboard: #24

Hal Blaine's greatest hits may be defined as the first through fourth beats of every bar. Not that they're any greater on 'Baby, I Love You' in particular than on any other Ronettes (or Crystals or Beach Boys or... you get the idea) record.

The rest of the record is one of Phil Spector's more purely confectionary creations, strings and sleigh bells pushed to the precipice of unquestionable schmaltz and Ronnie Spector's voice floating in the mix like the soul of Teen Dream incarnate. Although when you come right down to it, those repetitions of 'whoa-uh-oh-ooh' are more lustful than spiritual.

858: 'Why Do Lovers Break Each Other's Hearts' – Bob B. Soxx and the Blue Jeans

Produced by Phil Spector; written by Phil Spector, Ellie Greenwich, and Tony Powers
(Philles 110 1963) Billboard: #38

Bob B. Soxx was meant to be a *nom de studio* for Bobby Sheen, a good-enough R&B singer in the Clyde McPhatter mould, discovered first by Johnny Otis, then by Lester Sill, who sent him to Phil Spector. During Spector's brief tenure as East Coast A&R chief for Liberty Records, he cut a couple of sides with Sheen then brought him along as one of the first Philles acts.

But by the time they got to the studio, Spector was already (and justifiably) in love with the Blossoms, the Los Angeles female session group that featured Darlene Love. So 'Why Do Lovers', like the other Soxx hits, 'Zip-A-Dee-Doo-Dah' and 'Not Too Young To Get Married', revolves around Love's amazing singing. If Sheen's around, he can barely be discerned, except perhaps on some doo-wop nonsense syllables in the background at the start.

Despite a piano solo more rinky-dink than honky-tonk, the playing here is fine, one of the most spacious of the Wall of Sound productions, capped by a couple of explosive Hal Blaine fills on the final choruses. But it's really Love's show, one of the best of all the records on which she's featured.

991: 'Every Breath I Take' – Gene Pitney
Produced by Phil Spector; written by Gerry Goffin and Carole King
(Musicor 1011 1961) Billboard: #42

When Gene Pitney's self-made first single, '(I Wanna) Love My Life Away' failed to set the world on fire, his mentor, song publisher Aaron Schroeder, called in chips all over Broadway, getting songs and production help not only from Phil Spector, Gerry Goffin and Carole King but Burt Bacharach and Hal David – even the top dogs Jerry Leiber and Mike Stoller consulted on the project, though it was their one-time protégé, Spector, who drew the assignment.

Spector, whose Philles Wall of Sound wouldn't debut until the end of the year, placed Pitney's extraordinary high tenor in the centre of a musical maelstrom: huge booming drums, shuddering cascades of strings, a chorus big enough for *How The West Was Won*, and the dead-of-night studio psychodrama that went with it, so that by the time he actually stepped to the microphone, Pitney wasn't sure exactly what he was singing (which was nothing more complicated than any of Phil's other commissioned tributes to the holiness of teen romance), only that it was both Big and Important.

The result is too much music for the slight song, a premonition of 'River Deep Mountain High'. Somehow, the whole mess coalesces into a sound compelling for its very excesses. Pitney's vibrato and falsetto have never been employed more spectacularly (if often more appropriately), and Spector's kitchen sink has never been crammed so close to the brim.

The record flopped, of course. 'Love My Life Away' had edged into the Top Forty at Number 39. Spector's grandiosity saw the promised land from a perch at Number 42 and then sank quickly out of sight. But everybody lived happily ever after anyway. Pitney's career took off when he was teamed with Bacharach and David for his next two singles, a pair of movie themes. 'Town Without Pity' (Number 13) and 'Liberty Valance' (Number 4). Schroeder's Musicor label, which he'd founded as a vehicle for Pitney, also became a force in country, releasing some of George Jones's greatest hits. And Philles let Spector give full vent to his eccentricities and excesses with records that sold millions.

One of the more glaring absences from *The Heart Of Rock & Soul* is 'River Deep Mountain High', which Phil Spector produced for Ike and Tina in 1967. It isn't here because it sounds to me like a muddle, an album's worth of sounds jammed onto one side of a 45, with a little girl lyric that completely contradicts Tina Turner's true persona as the Queen of R&B Sleaze.

Of course, there aren't many other Ike and Tina records here, either, but that's mainly for the opposite reason: Ike Turner's productions with Tina were as undercooked as Phil's were overstewed. And for similar reasons, since Spector's need to prove his artistry was matched, if at all, only by Ike's complete disregard of anything that didn't result in a quick reward. So Tina's man slapped together live arrangements of good material and rushed them to market, without worrying exactly how well they'd translate to vinyl and the airwaves. The results are mainly as slap-dash as the process.

[Editor's note: Dave Marsh's top Spector selection was 'You've Lost That Lovin' Feelin'' which he placed at No. 5 on his top 1001 list. Out of interest, the records that he chose above it were, in ascending order: No. 4: 'Reach Out I'll Be There' by the Four Tops, No. 3: 'Papa's Got A Brand New Bag' by James Brown, No. 2: 'Johnny B. Goode' by Chuck Berry, and lastly at No. 1: 'I Heard It Through The Grapevine' by Marvin Gaye.]

15

Phil Spector: The Philles Years by Mike Callahan

In this second section of his piece from Goldmine, *April 1980,
Callahan looks at some of the varied issues from the golden Wall of
Sound era, and notes that not everything emerged in glorious mono.
(Note: terms like 'true stereo' as used here, and indeed notions of the
variety of early 'stereo' engineering, are ones that are subject to a
number of interpretations, and even to this day are often the subject
to much debate on internet chat sites.)*

'You see, I was never a stereo bug. I don't like stereo, maybe because
none of my old records were. I can't make stereo out of them now,
because all the whole track, that massive track, was cut on one
track, and I can't stereo it. I think in terms of a single record being
monaural. Stereo seems to take something away from it.'
Phil Spector, as quoted in Richard Williams' book Out Of His Head

The above quote sounds pretty final, so why am I writing this
column? Because I disagree with Spector's own statement. Many of
Spector's old records were released in stereo, and there are probably
many others that Spector could release in stereo, but hasn't as yet.

Phil Spector's stereo records for Philles are unlike almost any
others I've ever heard (might I coin a term 'Spectorstereo?' No, I'd
better not). 'That massive track' Phil speaks of is the rhythm track,
containing countless guitars, bass, pianos, drums, and percussion
instruments. Indeed, this track has always been on one channel in
Spector's Phllles records. But the voices and strings were recorded
at different times from the rhythm track and for that reason, can be
separated out for a true stereo sound. And Spector's use of echo and
bleedthrough keep the different parts of the song sounding integrated
in stereo, so they really make quite enjoyable listening.

Spector's first two hits on Philles with the Crystals were recorded
in late 1961 and early 1962 at Mirasound in New York. I don't know
of any songs recorded at Mirasound that early which have surfaced
in true stereo, so it's possible that 'There's No Other' and 'Uptown'
may have been recorded in mono. But Spector's next dozen or so

hits were recorded at least partly at Gold Star in Los Angeles, which by that time had a three-track stereo recorder. Spector used one track for the rhythm and the other two for the voices and strings. The LP *Phil Spector's Greatest Hits* (Warner-Spector 2SP-9104) contains an interesting stereo version of the Crystals' 'He's Sure The Boy I Love', recorded in October 1962 at Gold Star. The stereo version has the rhythm track on one channel. The instrumental track is essentially the same as the hit single, but the vocals sound different. First of all, Darlene Love (who was singing lead on this 'Crystals' record) can be heard singing over the 'sha-la-las' just after the spoken intro, and on the hit her voice is absent in this spot. This could be chalked up to being a stereo remix, but there is something else different about the stereo version. On the single, Darlene's voice is 'doubled' almost throughout the song (that is, she sings a duet with herself courtesy of overdubbing). On the stereo version, there is only one voice singing lead. Even after repeated listening, I can't decide whether the one voice on the stereo version is one of the two on the hit single, or whether the stereo version is a completely different take. Either way, the important point to be made here is that the song was recorded in stereo, and that Spector had just been sitting on the tapes for 15 years. Perhaps by 1990, we'll hear some more of the early Philles sounds in stereo.

None of the Crystals albums were released in true stereo, although a record collector friend claims to have seen one of their albums with a banner claiming it to be electronically reprocessed (I haven't been able to confirm this. Any help out there?). And none of the hit versions of the Crystals songs have appeared in true stereo on various artists' albums, either. In addition to the alternate version of 'He's Sure The Boy I Love' cited above, there are a couple of bogus versions of the Crystals hits which have appeared on various artists' LPs: 'Da Doo Ron Ron' is on *Monster Hits*, (English Pickwick STAR TRAX PDA-064) and 'Then He Kissed Me' is on *Young Love Era (*BU-4810). Both of these are reprocessed (!) and neither sounds as if Phil Spector had anything to do with their re-recording.

The first Philles album released in stereo was the Ronettes album (4006), which was quite a knockout. (The Christmas album (4005) has subsequently been reissued in true stereo.) Five of the classic Ronettes hits are on the album in true stereo, Phil Spector-style. On all twelve cuts the entire rhythm track is on the right channel, the lead singer in the middle, and the strings or back-up vocals on the left channel. There is quite a bit of bleedthrough of the rhythm track to the opposite channel, complete with echo (shades of the Teddy Bears album reviewed last month!). The Ronettes never sounded better. There are some pleasant surprises on the album, such as hearing the castanets and handclaps behind Ronnie's voice on 'Be My Baby' instead of being buried in the rhythm track. But one song in particular stands out on this stereo album. 'Walking in the Rain' has the usual rhythm – right, lead vocal – middle, back-up vocal – left, format, but it's the thunderstorm that *really* catches the ear! The first thunderclap booms in on the right, the storm rolls left and then stays on the left side through the first verse. For the second verse, the thunderstorm rolls across to the right channel. And near the end of the song, both thunder and rain slowly rumble from right to left and then back again. The effect is just subtle enough so that it doesn't detract from the song. Well done.

The stereo version of the Ronettes album on the original Philles label costs a small fortune these days, but to collectors' good fortune, the English reissue on Phil Spector International (SUPER 2307 003) is also in true stereo. The fact that the album is stereo is not immediately obvious by looking at the record jacket or label of the import. It's commonly available for under $10, and worth every cent.

The next three albums issued on Philles after the Ronettes album, were also in true stereo. All of them were by the Righteous Brothers, but only a few songs on each album were actually produced by Phil Spector. But what songs! 'You've Lost That Lovin' Feelin'' appears on the album of the same name (4007), and the stereo expansion really enhances the sound of this song. In fact, all of the Righteous Brothers hits sound particularly good in stereo. Again, 'Lovin' Feelin'' has the rhythm – right, lead – middle, strings – left, configuration.

Philles 4008 is *Just Once In My Life*, and contains both the title track and also a song I consider to be close to a perfect pop record: 'Unchained Melody'. They both get the topical stereo treatment from Spector. 'Unchained Melody' is a stunningly beautiful song in stereo, from Bobby Hatfield's soaring voice down to the almost subliminal horns playing miles away behind the strings. Phllles 4009 (*Back To Back*) contains 'Hung On You', 'Ebb Tide' and the non-chart 'White Cliffs Of Dover'. The stereo treatment is similar to the earlier Righteous Brothers albums, except the rhythm track is on the left for a change. All of the Righteous Brothers hits for Philles are in true stereo on *The Righteous Brothers' Greatest Hits* on Verve

(V6-5020). As a footnote to the Righteous Brothers, they supposedly recorded 'Soul And Inspiration' for Verve to prove Spector didn't have a monopoly on that sound. Interestingly enough, they copied Spector's production right down to the way he put stereo on records: rhythm-lead-strings separation.

Philles' last album (4011) was the Ike and Tina Turner album. It was re-issued (with one different cut) on A&M in 1969. With half the songs on the album produced by Spector and the other half produced by Ike Turner, the LP has a schizophrenic sound: the two production styles are so different that it only takes a few bars of a song to identify the producer. The recording quality of the album is sometimes a bit flakey, since it's fairly easy to hear vocal tracks being mixed in and out of many of the songs due to an odd hiss in either the tape or one of the mikes in the studio. The stereo version of 'River Deep Mountain High' is fairly impressive, with Tina's voice just barely escaping from being overwhelmed by a gigantic pulsating stereophonic blob. All in all, Spector's productions on the album are worth hearing.

Spector produced many records while he ran Philles, and most of them were hits. Contrary to what he would have us believe, most of them were also recorded on stereo equipment. The discography indicates the album availability of his Philles hits, and on which albums you can expect stereo and which mono.

How ironic that the man who disliked stereo would influence... trends in mixing!

16
Phil's Fillies by Geoff Brown

Spector has been, of course, long associated with the wonderful girl group genre, although many other producers provided us with memorable and varied examples of the style. However, Spector's groups remain the best remembered, and this overview from Geoff Brown, an experienced commentator on the whole pop and soul scenes, draws out the strengths and differences of the Crystals and the Ronettes. The piece first appeared in The History Of Rock *No. 26 in 1982.*

With the Crystals and the Ronettes, Phil Spector raised the girl vocal group style to a new peak. Such groups came to the fore in the late 50s and remained an integral part of rock and soul throughout the 60s. Their songs invariably concerned the virtues of a boyfriend past, present or future – virtues often visible only to the narrator herself. They told how he made her life special or how she made his hard life easier. He was, of course, frequently sought-after by other girls, but though sorely tempted, always remained loyal.

The first notable girl group in rock was the Chantels, whose 'Maybe' was a US Top Twenty hit in 1958. By 1961 the Shirelles had taken over through 'Will You Love Me Tomorrow', a number one in the States and a number three in the UK. It was written by Carole King and Gerry Goffin, two of the many Brill Building songwriters who, with Spector, were soon to develop the girl group style into an art form.

Spector's first female protégés were the Crystals, five Brooklyn schoolgirls who had formed a semi-professional singing group in 1961. Comprising three 17-year-olds: Dee Dee Kennibrew, Barbara Alston and Pat Wright – and 16-year-olds Lala Brooks and Mary Thomas, their pliable voices were perfect for the sound with which the producer wanted to launch his own label, Philles. They had previously been employed to cut demo songs published by Hill and Range Music; and two writers for Hill and Range, Bill Giant and Bernie Baum, offered the group to Spector in exchange for a financial interest in his label.

The Crystals were pleasant, though not breathtakingly attractive girls, and their first single, 'There's No Other (Like My Baby)', with Alston's lead vocal, was a ballad based on unquestioning devotion to a boyfriend – just the kind of contented, low-key passion one might expect from such girls-next-door. Released in October 1961, the single charted a month later in *Billboard*'s Hot Hundred, ultimately reaching the Number 20 position and giving both group and label a solid start.

Uptown Flamenco

The Crystals' next release was 'Uptown', originally written by Barry Mann and Cynthia Weil for Tony Orlando. Spector heard it first, however, and was rightly convinced that it was more suited to a female delivery. The mid-tempo ballad, its mood set by flamenco guitar, told a ghetto love story: the man goes downtown to demeaning daily toil, but when he returns uptown to his tenement slum his woman treats him like a king. Spector's use of strings and castanets reinforced the ghetto feel, a device learned when co-writing 'Spanish Harlem' with Jerry Leiber. 'Uptown' rose to Number 13 in the charts in the spring of 1962 and remained in the Hot Hundred for three months.

THE CRYSTALS   850 Seventh Avenue
                                New York, N.Y.

A gust of public indignation swept the Crystals' next single off turntables and record counters alike. 'He Hit Me (And It Felt Like A Kiss)' was a Goffin-King song and the premise of pain equalling pleasure was too near the knuckle for 1962. The lyric was no paean to sado-masochism, however, but rather a moral tale. The girl secretly goes out with another boy; when her original boyfriend is incensed enough to strike her, she realises the strength of his love and they kiss and make up. But as soon as the implications of the lyric sank in – not to say its tacit acceptance of violence – airplay was denied it and the record was quickly withdrawn. The track later surfaced on a Greatest Hits album.

Mary Thomas quit the Crystals in 1962 to get married, and the group continued as a quartet. Two months later, however, a far greater transformation occurred when Spector shifted from New York to Los Angeles. He took Gene Pitney's 'He's A Rebel' into the Gold Star studios with more enthusiastic, younger musicians and a fine session singer, Darlene Love. With this set-up he fashioned a brasher and far bigger sound than he had ever achieved back East.

'Rebel', with Love's assured double-tracked singing about a James Dean-like figure who only shows his soft, romantic side to the girl he adores, gave the group a US Number 1 in November 1962 and their first Top Twenty hit in the UK. 'He's Sure The Boy I Love' was the follow-up and the second consecutive 'Crystals' release to feature Darlene Love. The fact that her group, the Blossoms, provided the vocal backing did not deter Spector from issuing the disc under the Crystals name. The next release, however, unleashed the whirlwind. Spector, Ellie Greenwich and Jeff Barry collaborated on a song about love at first sight and set the lyric to music of a decidedly danceable tempo. 'Da Doo Ron Ron' fairly belted along, powered by Hal Blaine's booming drums, a clanging piano and a vast band creating an atmosphere of heady exuberance that contrasted with Lala Brooks' matter-of-fact narration. A Number 3 hit in the States in 1963, it reached Number 5 in the UK and re-appeared at Number 15 in Britain in 1974.

Pat Wright quit the group in October 1963 and was replaced by Frances Collins, who was in the line-up when the Crystals toured Britain in February 1964. By then they had achieved their biggest UK hit, 'Then He Kissed Me', which had reached Number 2 the previous year; it also made Number 6 in the US. But this was to be their swan song, as Spector had found a new act on which to work. Although the Crystals turned out more good singles such as 'Little Boy', 'I Wonder' (a UK-only release) and 'All Grown Up', a sparser, urgent sound, they gradually faded. The Crystals moved to the United Artists label where they cut a couple of poor singles before turning to domesticity. They reappeared in the early seventies to feature in Richard Nader's rock'n'roll revival show.

A Family Affair

Replacing the Crystals in Spector's plans, the Ronettes were something of a family affair. New York-born sisters Veronica and Estelle Bennett and cousin Nedra Talley started as a dance group, the Dolly Sisters, in 1959 and by 1961 were resident dancers at the Peppermint Lounge. During this Twist craze era they went on the road with DJ Clay Cole's Twist package and appeared with him in the film *Twist Around The Clock*. They were signed by Don Kirshner's Colpix label in 1961 but, renamed Ronnie and the Relatives, they had no success despite shortening their name after their first single.

Then fate took a hand. Legend has it that Estelle and Spector were connected by a crossed telephone line; they talked, and he invited her to sing on a session. (The girls had previously done sessions backing Del Shannon and James Darren.) Whether truth or fiction, the partnership became fact when the Ronettes signed to Philles in 1963. By August of that year their first single was climbing to the Number 2 position in the Hot Hundred and Number 4 in the UK. Spector had coached them for six months before its release.

'Be My Baby' had many of the producer's trademarks – booming tympani, whip-crack snare drum, swooping strings and clacking castanets. But what had as much impact as the sound of the record was the look of the Ronettes; these were no little girls next door, but wore their hair piled precariously high, their lips shining and pouty, their eyes hooded with mascara. Ronnie's high, throatily-squeezed voice was by no means classic, but was perfect for both vulnerable teen ballads ('The Best Part Of Breaking Up' and 'Walking In The Rain') and more up-tempo positive pieces ('Be My Baby' and 'Do I Love You'). In January 1964 they headlined a UK tour with the Rolling Stones.

Although the Ronettes never found the consistent chart success of the Crystals, it wasn't for lack of effort on their producer's part. 'Walking In The Rain', prefaced by thunder and a downpour, and 'Baby, I Love You', with its sweeping string arrangement sounding as though at least two orchestras were sharing the studio, had as much care lavished on them as any Spector record. The fact that Phil and Ronnie had fallen in love – they were to marry in 1968 – clearly had much to do with this.

However, after two fine songs by Spector, Pete Anders and Vinnie Poncia ('The Best Part Of Breaking Up' and 'Do I Love You'), two by Mann and Weil ('Walking In The Rain' and the blurry-sounding

'Born To Be Together') and a final small Hot Hundred hit with 'Is This What I Get For Loving You' (originally the B-side of 'Oh, I Love You'), Spector passed the group's production to Jeff Barry for a final Philles single, 'I Can Hear Music'. Their only LP for the label, *Presenting The Ronettes*, was rather better value than any of the three Crystals' sets, which each had four tracks in common.

Ronnie's career as a solo artist under the name Veronica took an early knock when 'Why Don't They Let Us Fall In Love', released on the new Phil Spector Records label, was pulled from the stores after a disappointing test market. When Spector moved to A&M in the late sixties, he brought the group back again with 'You Came, You Saw, You Conquered', the label crediting the artists as 'the Ronettes featuring the voice of Veronica'.

Working at Apple in London, Phil produced Ronnie's 1971 version of George Harrison's 'Try Some, Buy Some', but neither the song nor its treatment offered the singer the degree of emotional involvement so evident in the Philles material. The Ronettes surfaced with a revised line-up on the Buddah label in 1973. That was the year Ronnie and Phil separated; they were divorced in 1974.

Ronnie Spector subsequently made a live comeback with Southside Johnny and the Asbury Jukes, and a single recorded with Bruce Springsteen's E Street Band, the Billy Joel composition 'Say Goodbye To Hollywood', was released in 1977 to critical acclaim. Like so many girl vocal groups' lead singers, however, she failed to make a sustained impact as a solo star despite the obvious depth of her talent.

Though both the Crystals and the Ronettes faded after fairly brief, yet incandescent, spells in the limelight, the quality of their singles was high. From 'Uptown' and 'Da Doo Ron Ron' to 'Be My Baby' and 'Walking In The Rain', their records sound as fresh and exciting today as when they were first laid down.

17
The Crystals Wayne Jones Talks With Dee Dee Kennibrew

This short piece comes from the Goldmine *issue of December 1980, and is one of the rare occasions when one of the Crystals has aired her views of their all-too-short singing career.*

Dee Dee can you tell us how the Crystals first got together? I understand that you were all from Brooklyn.
We got together through mutual friends, really. The guy who put the group together had a niece who sang with two other girls in high school, so that made three. Then the guy who wrote our first song – his sister-in-law became the fourth member; my mother used to work where they all rehearsed, and so when they needed another girl I was number five.

How did you get together with Phil Spector?
We were rehearsing at Hill and Range publishing company and he happened to be there one evening. He asked us if we were signed to anyone; we said 'No', and it went from there.

Musically, everyone recognises the fact that Phil Spector was a genius – but personally, he was supposed to have been quite moody and temperamental. What was it like working for Phil Spector?
From the beginning he was just a normal, regular person who wore three-piece suits. I think he enjoyed taking people by surprise and he just got a little weirder and weirder and weirder.

The Crystals recorded their songs before the 'Wall of Sound' was added. How did you feel about the Wall of Sound?
Well, the Wall of Sound was very expensive – especially since we were paying for it. (Laughing.) I felt that a lot of it was not necessary and that you lost a lot of what you put down originally. The voices suffered a lot and it took away from our voices because they added in more music. If he wanted to make a wall of sound, why not make a wall of voices. He could have put in more voices instead of putting

in four pianos. I really felt it got to be a bit much after a while. I remember taking one of the songs to a writer to arrange the tune for us to do on stage and he couldn't figure out what the musicians were doing... it was just a muddle.

What about your musical influences?
When we first got started we just did it out of fun, without expecting to do any recording. To be honest with you I never saw a show until I was on one myself. There were certain groups I liked, like the Shirelles and the Chantels. And it wasn't that we patterned ourselves after any group – because we had never thought we would do any recording. We were basically just kids that were not looking at this from a point of being a profession. It was just fun to rehearse after school. Although our manager at the time had it in mind, we really never thought it would come to pass.

What about the tours? Did you encounter any problems, since on most tours there were very few girl acts and you had to travel with primarily male artists?
Not any serious problems. At our ages then it was easy to cope with the touring. I mean, doing 62 one-nighters was great. (Laughing.) No problems with the males. In fact, it was fun.

The Crystals had many great hits in the early 60s but perhaps your most controversial record was a song you did called 'The Screw'. I had heard that Phil Spector deliberately wanted a controversial-type song recorded in order to help get out of some sort of recording contract. What do you know about that?
That might have well been. I'm not really sure what his motive was for doing it but it was a haphazard thing. It was something we just went into the studio and did as opposed to rehearsing it to perfect it. Now originally we were supposed to be going on another label, I mean there was no Philles label when we first recorded. He was producing us initially for another label. But then he decided to get together with Lester Sill and put a company together after he had the record recorded. So, our first record became their first release on their label. Initially, I think we had been signed to Liberty or some other company and we were also with Thrill Publishing Company. So how he got out of that may have been because of 'The Screw'. And then again he had the 'He Hit Me' thing, too, which was another

one they had to pull off. But again I'm not really sure because at the time we were all just kids and weren't aware what was happening behind the scenes.

Someone else said that Phil Spector had to produce so many records by the Crystals and that he had supposedly run out of material. What Spector supposedly did next was to bring the girls (Crystals) into the recording studio along with his attorney, and that his attorney was the one on the record who sang the male part 'The Screw, Part 1'.
I don't really know who that male voice is but I do know it was not done while we were there. That was dubbed in later.

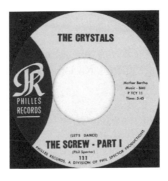

Who were the other original members of the group and what are they doing today?
Lala Brooks has four children and is living in Teaneck, New Jersey. Her husband is a drummer who has played with Roberta Flack. As a matter of fact she met him on tour many years ago and ended up marrying him. Patricia Wright – her husband was a serviceman and because she had a bad heart she left the group early because of the extensive touring. Mary Thomas now has two children and is living in Brooklyn. Barbara Alston has two children and, the last I heard, was living in North Carolina with her husband, who's also in the service.

Would you say that when Phil Spector fell in love with Veronica of the Ronettes that he seemed to neglect the Crystals and the Ronettes records were pushed more?
Yes, but you see, there was a lot of dissension between Phil and our group anyway at that point. It could have been because he started going out with Ronnie at the time but probably not the key factor.

Of the great groups in Spector's stable at the time, which one was the finest you worked with?
I never really worked with any of them with the exception of Bob B. Soxx and the Blue Jeans a little bit on the road, but Darlene Love was not there with them. Another girl had come in because Darlene was doing a lot of studio work. I would say Darlene Love was the finest singer he had.

Did Darlene Love ever sing with the Crystals?
No.

Who sang most of the leads?
Barbara Alston and Lala Brooks.

What is your favourite Crystals' recording?
I think I enjoy doing 'There's No Other' the best, but on stage it would be 'Da Doo Ron Ron'.

What about being called an 'oldies' act? Has it restricted you from progressing into other areas of music?
Yes and no. There are a lot of people who weren't from that era who aren't working at all – because they don't fit into that category. In other words, they're not really current, but not an 'oldie' either so they're just out of work. So, from that point of view, I don't resent it but yes, as far as going to record companies for new recordings I have to use another name. I went to one company with a tape and mentioned our name, the Crystals: they said no, because we were immediately recognised as an 'oldies' group. So, we brought the same tape to another company and used an entirely different name and got a record deal. So there are those in the record companies who will automatically turn you off. It's too bad, too, because there are some fantastic singers out there. For example Little Anthony sounds better than ever; Jackie Wilson, before his accident, was sounding just great – so these people will tend to stereotype you. This is one profession where they give you no credit for having learned anything. Instead of them saying, 'Oh, she's been around for some time so she must be good at what she's doing' their attitude is, 'The newer the better'. My feeling is who wants a doctor just out of med school? Wouldn't you prefer someone that's been at it a while?

Another one of the Crystals big hits was 'He's A Rebel', written by Connecticut's own Gene Pitney. What do you remember about that one?
Phil liked him a lot. The first that I remember of Gene was a song he did called 'Every Breath I Take'. When 'He's A Rebel' was made available to us, it didn't sit right at first. We wanted to keep doing the real funky stuff – but Phil said no and this song was one he wanted us to do. The darn thing came out and became #1. Songs that we like were mainly R&B hits but not nationwide.

The Crystals were also an important part of the classic Phil Spector-produced Christmas album. Did you have any inkling at the time that this album would go on to become a classic?
No, but I do feel that there were a couple of cuts from that album that, if released as singles, could easily have been hits on their own.

Which cuts?
One was 'Christmas (Baby Won't You Please Come Home)'; I thought it was an excellent tune. And the 'Bells Of St Mary's' I thought was very good, too.

Were royalties a problem for the Crystals as with so many others?
Yes. I think in those days they (record companies) felt the younger the better because when you're young you don't know a lot. By the time you wake up most record companies had made their bundle and that was it. So when you tried to find them to get your money, forget it because they had closed shop. It's always easy to rip off kids. And if you don't have a lawyer that really knows how to read show business contracts it won't do you much good either.

If someone ever wrote the definitive book on the history of rock music how would you like the Crystals remembered?
Well, I'll tell you. I'd like to write a book myself. (Laughing.) I would like to get together with all the groups I've worked with and interview them like you're doing me and from there, write a book on all of the unbelievable things that have happened to people who started off with stars in their eyes and finally woke up. This would be a good book for those who are just getting into the business... and let them know how many of us got ripped off and taken.

18
The Strange Story Of 'Please Be My Boyfriend'
by Kingsley Abbott

As with most other acts of the time, many tracks were recorded before the best single releases were decided upon. Spector's list of unreleased tracks was diminished when many great cuts appeared on the Phil Spector International label in the UK, but some remain in the can to this day. One such is the song 'Please Be My Boyfriend', which has become a minor 'cause celebre' of its own.

Spector productions, or productions purporting to be by Spector, or even sessions that are only linked to Spector by name or reputation have caused endless navel-gazing over the years. Foremost amongst these is the recording of 'Please Be My Boyfriend', which emerged as a bootleg vinyl 45 in Japan in the early nineties.

The song was first known about from an inclusion in the late Alan Betrock's seminal work, *Girl Groups – The Story Of A Sound* (Delilah Communications, 1982). On page 125 was a copy of a recording studio track sheet from 9th July 1964 for the basic session for the song. Added to the sheet were details of a second session on 4th August. Interestingly, the vinyl bootleg notes claim the second session was on 21st July with what may be some overdubs marked, but this is clearly marked as the billing date (though the billing, according to the pencilled additions close by, appears to refer only to the four and-a-half hour July session). The sheet is headed as 'Phil Spector Prod', with the 'Prod' subsequently pencilled over. The studio in question is Broadway Recording at 1697 Broadway, an address well known in the music business (see background piece in section 1). Although there is nothing on the sheet to suggest it, Betrock refers to the track in the caption as a Crystals session, and it was as such that it was bootlegged with an erroneous and misleading Gold Star acetate label. It is at least questionable if this was originally a Crystals session, as it comes after the time when Spector had appeared to have lost interest in them in favour of the Ronettes.

The story then seems to get more complicated – enter the Lovelites, a white East Coast trio, who had been introduced to Spector via the mentoring services of songwriter Doc Pomus. Doc had seen potential in the trio, and Spector appeared to agree as he teamed them with Pete Anders and Vinnie Poncia, with whom he had been composing for the Ronettes. Pete and Vinnie began some recording with the Lovelites, initially with 'Please Be My Boyfriend' in September 1964 at the same Broadway studio, utilising what is apparently the same track as was recorded in the July. A case of waste not, want not, it would seem. The Lovelites version was never released, and indeed group member Louise Robbins cannot recall ever getting as far as the background vocals for the song. She can however hear lead singer Joanne Clemente's voice at the end of the 'Crystals' version. The Lovelites did eventually get one release, '(When) I get Scared', the following year on Spector's offshoot Phi-Dan label (#5008).

A copy of the 'Gold Star' demo of 'Please Be My Boyfriend'. Barbara Alston sings lead

To further obscure its origins, 'Please Be My Boyfriend' has no writer credits. Aural evidence suggests that it is not an Anders/Poncia song. Their writing style of the time was already quite distinctive. Closer to the Greenwich/Barry style, this is also difficult to quite see, unless it was a work-in-progress or from their rejection pile. The song does not exhibit their usual strong sense of melody or hooks, though the timing is right that it would date from their association with Spector. The most likely scenario is that the song was lying around and was suggested as a try-out to see how well the very young Lovelites worked as singers in the studio. This of course does not explain the supposed Crystals version, nor how a Lovelite voice appears to be on the 'earlier' version.

The recording itself has the feel of a competent demo. Strong drumming and percussion drive it along, as does a strong lead, but the background vocals are poorly mixed and the arrangement leaves plenty of room for much more filling out. It can be easily dismissed as an actual Spector production, though it is far from being poor – rather more unfinished. It could therefore have been an Anders and Poncia produced session from the start, with them starting a Spector-feeling record, or it could have been a work by someone unknown, though the subsequent work with the Lovelites suggests the former.

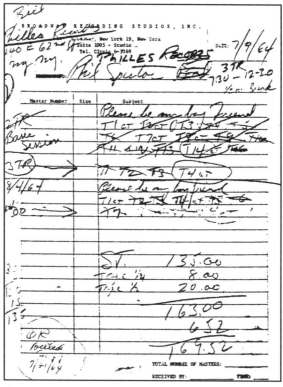

A studio sheet from the 'Please Be My Boyfriend' session

19
Ronnie Spector: Say Goodbye To Hollywood
by John Tobler

Ronnie Spector, née Veronica Bennett, is one of the most colourful and central figures to the whole Wall of Sound story. As well as providing the most distinctive voices associated with Spector, she also spent some years married to him, a time that is graphically detailed in her Be My Baby *autobiography. This interview, from the wonderful* Hot Wacks *fanzine, covers much of her career before and during her Spector connections.*

Phil Spector... Ah, the magic that name still evokes, but what of the former Mrs Phil Spector? Veronica Bennett, better known as Ronnie Spector, this is your story. The interview was conducted by the inimitable John Tobler when Ronnie was over here with Southside Johnny and the Asbury Jukes. The date is the 7th of April, 1977.

Your first meeting with Phil Spector; I have four different versions: a) he spotted you at the Peppermint Lounge b) you are introduced to him via Tony Orlando and Don Kirshner c) you talked to him on the telephone and d) your sister talked to him on the telephone...
Well, when he first saw us, when and where I don't know, but he must have seen us on the show or something. But as it turned out, the then editor of *16* magazine introduced us to Phil. They had a meeting and we met Phil one evening when we were suggested to do a background session for Phil and we came into the studio that evening and he heard my voice. He said 'that's it'. So that's how it actually started. I really can't remember now – it's been a long time.

What that meant was you cut 'So Young' and 'Why Won't They Let Us Fall In Love'?
The first time? 'Why Won't They Let Us Fall In Love' was my record before 'Be My Baby'. When I cut 'Why Won't They', they were writing 'Be My Baby'. Phil said, 'I don't want the first one, "Be My Baby" is it'. So 'Be My Baby' was actually my second recording with Phil.

What about 'So Young'?
That was done later. It was done maybe '64.

It still came out on the Phil Spector label rather than the Philles label.
Yes, because it was Veronica, it wasn't the Ronettes or things like that.

Look, I should really be asking about things going on now. How did you become involved with this Asbury Park scene?
John Lennon... he didn't actually have to do with the Dukes but he introduced me to his engineer and he called me and asked me would I like to come down to a recording session and hear the Asbury Dukes singer. I said 'who'? I had never heard of them, but I had nothing to do that evening and said 'why not'? So I went down there and I saw this little white guy with glasses on and sort of Nebraskan looking, and said well let me hear what they have to say... and when they played back that tape of Johnny's voice and what he was doing in the studio, I absolutely flipped... and Miami Steve, the producer, I just couldn't believe that there was a producer alive other than Phil that could do such work and that's how it actually all started. They asked me that evening would you like to sing on the record with John. I said 'great'.

Who is the engineer?
Jim Iovine. It's just that Miami Steve knew just how to do my voice so well because I retired in '74 'cos I just couldn't find a producer who knew my voice, knew how to handle my voice. When I saw Miami Steve and the way he handled me, boy he really knows how to handle my voice. I started semi-touring with the Asbury Dukes for a little while. Then it all sort of came together on its own.

Is Miami going to produce your album?
Yes, definitely.

He's good. When Springsteen came over I did a tape for the party afterwards and I put all these oldies on and even the ones he hadn't heard before he knew what they were. His Dion affiliation is obviously very...
He knows everything about the music business, he can play nearly every instrument; there's nothing the man doesn't know.

Have you actually recorded the album?
No, it's in the process of getting material, finding the right songs, 'cos he's being very choosy with my stuff because he's trying to find songs that fit me. Just like prior to what I did with George Harrison, several years ago, like 'Try Some, Buy Some'. All those things didn't fit me... so what Miami's trying to do is get absolutely everything that fits my voice so that the album won't miss something that the public would say 'that's Ronnie Spector.'

Are you going to record any of the oldies again or is there no going back?
I don't know, I wouldn't re-record ever any of the stuff that Phil did for me 'cos those are classics and I don't think they should ever be redone.

Not even something like 'When I Saw You', which didn't really get noticed properly?
'When I Saw You' was just a B-side, it was never meant to be an A-side. I don't think so.

When you played it at Biba's it was a storm!
Yes it was great... I don't know... when I came to London all I did was sing everything on my album and the audience loved it, which floored me. In the States I couldn't have got away with that.

Are you going to use the Asbury Dukes as back-up?
Probably the East Street Band. They are on my single, so they'll probably do my album as well.

Tell us about the single, what's behind it?

'Say Goodbye To Hollywood'... well the reason I love it is... Billy Joel wrote it and apparently had me in mind when he did. When I heard it, I said, 'that's for me'. I love it. It's just a great little number and it reminds me a little of my marraige – I lived in Hollywood. My new comeback. It's one hell of a song for a comeback for me.

You're probably the only person really that your ex-husband produced that is still recording.
Yeah, well I don't know, the Righteous Brothers are probably still recording.

But they were recording before Phil weren't they?
That's true.

They had a career of sorts. Somebody like Darlene Love, for instance...
I don't know what happened to her, someone told me that she's got a new single out and that it's great.

Should be, she had an excellent voice.
I loved it, out of all Phil's artists she was my favourite.

The Apple single, could you tell us how that happened?
That happened 'cos I was married and I guess Phil was just trying to make me happy. It was a George Harrison tune, he should have sung it, it wasn't for me. I didn't enjoy doing it. It wasn't in the right key as it wasn't written for me really. I even told George 'cos Phil wouldn't listen to me, I said 'what is he trying to do to me, this is just not me'. So during that time I was married I wasn't doing any recording. I was just happy do be in the studio.

Why weren't you? Was Phil preventing you?
Yes. That's 90% why my marriage broke up basically. I just found myself sitting at home, isolated from the world, not doing anything. My whole life is enslaved in singing and I just couldn't bear it any longer. Phil wanted me to be strictly a housewife – no recording, no performances. I thought that when we got married – I loved him dearly – we'd make an excellent team because we had that 'click'. I had the voice and the talent and he had the production part. I thought 'it can't miss'. But when I got married it all went into darkness. All of a sudden... Nothing.

That is a shame, because there was so much potential... Going back a little was it right you were called the Dolly Sisters before you were called the Ronettes?
That was something when we were 12 or 13 years old. My grandmother wanted us to be the three little Dolly Sisters and we were just called that for a little while... we never recorded as that.

Am I right in thinking that the name Ronettes came from a bit of each of the three names?
No, it actually comes from just my name. There were groups out then called the Marvellettes, Shirelles... taken from Shirley's name, so they figured Ronnie – my mother actually named us the Ronettes.

What about those Colpix records?
Well those I had done when I was in high school. Nothing happened with any of them.

How were you discovered to do them.
We used to hang around CBS in New York and we met a guy called Phil Halikus and he thought we were great and he's the one who sent us up to Colpix Records. I was a real baby when I made those records... I used to say, 'the little girl with the big voice'. But none of those records were hits.

What were they; cover versions... or what?
No they were all original songs, but none of them were hits because we had nobody like Phil Spector to handle us; most of those records were not put out until after 'Be My Baby' came out and was such a smash. Then they put a whole album out.

Tell me about the Peppermint Lounge. I mean, this is the Twist time, right?
That's when we really got started as far as performing. It was very big in New York – the Peppermint Lounge – so the three of us decided, because we were desperate to make it, desperate, because we didn't have a record out, we had nothing. The Shirelles and all the others had big hits by this time. So we went to the Peppermint Lounge and were standing outside, in line just like everyone else; we had to be in a line in those days – and the manager comes running out. We'd dressed alike, fixed our hair alike, and he came running

out, 'you're on girls, you're on'. They were expecting another girl group and they thought we were that group because they saw us all dressed alike and assumed we were the group. We didn't care, we said 'sure, oh yes' we got right up there on stage... and there was Joey Dee. First we started out more or less dancing and then I got hold of a microphone, which I couldn't resist and that's how it all started. So we started touring with Joey Dee... we were doing songs like 'Shout', 'Will You Love Me Tomorrow' and a couple of others like that. We only did 3 or 4 songs in his review. Then they shipped us out to Miami Beach, Peppermint Lounge and that's where we met Murray (Murray the K, who was from New York at the Brooklyn Fox) and he asked us to be his dancing girls. So we sang and danced on his shows and we didn't have any hit records but we went over the biggest because we were the first girl group to wear tight dresses, eyeliner – we were just different. The fellas sort of liked it too. We used to wear slits up the dresses because of the dancing, that's the story behind that one... I don't know where Phil saw us actually, he could have come to one of the Brooklyn Fox shows, but soon after that we went with Phil into the studios and that's how it all started.

Did you ever record with Joey Dee?
No. [Editor's note: it is almost certainly the Ronettes on Dee's 'Getting Nearer'.]

What about 'Twist Around The Clock'?
Someone else asked me about that – we never did 'Twist Around The Clock'. Was that a movie?

Yes. It was the follow-up to Rock Around The Clock *with Chubby Checker and Joey Dee.*
That was way before my time...

Ah well, that's another of those little rumours... is it true that your hair was actually 18" above your head?
Just about... No, it didn't take us that long to fix it that way. There was a lot of teasing involved. In those days that was the style, but 18" is a bit exaggerated, I don't think it was that high at all. It was the style then. It was a sort of Ronette trademark, if you like.

The singles you made for Phil, somebody has said they were all

songs about you and him.
Basically they were I suppose, about our relationship. Like, right after he wrote 'Be My Baby' because Phil and I were seeing each other, he wrote another song 'Baby, I Love You'. He was telling me he loved me, then it went from all those songs he wrote for me and I sang with all my heart to him.

How about 'The Best Part Of Breaking Up'?
Well, we never broke up, I think that was just one of the songs.

That wasn't specifically written...
About us? No.

What about 'Walking In The Rain'?
Well 'Walking In The Rain', I guess it was something that Phil and I did in New York together. All of the songs weren't written specifically about us because other writers were in on it too. So if Phil saw material – great material – we would do it. It was both. You could say that prior to 'Breaking Up' and 'Walking In The. Rain' it was songs about him and me.

How about 'I Can Hear Music'. It was a strange one (w. Jeff Barry) because a lot of people feel the Beach Boys did it far better than the Ronettes.
Well they did! When we did that I can remember being in the studio with Jeff and when we got to the studio – the last record at Philles that we did – I saw that there weren't a lot of musicians like I was used to on Phil's records. So Jeff took me to one side and told me that Phil said not to have a lot of musicians, he didn't want it that way. So I guess it was Phil's fault because he didn't want to make a big thing out of it... I thought it was a great song but it just didn't – it just wasn't produced right, weren't enough arrangements and production behind it.

What about the Christmas album? How long did it take you to record this?
Months, I remember it like it was yesterday because we had to stay in the studio and if necessary sleep on the stools outside. If one of the other groups were in the studio we would have to lay back for a while. It took months to do. Phil retired after this because it didn't do

what he expected it to.

Because it was released on the same day as John F. Kennedy was assassinated, right?
I think so, yeah. He put everything into it. It's quite a classic.

Was everyone on 'Silent Night', with all that chorus singing?
Yes, the whole lot of us.

Because that's about the only occasion that all you famous people recorded together... it's a shame that there weren't more like that, because it could have been excellent album-wise.
Phil's such a moody person to work with, he was so... er, 'I don't want this, I don't want that', and he has his rights because he's a genius, he really is. I guess he knew what he was doing but it's so often like material that I've got to do and we couldn't understand after recording it why he wouldn't put it out. He had his own personal reasons. It would just drive me crazy.

Is there still a lot of stuff that hasn't come out yet?
You know, it's been so long that I don't know if he has more because Phil is always so full of surprises. But I would say Ronnie has more songs because I was in the studios an awful lot in those days.

These reissue albums, there's an awful lot of stuff that has been previously unavailable. Did you remember it before?
Yes I remembered every song. Like, there was 'Paradise', 'A Woman In Love', 'Keep On Dancing' all these songs. I can't remember any other songs unless they came out.

How did Phil get all those musicians? They weren't very well known at that stage (RS: That's how he got them). He must have had some magic touch there because most of them became very famous afterwards.
It just used to amaze me. There I was 15 years old sitting in a studio and I'd see Leon Russell, Harry Nillson, Sonny Bono, Glen Campbell and Herb Alpert, all these people and they'd be in the studio for hours and hours and Leon Russell's hands were falling off and I'd say how do those guys take this from Phil? I figured it out that they were all learning, that's why they're all big today... because they all learned from Phil.

Are there any of these people that didn't come through when you feel they should have done? I mean someone like Steve Douglas is not as famous now as he might be. Another one is Nino Tempo.
Ah well, he sort of vanished; he has great talent. I used to see him a lot during my married days and he's great. He just didn't click.

What did you do in the meantime? Your marriage broke up in 1974, so what have you been doing for the last three years?
Just getting my own head back together, relaxing myself, trying to wind up my whole inner thoughts and just trying to be me, instead of Phil Spector's wife or one of the Ronettes. Just finding myself.

It must have been difficult to have lived as Phil Spector's wife?
Oh it was amazing...

Does your sister still sing at all?
No, neither sister nor cousin, they're both very happily married and have kids and they like that; and that's great. We have a five-year-old child too, I love that life too but I also love my performing and I didn't understand why I couldn't do both. He didn't understand why I wanted to sing and I didn't understand why he didn't want me to sing. That's why we didn't see eye to eye.

So when you played at Biba's, why did you?
I was so desperate to perform again I knew that if I came over to London I still might have a chance. It was just after my divorce and when I was offered a tour in London I naturally couldn't refuse. That's why I did it. I wanted to perform. After five and-a-half years of marriage and never having seen the stage in that time I grabbed the chance just to get on that stage.

Who were the people who backed you? Were they just people?
People I just picked up, no one known especially.

English?
No, from America.

They did reasonably well.
Yeah, considering the Phil Spector sound, there were only three of them, I thought they were excellent and just the two girls.

You made some records for Buddah, didn't you?
I made a couple but they were never distributed because during that time I was just separating from Phil and he sent them a letter saying, 'that's my wife' sort of thing. They got scared so the Buddah thing never took off.

Were they ever released though?
I don't think so. [Editor's note: two singles were released as by Ronnie Spector and the Ronettes, though they are more often found as promo mono/stereo A/B-sides, rather than the fully released singles with different B-sides. They have also been bootlegged.]

So they're enormous collectors items?
That's another thing I did, as soon as I got my separation I just ran into the studio, that's why I retired after 1974 because I just refused to have any producer. I'll just wait until the right one comes along. Miami Steve's just so great, knowing my voice so well. He knows how to handle it; he knows what key I sing in, he's great.

Did it never occur to you to at least restart a business relationship with Phil?
It wouldn't have worked because we had too much romance going. Romance and business don't fit. We never had a business together.

Having gone that long time without a record, just to say to Phil, 'well look, do you want to produce it?'
I said that several times, but he wouldn't do anything with me. I guess because he loved me a lot and wanted me home as a wife. He didn't want me travelling and singing and that.

One gets the impression from the very few interviews done with Phil that the Spector house is very quiet. A house that very few people arrive at?
Dreadfully quiet, dreadfully boring. It's like a mausoleum to live in; 23 rooms, 5 people in the household staff, it's very boring for me after a while. The first year it was great, because of this castle-like thing, all my little personal servants and a Rolls Royce to drive around in, but after that, you go crazy. No company ever. How much of that can you take? We went out annually – on my birthday.

When you divorced, you moved back to New York.
These are my roots. I hated Hollywood because it was a very stereotyped life – no buses, no one walking and so forth. I was too young for that. That's why I love New York and London; you see buses and planes and people bustling, and I love that and grew up with it. In LA and Beverly Hills, 6 o' clock and everything was deserted.

Was there ever any relationship between Brian Wilson and Phil?
Yes, Brian used to come to a lot of the sessions. As a matter of fact he wrote the next... what was it called? [Editor's note: 'Don't Worry Baby', subsequently recorded by Ronnie with Joey Ramone producing, and released in England on Creation Records CRESCD 305 in 1999, and now a hard to find collectable in its own right] ...ah well, they wrote it for me. They wrote it for me in early 1963/64, right after 'Be My Baby' but Phil turned it down for 'Baby, I Love You'. I think right now, Brian and Carl are writing material for me, on the QT. They're great – it's a shame Brian had to go on drugs and get messed up. He's a genius, he really is. Now he's getting on, coming through.

The two sounds of California were Phil Spector and the Beach Boys and the other ones just sort of vanished like the Byrds... so you have no idea what any of the rest of these people are doing?
I haven't seen Bobby Sheen in 10 years. I haven't seen Darlene in maybe 7 or 8. I don't know what any of these people are doing.

Not the Crystals either?
Well the Crystals are doing all these shows in New York. I did one Dick Clark show in Madison Square Gardens and the Crystals were on that show. I don't know if they're still working or not.

Are they the same people?
No, just one of the original Crystals is left.

Is it right about Darlene Love was also one of the Blue Jeans as well as being Darlene Love?
Yes.

Do you remember who the other one was?
Venetta.

Venetta Fields?
I forget her last name.

Because there's a lady called Vernetta Fields who's a big session singer.
Venetta's a good session singer too, that's what they did mostly.

Were you surprised when all those things started coming out here?
Yes, because I thought Phil would never put out that stuff again – I thought he had waited a little bit too long.

I think that those who have them appreciate them enormously. I presume it's of no financial interest to you?
No, Phil gets all the money anyway.

Why hasn't he done it in America do you think? The records aren't released in the States are they?
I don't know if it's because he doesn't feel that they're ready for them or whether they'll be accepted because Britain gave him a number one with 'River Deep Mountain High' and in America it didn't sell two copies, so maybe that's why, maybe he's testing them out here to see what they do and then put out some of them in the States (Warner/Spector did issue a 20-track double a year or so ago, but the splendid UK Rare Masters and Wall Of Sound series never surfaced). I don't know what Phil's doing now. I don't see him that often.

20
Wall Of Sound by Mike Callahan

In the third part of Callahan's piece (published in Goldmine, *December 1980), Mike considers the famed Christmas Album and some of the Beatles' work.*

This is the third and final part of the series in Both Sides Now about Phil Spector and stereo. The first two parts appeared in Issues #46 and #47 of *Goldmine*, and covered the pre-Philles and Philles years, with the exception of the Philles Christmas Album. Between the time Spector recorded the Christmas Album and the time he produced 'Happy Christmas (War Is Over)' for John and Yoko, his stereo productions underwent a dramatic change: Spector developed the stereophonic 'Wall of Sound'. This month, let's listen to the Christmas Album and the Christmas single, and follow what happened between.

   The Christmas Album's first title, back in its original incarnation as Philles PHLP-4005, was *A Christmas Gift For You From Philles Records*. The album was recorded in the fall of 1963 at Gold Star Recording Studios in Los Angeles. Spector had his usual cast of thousands on hand: four horn players, four guitarists (including Tom Tedesco, Bill Pittman, and Nino Tempo), three pianists (including Leon Russell and Al DeLory), two bassists, Hal Blaine on drums, Frank Kapp, Sonny Bonn, Jack Nitzsche, and apparently Jeff Barry on percussion, and the Johnny Vidor Strings. Larry Levine was engineering and Jack Nitzsche was arranging, as usual. Normally, Spector paid little attention to albums, concentrating his energy on singles, and only the A-side of singles, at that. The Christmas Album was different. Each cut was produced as if it were a single; everything had to be perfect. The result was a six-week recording marathon that tried the patience of everyone involved. In his book *Out Of His Head*, Richard Williams quotes Jeff Barry and Larry Levine: 'Barry and Levine remember the sessions with a shudder. Levine: "It went on for months, and I never wanted to see him again after that. Day and night for months ..." Barry: "I stood there for days and days and days, just playing shakers."' To record collectors, it seems to have all been worth it.

As were many other of Spector's Philles records, the Christmas Album was recorded on Gold Star's three-track stereo equipment. Spector put the entire rhythm section, the 'wall of sound' consisting of the bass, drums, guitars, pianos, horns, bells, and other percussion, on a single track. Recording the 'wall' in mono was typical of Spector's Philles records. The other two tracks on the studio recorder were used for voices (and handclaps and some special effects) and for the strings. But even though the album was recorded in stereo, it wasn't until over ten years later that it was finally released that way.

The original issue on Philles 4005 was monaural only. The record jacket featured pictures of all the artists in a Christmas setting. In 1972, Spector reissued the album on Apple SW 3400, also in mono, but the reissue contained a completely different album jacket. On the front of this new jacket was Phil himself dressed as Santa Claus, complete with 'Back to MONO' buttons adorning his suit. The abbreviated liner notes on the Apple reissue were paraphrased and condensed from the original liner notes on Philles, with an interesting change. On the Philles album, Spector had said, 'Because Christmas is so American it is therefore time to take the great Christmas music and give it the sound of the American music of today...' On the Apple reissue, this claim had been changed to 'Because Christmas is so international...' Two years later, when Spector had arranged for Warner Brothers to distribute his new label, the Christmas Album was again reissued, this time as Warner-Spector SP-9103. As with the Apple release, the album was titled *Phil Spector's Christmas Album* and featured a cover nearly identical to the Apple release. On the bottom of the front of the Warner-Spector issue were two words with which we had grown familiar when it came to Spector: 'Authentic Mono'. Nothing was further from the truth. The Warner-Spector issue was 100% true stereo! Nowhere on the jacket or label did it give us a clue to the surprise inside! Finally, still later, Spector issued the album again on Phil Spector International (Super 2307005), but this time the album front had a small sticker, which read, 'Now In Stereo'. Both stereo reissues still have Phil on the cover with his 'Back to Mono' buttons.

The stereo format on the album is typical of Spector's Philles recordings. On almost every track, the rhythm instruments and strings are on opposite channels, with voices in the middle. A few places on the album, Spector breaks out of this by using strings on more than one track, such as the intros to 'Marshmallow World' and 'I Saw Mommy Kissing Santa Claus'. 'Silent Night', on the other hand, has Phil's voice in the middle bracketed by strings and back-up voices.

The stereo on this album has made a great album even better. In the opening moments of 'I Saw Mommy Kissing Santa Claus', we hear footsteps walk from one channel to the opposite channel, where a door opens, a kiss is heard followed by the door closing, and then the footsteps walking back across the original channel. And there are stereo oddities on the album, too. For example, on the 'strings channel' near the beginning of 'Rudolph The Red Nosed Reindeer', there is a sound like someone answering 'uh-uh' in negative reply to an unheard question. This sound is also on the mono version of the album, but is so buried under the rhythm track that it is essentially unnoticeable. And occasionally throughout the album, there are other sounds (instruments) on the empty strings tracks.

Everyone seems to have their own favourites among the songs on the album; mine are 'Parade Of The Wooden Soldiers' (which I can't get out of my head for weeks after I hear it) and 'Sleigh Ride'. Every time I hear the Ronettes do 'Sleigh Ride', I inevitably think about Leroy Anderson, who wrote 'Sleigh Ride' as an instrumental in the 1950s. At first glance, there doesn't seem to be much similarity between the orchestra leader of the 50s and the producer Spector, of the 60s, but they are alike in at least one important way. Anderson was an absolute master of taking relatively commonplace scenes (a clock ticking, a typewriter, using sandpaper, a horse and buggy ride) and painting such a vivid musical picture of them that the music almost physically projected the scene right in front of you (listen to Anderson's 'The Syncopated Clock', 'The Typewriter', 'Sandpaper Ballet', and 'Horse And Buggy', for example). So it is with Spector, and especially here on the Christmas Album. Play the album and it is Christmas, no matter what the weather is like outside. Spector uses sound effects masterfully here, including the almost subliminal horse hooves clopping along in the background of 'Sleigh Ride'. The choice of the spirited horse for the sound effects at the beginning and end of the song was an inspiration; I can just see the horse rearing back with white puffs of smoke coming out of his nostrils! All throughout the song, the music generates the feeling of sailing along over the snow on a winter evening. And in the end, the sleigh slows down and the ride is over. We all get out, and the bells go jingling off into the distance. What a trip!

If the Christmas Album was a typical example of Spector's mono 'wall of sound', eight years later Spector produced another Christmas record which was just as typical of the stereo 'wall of sound' of the 1970s. By 1971, when John Lennon and Yoko Ono sang 'Happy Christmas', the Christmas Album seemed to belong to some prior lifetime many, many years before. A lot had happened in the meantime. Let's follow some of the events.

*The favourite Christmas song on the
UK Warner-Spector label from the 70s*

Although the Christmas Album on Philles was a critical success, it was not exactly a barn-burner in sales (most Christmas albums aren't, but this one also came out the same time that the US was picking up the pieces after President Kennedy's assassination). Bigger successes awaited Spector with the Righteous Brothers. Bigger failures awaited him also; after Ike and Tina Turner's 'River Deep Mountain High' bombed in the spring of 1966, Spector threw in the towel and temporarily retired; but like a lot of other talented people, Spector couldn't stay retired forever.

About three years later, we noticed a little man dressed in black starting to appear on certain A&M records, along with the words 'Phil Spector Productions'. Spector had un-retired. The first single was 'Baby Don't Get Crazy'/'Spanish Harlem' by The Checkmates Ltd (A&M 1006). After DJ copies were distributed, the single was withdrawn: Spector started right off by announcing that he hadn't changed. Withdrawing records and using old material for flip sides was classic Spector. Actually, though, this version of 'Spanish

Harlem' was no throwaway; although given a substantially different treatment from the Ben E. King original, it was every bit as good.

But one thing had definitely changed. Rather than using three- or four-track recording equipment, Spector was now using 8-track recorders, and his stereo took on a more conventional sound. The 'wall of sound' was there to a certain extent, but now it was spread out over two channels instead of just one. It was beginning to sound like one was inside the wall instead of just standing in front of it.

After the initial A&M single came several more by the Checkmates: 'Love Is All I Have To Give', 'Black Pearl', and 'Proud Mary'. All of these made the charts, but 'Black Pearl' turned out to be a hit of sizeable proportions. All of these songs are in true stereo on the A&M album *Love Is All I Have To Give* (SP-4183). Disappointingly (but not surprisingly, given Spector's dislike for stereo), these cuts have appeared on several other albums in mono only. The original LP disappeared from the cutout bins years ago, making the stereo versions tough to find these days.

Spector didn't spend too much time with A&M. In addition to the Checkmates records, Spector released the Ronettes' 'You Came, You Saw, You Conquered' on A&M (1040) and reissued several records by Ike and Tina that originally had been done for Philles. Another Spector trait that has become evident over the years is his liking certain songs and having different artists record these songs. This was seen with 'Unchained Melody', 'Be My Baby', and several other songs. One of the Ike and Tina reissues on A&M was 'A Love Like Yours (Don't Come Knockin' Every Day)', which Spector had originally issued on Philles. The song was a Holland-Dozier-Holland tune, which had first appeared on Martha & the Vandellas' debut LP (Gordy GS-702, *Come And Get These Memories*) as a nondescript Motown album-filler with a 'You-Beat-Me-To-The-Punch' beat. Spector slowed the song down considerably, added strings at the beginning, and turned it into a powerhouse by playing Tina Turner's voice off against the 'wall of sound'. Later, Spector tried the song again with Nilsson & Cher (Warner-Spector SPS-0402), but the later version didn't even come close to the power and realism of the Ike & Tina version. The Ike & Tina version was the last single issued on Philles (136) and ironically was also the last Phil Spector single for A&M (1170).

Near the end of 1969, Spector met the Beatles for the first time since the Philles heyday, and this started an association with John and George that would last for years. The Beatles had recorded an album called *Get Back* some time earlier, but it had not been released due to the group's dissatisfaction with the way it sounded. Spector was given the album to remix, and shortly thereafter it emerged in quite different form as *Let It Be*. Four tracks in particular are indicative of what Spector did to the album:

'The Long And Winding Road', in its original form, might have instead been called 'The Long And Boring Song'. It featured Paul banging away on the piano with simple instrumental back-up. Spector's addition to the song can easily be heard using out-of-phase stereo: he added a small symphony and a few dozen voices in the background, changing it from an ordinary song into three minutes and forty seconds of melancholy that rocketed straight to #1.

'Across The Universe' was another song to which Spector added a chorus and strings. Again, by using out-of-phase stereo (see *Goldmine* 052), Spector's additions can be heard alone. Here Spector changed a song with which John was very dissatisfied into something memorable.

Both 'Let It Be' and 'Get Back' were issued here in their original George Martin productions first, and then later also as the Spector-produced *Let It Be* LP cuts. It's difficult to call either the Martin or the Spector versions of these songs 'better' but they are certainly 'different'. Martin's versions are more spread out and inventive for stereo listeners, with stereo drums and moving choirs on 'Let It Be' and stereo drums on 'Get Back'. Spector's versions have some of the instruments on different channels and are more basic stereophonically. On the other hand, Spector's *Let It Be* is much closer to rock and roll and less 'churchy'.

About the same time Spector was working on *Let It Be*, he produced a couple of songs for Derek and the Dominos. 'Tell The Truth' and 'Roll It Over' were released on a mono DJ single (Arco 6780), but again we saw a Spector single withdrawn. Later, the Spector production of 'Tell The Truth' was included in stereo on *The History Of Eric Clapton* (Atco SD 2.803), but the Spector version of 'Roll It Over' has only endeared on the single, in mono. (Both these songs were recorded more than once by Derek and the Dominos, so the titles are easy to find, but not the Spector versions.) Both sides have the Spector sound to them, with dense instrumental backgrounds, and 'Roll It Over' uses tape echo prominently on the vocal. The stereo on 'Tell The Truth' is modern-sounding, but the 'wall of sound' is there, also.

After the *Let It Be* assignment and the diversion with Derek and the Dominos, Spector co-produced George Harrison's three-album set, *All Things Must Pass* (Apple STCH-639). It was on this album that the groundwork for what ultimately would become the stereo 'wall of sound' was done. One of the ingredients of the mono wall was doubling, that is, having more than one musician simultaneously playing identical parts on the same instruments. This is what was responsible for the unique drum sounds which Spector obtained in his early Phllles' productions. On the *All Things Must Pass* album, Spector for the first time uses extensive doubling in stereo. 'My Sweet Lord' starts out with doubled acoustic guitars, which really sound nice in stereo. And 'What Is Life' used a double fuzz guitar. There are two versions of 'Isn't It A Pity' on the album; one sounds so conventional that one is tempted to speculate that George Harrison did it alone. The other (hit) version is probably the earliest example of the full-blown stereo 'wall of sound'. There is so much happening in the background of the song, so many things being doubled, that the individual instruments become almost indistinguishable. This new wall was more powerful than the mono wall, since now it was like hearing the rhythm section in front of you instead of off to one side.

For John Lennon's records, Spector was also using doubling, but on a much simpler scale. Instead of a 'wall of sound', Spector used a liberal portion of tape echo for Lennon. On Lennon's first album, *John Lennon/Plastic Ono Band* (Apple SW3372), Spector was up to his old tricks, since about half the album is essentially mono ('God', 'Remember', 'Love', 'Look At Me', 'Working Class Hero', and 'My Mummy's Dead'). 'Isolation', however, features a neat stereo trick based on doubling. Most of the song is mono, but during the bridge, John's voice is doubled and split out onto opposite channels. As the bridge ends, the voices smoothly fold back down to one voice in the middle.

A similar sound is used for the title cut of Lennon's second LP, *Imagine* (Apple 5W3379). The song starts with a single piano in the middle, but quickly splits into doubled pianos on opposite channels, a nice effect for stereo headphones. Other songs on this album also feature instrumental doubling in stereo.

By the fall of 1971, when Spector finally got around to producing another Christmas record, he was riding the crest of his most successful year on the charts since 1963. He had also been experimenting in stereo for the previous couple of years, developing a stereo sound that was the equal of his old mono 'wall of sound'. 'Happy Christmas' was a good example of the new sound; guitars, drums, strings, bells, and voices all flood out of the speakers in uncountable numbers, giving the impression of a huge outdoor singalong with an immense orchestra. Considering that the Vietnam War was still in progress in 1971, the record arrived just in time to put a warm spot on the radio amid otherwise gloomy news. It was an up-to-date Christmas gift to us from Phil, John, and Yoko. As a finishing touch, the record was pressed in green plastic.

Since that Christmas, Spector has been involved with many artists. A few more albums for Lennon and Harrison, and then Spector was off to start his own label again. Overseas, Spector set up the Phil Spector International label, while in the US, his material was on Warner-Spector and then Big Tree-Spector. During the 70s, he worked with Nilsson, Cher, Dion Dimucci, Kim Fowley, Leonard Cohen, and even the Ramones. Throughout these later works, the stereo wall of sound has been Spector s mainstay. Interestingly enough, there has been a trend in the music industry lately to mix stereo with less separation than was common in the 1960s; the trend is toward Spector's stereo sound. How ironic that the man who dislikes stereo would influence an industry trend in stereo mixing.

21
[Up]Dating Ronnie by Kingsley Abbott

*As a companion piece to the preceding John Tobler/*Hot Wacks *interview, this covers Ronnie's Phil era rarities and her post-Spector recording activities, many of which have become highly collectable in their own right, but also inevitably by association. This piece and interview first appeared in* Record Collector *magazine No 234 (Feb '99).*

Before the summer of 1963, girl groups had been sweet and demure with hair approved by their mums and party dresses with the correct number of petticoats. Then, suddenly, there were the Ronettes – Ronnie, Estelle and Nedra, who looked as if they would walk off the street, pin you up against the wall and have their evil way with you. Here were dangerous girls with outrageous bouffants and thin, slinky skirts with slits that went all the way to fantasy land.

The packaging of the girls – all controlled by men, of course – was perfect. But so was the musical content, as their mentor and producer Phil Spector unleashed a string of hits that remain some of the most perfect pure pop ever made. 'Be My Baby' struck worldwide like a thunderclap, closely followed by 'Baby, I Love You', 'The Best Part Of Breakin' Up', 'Walking In The Rain', 'Do I Love You?', 'Born To Be Together' and the wonderfully understated 'Is This What I Get For Loving You?', on which Ronnie made men weak at the knees with a single sigh. For a couple of years, the girls were queens of pop, and everyone from the Beatles and the Stones downwards came to pay court.

Throughout the Ronettes' recording career, the accent was on Ronnie Bennett (as she was then). Her vocal, with its built-in vibrato, was mixed way above the other background voices. No one could tell if the other girls were actually in the mix. In fact, they were not always there, as Spector sometimes replaced them with other members of his studio entourage, and usually augmented them with people like Cher.

Soundscapes
Everything was subservient to his grandiose soundscapes. The

lead voice had to be strong enough, and distinctive enough, to cut through the Gold Star echo chamber, which enabled Spector to take his retrospectively named 'Wall of Sound' to undreamed-of heights. In Ronnie's voice, he found his perfect spearhead. It was more immediately recognisable than LaLa Brooks of the Crystals or Darlene Love, the two female leads he'd favoured before then. Spector was convinced that Ronnie was the piece that completed his personal jigsaw puzzle, and his concentration on her became absolute – and gradually more personal.

In time, the group's hits became smaller and the 'Wall of Sound' bubble burst. Phil Spector had married Ronnie and, for a while at least, paid total attention to her and marginalised the other two group members. This close focus on Ronnie first showed itself when Spector issued two solo singles by her in 1964, on his offshoot label (modestly called Phil Spector Records). 'So Young' was a revival of the old doo-wop song by the Students, and was probably a tune that Ronnie had enjoyed in her early teens, given her love for the high tenor groups who followed Frankie Lymon's hits in the late 50s.

The second solo release was a contemporary song by the Spector/Greenwich/Barry writing team. 'Why Don't They Let Us Fall In Love?' also appeared later as a Dixie Cups issue on Red Bird, retitled 'Gee The Moon Is Shining Bright'.

Both of Ronnie's records, issued under the name of Veronica, were great examples of Spector's production craft and Jack Nitzsche's arrangements, but neither did much sales-wise, ensuring that they're now highly collectable items in their own right.

The Ronettes survived as a working unit until autumn 1966, when they undertook a tour of Germany, playing mostly to American troops. Two shows were scheduled in the town of Glenhausen. The first went smoothly, with a packed house of very satisfied GIs (one of whom took this very literally, inflamed by a close-up view of Ronnie's hitched-up skirt). The second show was marred by rioting soldiers outside the Moonlight Lounge club, and the girls were forced to abandon the stage.

At this point, Estelle and Nedra decided enough was enough, preferring to stay at home with their long-standing boyfriends. 'It hurt in some ways,' Nedra Talley said later. 'It wasn't cold and callous, but we did split at that point.' It didn't alter the group's recording methods, but without the three faces to promote their records, the Ronettes' days as a hit act were over.

By 1966, Phil Spector's recording attention had switched to Tina Turner, anyway, and the Spector/Barry/Greenwich writing team were tailoring material for her voice, rather than the pure pop style of old. Meanwhile, the Ronettes were only allowed one release that year. 'I Can Hear Music' only managed to scrape into the US Top 100, despite being a marvellous song and performance. It has the distinction of being one of the few releases on the Philles label not to have been produced by Spector himself, who delegated the task to Jeff Barry – underlining the fact that he'd been forced to jettison his original plans for Ronnie.

There followed a period of three years when, apparently at Spector's insistence, Ronnie dropped out of sight. She was occasionally allowed into the studio, but nothing new appeared until 1969, when 'You Came, You Saw, You Conquered' was released on A&M. In the meantime, Philles had gone out of business, and Spector's traditional haunt, Gold Star Studios, had closed. Ronnie wrote later that she felt Phil wasn't at home with A&M's state-of-the-art equipment: 'I think he felt a little intimidated around all these space age recorders and microphones. Unfortunately, instead of admitting he was out of his class, he tried to make up for his ignorance by taking his anger out on people. Especially me.'

Relationship

She also noted that Phil's relationship with the studio personnel was different: 'These guys at A&M didn't depend on Phil for their jobs, so they treated him like the nut that he was. They even had a picture of him that they threw darts at.' Spector apparently saw this as a great compliment, thinking that they were threatened by his abilities. But, with Ronnie at least, the old magic was no longer there. The A&M single was a complete flop, and Ronnie suspected that her recording career was over.

For a couple of years, it was. Then in 1971, out of the blue, Phil told her that she was going to London to record. He had maintained intermittent contact with the Beatles since their original breakthrough in the States, and in 1970 he had finally begun to work with them for the first time, notably on singles like John Lennon's 'Instant Karma!' and George Harrison's 'My Sweet Lord', and the controversial *Let It Be* album.

Ronnie had been kept rather further away from the Beatles, as Phil always considered John Lennon a threat where she was concerned.

But now there were plans for her to record an album for the Apple label. The Spectors flew to London and went to Abbey Road, where Ronnie met George Harrison. He had written a new song especially for her, called 'Try Some, Buy Some'. Ronnie listened – and hated it from the start. Melodically and lyrically, it was far removed from the material that she was used to singing. She was persuaded to give it a try, but found the entire process difficult, as she believed the song had been arranged in the wrong key for her. Harrison later recalled that he had another proposed song for the project, called 'You': 'I tried to write a Ronettes sort of song... but we never got to make a whole album.' The backing track was recorded at the time, with Leon Russell (from Phil Spector's old Wrecking Crew) on piano, and eventually surfaced on Harrison's *Extra Texture* album. 'Try Some, Buy Some' was released under the name of Ronnie Spector, and – as she expected – did nothing, except to provide her with the stage name which she has used ever since.

Meanwhile, her marriage to Phil was steadily deteriorating, to the extent that she filed for divorce in June 1972. It was a messy and drawn-out affair, at the end of which Ronnie emerged with very little. A chance call to her old boss from her 'dancing girl' days, Murray the K, brought her into contact with someone who was promoting an oldies show at the Brooklyn Academy of Music, who was very keen to include the Ronettes. Ronnie quickly contacted the other girls, but her sister Estelle had put on a good deal of weight and could no longer cope with the dance moves, while Nedra Talley – now a minister's wife and the mother of a young family – was just not interested.

Still keen to do the show, Ronnie recruited Chip Fields and Diane Linton as new slim'n'slinky Ronettes. The concert was a great success, and it brought her into contact with 60s hitmaker Billy Vera, who organised a band for further shows. But this stage of her career was dogged by alcohol problems that had surfaced during the collapse of her marriage.

Contract

Ronnie signed a two-year recording contract in 1973 with Buddah Records – the only label prepared to take her on, as everyone else assumed she was only an oldies act. She recorded two singles with producer Stan Vincent, 'Lover Lover' (which Ronnie remembers as 'awful') and a remake of a favourite of hers from the Philles era,

'I Wish I Never Saw The Sunshine'. The Vincent-produced version was weak, totally losing the power of the song – and Ronnie knew it. Both singles deservedly flopped, ensuring that although promo pressings with mono and stereo versions of the A-side used to be fairly common, commercial copies featuring the B-sides as well were much rarer, to the point that the four tracks were later bootlegged as a 7" EP.

March 1974 saw Ronnie play Richard Nader's Madison Square Garden revival show, with another new Ronette, Denise Edwards, replacing Diane Linton. This line-up performed throughout 1974, including a legendary show at the gay venue, the Baths, which convinced Ronnie that she was still in the right career. But her recording activities were still in the doldrums. There was a one-shot single, 'You'd Be Good For Me', on Tom Cat in 1975, but despite an extended mix to tempt DJs, it completely flopped.

Meeting

A chance meeting with May Pang in New York in late 1974 brought Ronnie back into contact with May's boyfriend at the time, John Lennon – who was accompanied by producer/engineer Jimmy Iovine. He invited her down to meet an act he was working with, Southside Johnny & the Asbury Jukes, who were being produced by Stevie Van Zandt. They had already recorded the backing track to a song called 'You Mean So Much To Me', written by Bruce Springsteen. It was only when Van Zandt told her that he wanted to record the song as a duet that Ronnie realised she had been invited as anything more than a bystander. When she heard Southside Johnny sing, she immediately went for the idea.

Bruce Springsteen was quickly summoned down to the session and completed a lyrical rewrite. The recording was quick, painless and successful, and turned out to be the hottest track on the Asbury Jukes' debut album, *I Don't Want To Go Home*. The band even took Ronnie out on the road with them, and on some dates they opened for Bruce Springsteen & the E Street Band – who were themselves heavily influenced by the old Phil Spector sound.

She toured with the Jukes for about a year and-a-half, after which she got a call from Epic Records, who played her a new song that Billy Joel had written specially for her. 'Say Goodbye To Hollywood' was cut with the E Street Band, with Stevie Van Zandt producing. It sounded like a 70s take on her classic 60s sound, with the song to match, and the result was a fabulous record, featuring her best vocal performance in years. She promoted the song in America and in Britain, turning up here on a late night TV arts show to give a mimed (but still amazing) performance that fairly burst out of the screen.

US copies of the single stated that the song was taken from a forthcoming album by Ronnie and the E Street Band, even giving the projected catalogue number. But despite wonderful media reaction, and plenty of radio plays, the single failed to become a big hit, which in turn meant that the impetus to complete the album was lost.

Ronnie's original contact at Epic, Steve Popovich, stuck with her, and co-produced some more tracks with Kyle Lehning in the late 70s. Two of them, 'It's A Heartache' and 'I Wanna Come Over', were released on the Alston label in 1978. Other songs, co-produced around the same time with veteran Four Seasons arranger Charlie Calello, were canned, including 'You Light Up My Life', 'And The Music Plays On' and another Lehning track, 'Cry Like A Baby'.

Drifting from one producer and short-lived deal to the next was the pattern of Ronnie's career during this period. There was no shortage of people wanting to work with her, but a hit single was as elusive as ever. If the ultra-commercial 'Say Goodbye To Hollywood', couldn't chart, then it was difficult to imagine what would. Her name was kept in the public eye, at least in Britain, when her ex-husband launched the Phil Spector International label, and unveiled vintage Ronettes masters like '(I'm A) Woman In Love' (issued as a single), closely followed by 'Soldier Baby (Of Mine)' and 'Paradise' on the album *Rare Masters Volume 1*. 'Everything Under The Sun', 'Here I Sit' and the original version of 'I Wish I Never Saw The Sunshine' appeared on a second Rare Masters set, while the mysterious 'Lovers' surfaced on a later box set.

Meanwhile, Ronnie had teamed up with a female producer for the first time, Genya Raven – better known as Goldie of Goldie & the Gingerbreads fame in the early 60s. In the late 70s, Raven had become caught up in the New York punk scene centred around CBGBs and Max's Kansas City, and she was determined to shake off Ronnie Spector's 60s tag. Together they worked on an album called *Siren*, which featured a much harder edge than anything Ronnie had recorded in the past – not entirely to her liking. Despite the punk input, the album featured some surprisingly retro moments, adding up to a hotchpotch that pleased no one. Ronnie did her best to promote the most commercial track, 'Darlin'', as a single, but soon discovered that audiences preferred to hear her 60s hits.

In 1982, she remarried and subsequently raised two children with husband Jonathan Greenfield. But just when it seemed that she was set for a life of domestic bliss, she had a call from Eddie Money, who wanted her to sing a section of 'Be My Baby' on a song called 'Take Me Home Tonight'. Ronnie happily agreed, and the record roared into the US Top 10, her first taste of real chart action in more than 20 years. Suddenly she was back on major TV shows, and being asked to co-host awards ceremonies.

Solo Deal

The public reaction was so strong that Money's label, Columbia, offered her a solo deal. To complete the fairytale, the *Unfinished Business* album ought to have been a soaring artistic and financial success. But the record let her down, both by its lack of a cohesive sound (more than one producer worked on the sessions), and its unimaginative song selection. It also featured a spectacularly dull cover, which was quite an achievement given that it featured a picture of its star! Eddie Money returned her earlier favour by guesting on 'Who Can Sleep', which was picked as the single, but to no avail – and Ronnie's fourth comeback fizzled out.

Later in the 80s, Ronnie cut some tracks with rock journalist turned producer, Alan Betrock, but 'Communication', 'For His Love', 'Whenever You're On My Mind' and the ironically titled 'Something's Gonna Happen' remain unissued.

Everything remained quiet for another decade, until early last year, when it was revealed that Ronnie had recorded Brian Wilson's 'Don't Worry Baby' – a song originally written for her as a possible follow-up to 'Be My Baby'. The rumours were confirmed by Creation Records, who have released a four-track EP, co-produced by Joey Ramone. Besides 'Don't Worry Baby', it includes 'She Talks To Rainbows', 'You Can't Put Your Arms Around A Memory' and a duet with Joey called 'Bye Bye Baby'. Maybe this time... but it was not to be.

Ronnie Spector Interview By Kingsley Abbott

The key relationship throughout your musical career has always been with your producer.

Well, the Ronettes started way back at my grandma's house, really. We were very young and naive, so when we got together with Phil

Spector, he was definitely the boss. He really wanted to make hits. He was obsessed with my voice. He would sit in the control room with his eyes closed, listening to things over and over. He worked us hard all the time.

Then he would want the other girls to go out and do all the shows, and have me in the studio all the time – making the hits, he said. The other two had a real problem with this. They said to Phil, 'How can we go out without our lead singer?' Phil didn't see this as any sort of problem, and just said for them to go out with one of my look-a-like cousins. That's what they did for the Beatles' tour in the US. Phil kept me working in the studio, while they went out with my cousin. It was also because Phil was not comfortable about my being out on the road with John Lennon. I had had some dinner dates with John when the Ronettes were in London.

Anyway, Phil made sure that I stayed in the studio. He worked me so hard that sometimes we wouldn't get out of the studio until the sun was coming up. He tricked me. He kept on telling me that we were making new hits, but then he didn't release things.

I always wondered why there was never a second Ronettes album.
Exactly. Phil said that we had to be cutting tracks for a second album. It was clear that there should have been one. We cut so many songs. Most of them are still unreleased.

Some tracks were released years later, but are there still some more?
Oh, I'm sure Phil has others. We did so many. As I said, Phil sort of squished my career. He decided that I wasn't going to be released anymore. I didn't really question it enough at the time. Things were very different then, in the first half of the 60s. It was always the men who called the shots. They did it all. Women were sidelined and got to sing. Women could write, like Ellie Greenwich and Carole King, but it was usually the men who the business was built around. So I was young and naive, and I couldn't do too much at the time.

Later, in the early 70s, Stan Vincent produced me. We did some songs as demos. He didn't have a deal for them, so they were done cheaply, and they sound like it. I didn't like 'Lover, Lover', and the version of 'I Wish I Never Saw The Sun Shine' was weak compared with the power of the earlier version. Stan couldn't get any deals with any of the majors, so the demos were eventually issued on Buddah.

What about the tracks you did with Stevie Van Zandt and Springsteen? 'Say Goodbye To Hollywood' was a real high point.
That song was great! (She sings a little from it. Her voice sounds wonderfully full and sexy, transporting the interviewer, unashamedly back to teenage adulation.) It was written specially for me by Billy Joel, and it really said what I was doing, leaving Hollywood. The problem was that it came at a time that was really difficult for me. I had to keep going back to Hollywood to visit the kids in foster homes while things were in a difficult state. Bruce would call and want me to come and finish a track, but I'd have to say I couldn't. I couldn't give 100 per cent, so that's one of the reasons that there wasn't an album at that time. I'm pretty sure that Bruce would still have some other unreleased tracks. I can't really remember exactly.

What about the Genya Raven sessions for the Siren *album?*
Oh, I had forgotten about her! That was another era when I couldn't fully concentrate. We did the album and then she looked for a deal. Phil probably blocked me from the majors, so it ended up coming out on a really little label. I never play that stuff today.

We touched on the songwriters earlier. Can you tell me who your favourites were?
Phil had all the early songs from Ellie and Jeff Barry. He wrote with them, and all their songs were great for me. Later, when he stopped using them so much, some of the songs that they wrote originally for me ended up going to the Dixie Cups and the Shangri-La's. Ellie and Jeff wrote really well for females, whereas Phil's next writing team didn't do so well. He turned to Pete Anders and Vinnie Poncia, but I never thought that their songs were so good for me. They were great at what they did, but they wrote better for guys. My favourite song of all of them is still 'Walking In The Rain'.

Can you remember anything about the song 'Lovers', which turned up without a writing credit on the first Wall of Sound vinyl box set.
Oh, do you mean (sings) 'Come on baby, let's be lovers...'? Yes, I think that was one that Phil wrote by himself. There was another one about the same time called 'When I Saw You' that he wrote just for me. That was a very personal song.

Can you tell us about the new Creation project?

It's *great*. It's *wonderful!* I *helped!* Really, for the first time ever, I'm properly involved. It's the first time that I've had proper input. With Phil, if I put in a couple of lines or suggestions, he wouldn't pay any real attention, or at least I never got any credit. Now I'm helping some with the writing, the production sound and the endings. Like on one new track, 'She Talks To Rainbows', there's a bit at the end where I said it should go 'Don't talk, don't talk', and we did it.

It's a real collaborative effort with Daniel Rey and Joey Ramone, who have co-produced these four tracks on the EP. It's a very good relationship, and I think that it's the best ever production situation for me.

Hey, listen, just five minutes ago Alan McGee came in and said that we are going to make an album! Wheeeee! I'm really happy about that!

You've also done 'Don't Worry Baby' on the EP.
Yes. It was originally written by Brian Wilson as the follow-up to 'Be My Baby', but as Phil didn't co-write it, or have any of the publishing, we didn't ever record it at the time. Phil was always a little greedy. I have always loved the song, throughout all the difficult times. It talked to me to keep me going, and I'm so happy to have recorded it. I think our version has turned out real well. We didn't change any of the car race lyrics, just 'she' to 'he'.

We're really looking forward to an album that you are really happy about and fully involved with. Thanks for talking to us.
Thank you. Believe me, I'm loving it too!

22
End Of The Century by Dee Dee Ramone

One of the more colourful episodes in Spector's recording history is the work that he did with New York's brudders, the Ramones. Though the sessions yielded a big UK hit in the shape of their version of 'Baby, I Love You', the work was not really considered a success by either party. Excerpted from his book, Poison Heart: Surviving The Ramones *(Firefly 1997), the late Dee Dee Ramone recalls the sessions in graphic detail.*

The first time I met Phil Spector was at a club called the Whisky A Go Go on Sunset Boulevard in Hollywood, California. Phil was there to see Blondie who were playing that night. Somehow I got lucky enough to have a day off from touring and be in Los Angeles at the same time.

Blondie and Deborah Harry were friends of mine and were starting to have some success with a song called 'Denis', which Richard Gottehrer had produced. But Phil had the idea he could do better, and I think he was obsessed with stealing Deborah Harry away from Blondie, producing a record for her and making her a major star. Perhaps he was in love with her and secretly wanted to marry her, who knows?

Blondie were really good that night, and I was having a great time. Deborah Harry was smashing, and wearing one of the shortest mini-skirts I had ever seen her wear. All the boys were crowding the front of the stage, trying to get a look up her skirt at her white bikini briefs. It was all quite enjoyable and I was making it better for myself by buying round after round of drinks for all the patrons in the club. I was already so drunk by the time I got to the Whiskey that when Blondie came on stage I had very little idea of what I was doing.

As excited as Los Angeles was to have Deborah Harry and Blondie finally playing in their city, I could sense that there was one sourpuss in the audience that did not appreciate what was going on. My psychic intuition was later to prove accurate, as I found out after the concert when I tried to go backstage and mingle with the band. I was stinking of rum and very tipsy. But it was no great challenge for me to find my way up the stairs to the Whiskey A Go Go's backstage dressing room, as I had been there so many times before. But, as I was walking up the stairs, my way was blocked by a man holding the red velvet curtains at the top of the staircase together so as not to let me pass through. This man I can only describe as resembling Count Dracula himself. He was dressed in a batwing-type cloak, he had a black beard and moustache which gave him a devilish appearance, and his dark aviator shades gave him an aura of menace and mystery. Later I discovered that this man was the crown prince of darkness himself, Mr Phil Spector.

'Where do you think you are going?' he addressed me. 'I'm going to see Debbie now', I told him.

'Not on your life', he told me.

But at just the right moment, a drunken and stoned Jimmy Destri opened the dressing room door and everyone spilled out towards the entrance-way past Phil, sweeping us inside. There was little he could do. Phil was furious, because a hot and sweaty Deborah Harry was sitting there in the dressing room, clad only in her bra and panties – she hadn't had time to change yet. I don't know if Phil had ever seen Debbie in this state before, but I sensed he didn't want anyone else to. So he was really pissed off and when he entered the dressing room and saw Debbie, freshening up her lipstick and being very friendly to me, he formed an instant bitter dislike to me, before he even knew me.

The name Phil Spector was mentioned to me again shortly upon my return to New York. Danny Fields informed us that Seymour Stein had decided that it would be good if the next Ramones album were to be produced by Phil Spector. This was around the time the Ramones were involved with the *Rock'n'Roll High School* movie, 1978 or 79. I think the original idea for working with Phil was for him to produce the song 'Rock'n'Roll High School' for the movie soundtrack. Maybe the record company thought that they could make a hit out of punk rock in the US by having Phil produce us.

By this time Seymour had really gone out on a limb for the Ramones. We still hadn't scored a hit, but no one was giving up on us and it made sense that perhaps a movie with music by Phil Spector and the Ramones would be a success. So Danny and Linda Stein invited me for a lunch/business conference at the Russian Tea Room on 57th Street, which is across the street from their management office and not too far from Studio 54.

187

My memory about dates and specific events is fuzzy. I was heavily into sedatives and prone to falling asleep at any time. It was hard to communicate with me – I had no interest in anything. I don't even remember the plane ride that brought me to Los Angeles for those fateful Ramones-Spector sessions. I may have already been in Los Angeles for a couple of months working on the *Rock 'n' Roll High School* movie, which makes sense because I can imagine that Danny and Linda would have thought it best for us to do the album and movie simultaneously, to make the most productive use of our stay in Los Angeles.

I think I remember being in the Gold Star studio with the Paley Brothers, trying to record a song called 'Come on, Let's Go' and I couldn't remember how to play it. I had done the simple bass part hundreds of times and each time I made a serious mistake. Maybe the Gold Star studios were just too historic a place for me. This was where Phil Spector created his Frankenstein experiments and the Beach Boys supposedly blew their minds.

In the studio there were many large hospital-type oxygen tanks, complete with face-masks and valve regulators for use either as a hangover cure or to aid alertness. This was supposedly invented by Brian Wilson. Underneath the studio floor was a swimming pool which was used as an echo chamber – when Phil Spector started recording, studio techniques were still too primitive to achieve these effects normally, so he had to do things this way to get what he wanted.

I guess that's why there was an aura of underlying threat. Maybe my imagination was set off from hearing so much talk about handguns and personal bodyguards and karate techniques. Finally I finished 'Come on, Let's Go', and amazingly despite the recording conditions and my immediate surroundings, the song came out quite cheerful.

Later, after I left Phil's laboratory at the Gold Star Studios, with Monte and the band, we went to meet Phil. Ed Stasium the co-producer of *End Of The Century*, escorted us to an out-of-the-way rehearsal studio in Hollywood somewhere. We tuned the guitar and bass and started struggling through 'Rock 'n' Roll High School'. The stage was at the end of a big, long room with a very highly polished floor. As we were halfway through the song, Phil appeared and walked confidently to the centre of the empty room, placed his briefcase in an open position, and, as there was no chair, crouched on the floor, peering at us from behind his briefcase. Needless to say, it had been a long day and I was losing my sense of humour and really feeling like I could use a good sleep. I don't know what Phil was doing behind his briefcase, but something seemed very suspicious to me about this type of behaviour. When we finished playing the song, Phil walked over to us and congratulated us on how good the song sounded, but I still felt very ill-at-ease.

I guess this was all just one of Phil's tests to scrutinise us before agreeing to produce us. I guess the next step was for Phil to see if he could enjoy being around us. After all we would be in each other's company for quite a long time, as it takes Phil a long time to complete an album. Everybody looked beat, probably from partying every night, so we all made a polite excuse to part our separate ways and meet again the next day at Phil's mansion in Beverly Hills.

The drive to his house was up a steep highway. When we arrived the place was like a heavily fortified mansion and we had to press a button and wait until we had cleared a security check and the roadblocks from the gateway to the house. His estate was a bit shabby and not very well kept. Maybe it was because he was a bachelor and lived there alone with his huge St Bernard and two bodyguards. As far as I could see, his only other friend at the time seemed to be disc jockey Rodney Bingenheimer. We knew Rodney as he had the Ramones on his first show for KROQ in Los Angeles in 1976.

Once inside his home, Phil took us for a brief tour. I'm a big fan of Phil Spector's music and, as out of it as I was at the time, I was aware that I was in the presence of a great rock'n'roll legend, but he was really making me nervous. After the tour of his mansion, he left me, John and Marky downstairs in the piano room, while he took Joey upstairs for a private conference. After about three hours I was getting restless, sitting there in that room with nothing to do except stare at John and Marc. Finally I got up off the couch and tried to find Phil and Joey to see what was up. Phil must have thought I was an intruder. I really don't know what provoked him, but the next thing I knew Phil appeared at the top of the staircase, shouting and waving a pistol. Then he practically field-stripped the thing in two seconds flat, put it back together in two more seconds flat. He had all the quick-draw, shoot-to-kill pistol techniques. Like Jimi Hendrix only with a pistol instead of a guitar.

'I can't believe this', I thought to myself. 'I'm bored to death, I've got to get the fuck out of here'.

'Phil', I challenged him, 'I don't know what your fucking problem is, waving that pistol around and all that stuff, and trying to steal

Joey away from the Ramones? I've had it, I'm going back to the Tropicana', which was the hotel on Santa Monica Boulevard where we were staying.

'You're not going anywhere, Dee Dee', Phil said.

He levelled his gun at my heart and then motioned for me and the rest of the band to get back in the piano room. Everybody sat down on the couch and had another beer. We were all very drunk by then – I was fed up, confused and hungry. Phil was a merciless host. He only holstered his pistol when he felt secure that his bodyguards could take over. Then he sat down at his black concert piano and made us listen to him play and sing 'Baby, I Love You' until well after 4.30 in the morning. By 5.00 a.m. I felt as if I was going to completely lose my mind.

Two weeks later Johnny Ramone, Marky Ramone, Joey, me, Ed Stasium and Phil Spector were in a studio in another secret location in Hollywood. We had been working for at least fourteen or fifteen hours a day for thirteen days straight and we still hadn't recorded one note of music. I can't imagine why, but I was getting impatient. Phil would sit in the control room and would listen through the headphones to Marky hit one note on the drum, hour after hour, after hour, after hour. It sort of reminded me of being back in Forest Hills, in Birchwood Towers with Joey Ramone in his mother's apartment, dribbling a basketball for hour after hour while Joey got it on tape.

During one lunch break a couple of days later, I asked Ed, 'Where's John now?' and Ed replied 'Oh, John left five hours ago. He flew back to New York.'

'That's crazy', I said, 'we haven't even begun recording the album.'

'Well what can I tell you?' Ed told me, 'I think he was trying to hide a lot of anxiety.'

I went back by the soda machines and lounge area and saw Marky. 'Marky', I said, 'John left. He went back to New York. What do you think we should do?'

'Let's go home', Marky said.

I don't know how we did it, but somehow Marky and I managed to book a flight back to New York that evening at seven o'clock. The next morning we arrived at JFK airport. To this day I still have no idea how they made the album *End Of The Century*, or who actually played bass on it.

23
Rebuilding The Wall Of Sound by Richard Williams

Richard Williams has long been one of the most respected of British music writers, even though he has been sidetracked into sports writing with his top job at The Guardian *newspaper. This piece has come from his book* Long Distance Call: Writings On Music *and he has allowed its use here. It is one of the very best pieces to paint an eye-witness picture of Spector working in the studio doing what he did best, which is why we are delighted to include it.*

Up on the seventeenth floor of the St Regis Hotel in New York City, a highly traditional establishment where the majestic Mabel Mercer serenades drinkers in the lounge with the songs of the great Broadway composers, John Lennon is wading on his hands and knees through a pile of Elvis Presley singles. Their bright red labels litter the deep-pile carpet, forming a river that flows under the big unmade bed, in which Yoko Ono is reclining. He sorts the 45s out into three piles – the good, the mediocre, the crap – with the intention of making a selection for the jukebox in his new apartment in the West Village.

It's the afternoon of Thursday, 28 October 1971. John is talking about his plans to hit the road with the Plastic Ono Band in the next few months. 'I've got a lot to learn,' he sighs. 'It's been seven years, you know.' Seven years since the Beatles wound up their last tour at Candlestick Park, San Francisco, and retreated into the recording studios. 'It's been fun turning up at odd gigs like the Toronto Peace Festival and the Lyceum and the Fillmore, but I'm sick of having to sing "Blue Suede Shoes" because we haven't rehearsed anything else.'

The band will have a nucleus of himself and Yoko, Nicky Hopkins on piano, Klaus Voorman on bass and Jim Keltner on drums. With a bit of luck, he adds, Phil Spector will be along to sing and play guitar, on stage for the first time since the Teddy Bears toured the Southern California high-school prom circuit in 1959, when 'To Know Him Is To Love Him' was climbing the charts.

John's plan is to turn the band into a troupe, a circus-cum-carnival, with room for participation by street theatre groups and bands from wherever they happen to be playing. He wants to send Jerry Rubin, the leader of the Yippies, on ahead of the main caravan to get things organised, although sending an anarchist to sort out logistics seems a bit optimistic.

Scratching his head, undecided over which pile should get 'Love Me Tender', he starts talking about his own songs, and how he pinches ideas from the old rock and roll songs he grew up with. Finally he throws 'Love Me Tender' onto the 'wanted' pile, picks up his guitar, and sings a song he's just written about Chuck Berry and Bo Diddley, two of his early idols. The middle-eight, he remarks, is nicked from 'Quarter To Three' by US Bonds, probably because he heard it on the radio the previous day.

This very night, he and the Plastic Ono Band are scheduled to record another song, a Christmas single. It's called 'Happy Xmas (War is Over)'. 'The "War is Over" bit's in brackets,' Lennon points out. He likes songs with brackets in the title, two sets if possible. Being an ex-Beatle with a sense of irony, he'd like to write a song called '(Yeah) Yeah (Yeah)'. When he first played the Christmas song to Spector, the producer commented straight off that the tune was a direct lift from 'I Love How You Love Me', the Paris Sisters' hit from 1961. And Spector should know, since it was his first big hit after the Teddy Bears. That made Lennon like his new song even more.

He rolls back into the bed, next to Yoko. It's three o'clock in the afternoon, the session is at seven, and he needs to catch up on the sleep he missed last night while staying out conferring with Rubin. Elvis can wait.

Four hours and ten minutes later, John sits with his jumbo guitar on the fringed carpet of the Record Plant, a small, dark, comfortable studio complex on West 44th Street, between Eighth and Ninth Avenues. He's teaching the chords of 'Happy Xmas' to the five acoustic guitarists sitting in a circle around him.

Why all those rhythm guitarists? Well, Spector had called the previous day from his office on the West Coast, wanting to know who was playing on the session. When Lennon's assistant, May Pang, told him there'd be John, Yoko, Nicky, Klaus and Keltner, Spector exploded.

'Listen,' he screamed, 'I want five rhythm guitars. And this is a Christmas record. Get me some percussion. Bells, celeste, chimes...'

Most of the guitarists are young and inexperienced, the friends of someone John met in a local guitar shop, but among them is Hugh McCracken, the brilliant session guitarist who recently played on

Ram, Paul McCartney's second solo album. John doesn't know this yet. He asks their names. 'Chris.' 'Stu.' 'Teddy.' 'Hugh.' John turns to Yoko. 'Hey, Yoko,' he says, 'doesn't Hugh look like Ivan?' Yoko doesn't respond. 'Hugh, you look just like a mate of mine from school. A cross between him and Paul.'

There's a little break, and someone takes the opportunity to tell Lennon about McCracken's past accomplishments. 'Oh,' he says, and can't resist a crack. 'So you were just auditioning on *Ram*, were you?' The younger guitarists laugh. Whatever tension had existed among them in the presence of the ex-Beatle is gone.

They get back to learning the feel of the song. 'Just pretend it's Christmas,' John suggests. 'I'm Jewish,' one of them shoots back. 'Well, pretend it's your birthday, then.'

At the doorway, there's a sudden flurry. It's Spector, just in from the coast, with big aviator shades and neatly pressed jeans, and a denim jacket with a red and white button reading 'Back to Mono' above the left breast, which amuses Lennon and the engineers in the control room, where the full panoply of state-of-the-art 24-track recording apparatus is in readiness.

Within seconds, it seems, the session has switched from playtime to worktime. It takes Spector, who is running at a different speed from everyone else in the building, roughly one minute of supervising the control board to transform the guitars coming through the monitor speakers from a happy hootenanny-style rabble into a brilliant wash of colour. And they haven't even worked out the microphone placement yet.

'Play that back to them,' Spector tells Roy Cicale, the chief engineer. 'It'll get 'em relaxed.' During the playback, Spector leaves the control room and enters the studio. He and John dance together, arms around each other's shoulders.

They run through the chords again, with Hopkins on piano this time. Spector leans down to the intercom, presses a little green button, and commands: 'Guitars, play the basic rhythm. Don't play anything else, nothing across the beat. Just keep it simple and play together. Nicky, I'd like to hear more of that in octaves in the right hand. Make it more dramatic.'

Leaning down to his guitar microphone, John shouts: 'Don't start dictating yet, Phil. Let's get comfortable first.'

'OK,' Spector responds, visibly trying to contain his energy. Spector is already in the groove, the one he patented ten years earlier.

He's thinking not just of sound, but of arrangement and drama. He's thinking of production. His weird little head is taking the simple guitar chords and moulding, blending, and transforming them. It's his familiar pattern. It's the one that gave the world 'He's a Rebel', 'Da Doo Ron Ron', 'Then He Kissed Me', 'Be My Baby', 'Baby, I Love You', 'You've Lost That Lovin' Feelin'' and 'River Deep Mountain High'.

He's serious about this stuff. He called his hit records 'little symphonies for the kids', and he fought people who belittled them. 'Making something good was always much more important than success,' he told me. 'The fact that it was successful was just the icing on the cake. It wasn't the main purpose at all. It was always to try and make something that was good, and moving, and important. Because if I didn't make anything that was better, I might as well have left it to Fats Domino, because he did it all, by himself. The business didn't need me to come along. I had to progress. "Little Star" by the Elegants... I mean, that was *great*. What need was there for Phil Spector to come along and make his records unless they were going to represent a contribution?'

Jeff Barry, who was once married to Ellie Greenwich, with whom he wrote some of Spector's biggest hits, told me how it had worked in the sixties heydey of Philles Records. 'It was basically a formula. You're going to have four or five guitars lined up, gut-string guitars, and they're going to follow the chords, nothing tricky. You're going to use two basses in fifths, with the same type of line, and strings. There would be six or seven horns, adding the little punches, and there would be the formula percussion instruments – the little bells, the shakers, the tambourines. There might be certain breaks that Phil had come up with, or we'd come up with, and those would be written out. Then Phil used his own formula for echo, and some overtone effects with the strings. But by and large there was a formula arrangement to create a formula sound, which you can hear develop if you play the records in sequence.'

Now it's five years since his last big hit, unless you count his post-production work on the Beatles' *Let It Be* or the singles he's done with John, 'Instant Karma' and 'Cold Turkey'. Until Lennon hooked up with him, it looked as though the world had passed him by. But now he's sitting here, his mind running at full throttle, imagining the sound of this record coming out of a million tiny transistor radios. And all he's got so far is a chord sequence played by five acoustic guitars and a piano.

At this point they add the bass and drums. Keltner settles behind his kit in a small area to one side, fenced off behind acoustic baffles. One of the guitarists is asked if he minds playing the bass instead – Klaus Voorman's flight from Germany has been delayed, and he's going to miss the session, but the song can't wait.

They run the tune down a few more times. It's sounding good, the tapes are rolling. Every so often they put their instruments down and crowd into the booth to hear a playback.

'I like the ones,' John says, 'that sound like records...'

'... Before you've made 'em,' Phil adds, jumping in to complete his thought. At the level of the classic three-minute pop single, they seem like the perfect double act.

Almost imperceptibly, they slip into recording proper takes. During the third completed take, the sound really begins to lift off. Spector sits at the centre of the board, firing instructions to the engineer beside him, his voice rising in volume as the take continues and it becomes obvious that something is happening.

'More echo on the piano, Roy. More echo. More... more... more. MORE ECHO! C'MON! That's it. Beautiful!'

During the second verse, Spector leaps to his feet. The thick soundproof plexiglass window between the control room and the studio is split into three panels, set at angles, like an old-fashioned car windscreen. From the room you can see the musicians, with a triple image of Spector, arms spread, superimposed on them.

His arms are windmilling with the beat. He's practically dancing. And as the climax approaches he stares over the heads of the guitarists, straight into Keltner's eyes, willing him to lay into his tom-toms, to make the fills explode just like Hal Blaine and Earl Palmer did on those old Ronettes and Righteous Brothers sessions at Gold Star in Hollywood. Keltner knows exactly what he wants. He grimaces and strains to oblige, and the take ends in a blaze of glorious noise.

'Great!' Spector screams. That's the one.

The overdubs start, and again the Spector magic is even more apparent. At John's suggestion, they begin with guitars playing a mandolin-like line which wanders behind the verse. It takes a mere ten minutes to get them on the track. This is record-making the way it used to be, when you had three hours to get the A-side and B-side down, and maybe the follow-up as well – the days before musicians went off to a country cottage to get their heads together.

They try out all sorts of percussive effects, finally settling on Hopkins playing chimes and glockenspiel, while Keltner adds a four-to-the-bar jangle on a handy set of sleigh bells.

'How can you make a Christmas record without sleigh bells?' Spector had asked. Now he smiles and mutters, as if to himself, 'I know something about Christmas records, you know.'

After recording *A Christmas Gift To You*, the album featuring the Crystals, the Ronettes and Bob B. Soxx and the Blue Jeans on material like 'Santa Claus Is Coming to Town' and 'I Saw Mommy Kissing Santa Claus', he probably knows more about Christmas records than anyone alive. But it's not an unmixed memory. Lavishly recorded in Los Angeles in the summer of 1963, full of bells and chimes and ersatz good cheer, it was released that November, just a few days before John F. Kennedy was assassinated in Dallas. After which, of course, no one was remotely interested in merry seasonal pop records. The Christmas album became a bit of a legend, until radio started picking up on it almost ten years later, when it became recognised as a kitsch classic (although Bob B. Soxx's version of 'The Bells Of St Mary's' has a tidal wave momentum that would give even 'River Deep Mountain High' a run for its money).

Now it's time for the vocal, so John and Yoko clamp on the headphones and start practising, while Phil has the engineer run the track for them. John sounds wheezy and is unable to hit the high notes. Phil shouts through the talkback: 'Yoko's outsinging you, John!' He flips off the mike and turns away, shaking his head in disapproval. 'He's smoking his ass off while he's singing.' Bobby Hatfield would never have been allowed to get away with that when the high notes on 'Unchained Melody' or 'Hung On You' needed singing. But this is John Lennon, after all, and Spector turns his attention to finding exactly the right amount of echo for the voices. Meanwhile, with the aid of tactful prods in the back, John gets Yoko to come in at the right places. They get a take they're happy with.

Now they start talking about what to do with the strings and the children's choir, scheduled for overdubbing over the next few days. Phil thinks it's a good idea to have the violins playing 'Silent Night' over the fade. John suggests a cello figure to go against the chorus.

Once again, they do a rough mix. But it's four o'clock in the morning. Time to go. Spector and the Lennons say goodnight. Their two Cadillac limousines sweep down 44th Street and into the night.

The following evening, the band runs through 'Snow Is Falling', a Yoko composition scheduled for the B-side of 'Happy Xmas'. It's five years old. It was, she says, the first song she showed John when they got together. To be blunt, it's probably not the reason he left Cynthia. But Yoko is happy because she's getting the chance to record it at last.

Spector is there with his brother-in-law, Joe, whose Brooklyn accent could be cut with a blunt switchblade. In the grand tradition of Phil's 'assistants' Joe stands by the wall all night, not saying a word, moving only when Phil mutters a request for a Scotch. Joe then rummages in a blue flight bag for the bottle of J&B, and mixes the drink with water in a studio glass. When they run out of ice, Phil gets shirty. Then Joe starts worrying. He wanders around the studio, murmuring: 'I gotta find da ice.'

In the studio, an argument starts. John and Yoko can't agree on the tempo. John has been amusing himself by picking out rockabilly riffs on his guitar, with the amp's reverb turned way up. 'I'm not gonna play on this,' he says, putting his instrument down.

'I asked you to play organ,' Yoko says, with an edge of peevishness in her voice. 'I've been asking you to do that all along.'

John goes back into the control room and shuts the door.

'I thought this was supposed to be a light thing,' Spector says to him.

'It was,' Lennon responds. 'But she says "Faster!" and they all start rocking like shit.'

Yoko, exercising the composer's rights, tells Nicky Hopkins to play with a lighter touch on the intro. 'Pretend that it's snowing,' she suggests. 'Pretend that snow is melting on your fingertips. Not that banging.'

Hopkins gets it right this time, while Klaus Voorman, whose plane finally arrived, and Hugh McCracken, who has been invited back, work out little background licks strongly reminiscent of Curtis Mayfield's 'People Get Ready'.

But within a couple of minutes Yoko and Klaus, who knew the Beatles back in Hamburg, are in a shouting match over the placement of chords at the end of the song. Voorman gets up, unstraps his bass, and appears to be on the point of walking out. John goes into the studio and placates both of them. It makes you wonder how many times such things happened in the seven-year recording career of the Beatles, and whether John was often cast in the role of peacemaker. Probably not. But he must have learnt something from the experience, because Klaus has his bass back on, Yoko is in front of the vocal microphone, and they're trying it again. This time it works. They get a good take straight away.

John (relieved): 'Fantastic...'

Phil: 'Great. Great echo.'

Yoko: 'How was my voice?'

Phil: 'Great. Great echo.'

The track sounds pretty enough in its unadorned simplicity, but within minutes they're talking about adding organ, chimes, more guitar, even sound effects. What they want is the sound of a celeste, but they haven't got one. The engineers set to work to find a way of getting a celeste sound out of the electric piano. As they're working, Hopkins and Voorman and Keltner start to play a medium-tempo blues.

'Oh-oh,' Spector says. 'They've started jamming. Now we'll never get anything done. Let's put a stop to that.'

He moves to the connecting door, but Yoko pre-empts him.

'STOP JAMMING!' she screams, her finger jammed down on the talkback button, her voice almost bursting the speakers. The musicians halt as one, in mid-note.

Yoko is obviously more than a little tense. Earlier, she confided her fear that the musicians don't take her songs as seriously as she believes they deserve to be treated. But this is a nice little song, no doubt about it. It's not 'Norwegian Wood' or 'Happiness Is A Warm Gun' by any means, but it sounds quite commercial. She flutters her hands with delight when, during the overdubs, someone says it sounds more like a Top Five smash than the A-side.

They finish off, as promised, with the sound effects. One of the engineers digs out the album of effects that all studios keep for such occasions. They decide to open the track with the sound of 'Feet in the snow' and close it with 'Strong wind'. The lights are turned off for the final playback. 'Listen... the snow is falling everywhere.' Outside in midtown, there's still a vestige of summer warmth in the night air.

On Sunday afternoon the session starts early. The choir is there, and the choir has a strict bedtime.

The choir consists of about thirty black kids, aged between about four and twelve, plus four adolescent girls whom Lennon affectionately refers to as the Supremes. A few of the singers' mothers shush and cluck around the studio, making sure that ribbon-bows aren't crooked.

John and Yoko get the children singing 'Happy Xmas' from the words that Lennon has scrawled on a blackboard, with Yoko singing lead. They get it after a handful of run-throughs, and their voices are superimposed on a track that has already been mixed down. Spector insists on one more take from the singers. Nothing wrong with the first effort, he says. Just give me one more. He records both, and dubs them both on top of the track. Now there are sixty voices, for the price of thirty. A trick from the old days.

The only thing left to do is the strings. That's scheduled for another day, and what Spector will do is record them but only put their echo on the track. That's another of his oldest tricks. If you use the echo rather than the original signal, it lends the string line a more ethereal, more romantic quality.

The Lennons, the children, the mothers, the Supremes, the band, the engineers, the studio secretary, Phil and the reluctant Joe gather round to pose for a picture for the bag of the 45. A green plastic Christmas tree with dangling lights, specially bought for the occasion, towers over the group.

The photographer is a little slow. He can't seem to fit everyone into the frame. So Phil takes over.

'C'mon,' he cajoles the photographer, who is fiddling with his tripod. 'When I say "One – two – three", everybody's gonna shout "Happy Christmas!" and you take the picture. Right? One – two – three!' *Happy Christmas!* 'One – two – three.' *Happy Christmas!* 'One two – three.' *Happy Christmas!* 'OK. You got it.'

Shortly after midnight, the two black Cadillacs pull away from the kerb outside the Record Plant and swing into Eighth Avenue. They travel one block in convoy before the first car peels off left into 45th Street, towards the St Regis.

The second car carries on along Eighth, heading uptown. The partition is shut. Sitting right in the middle of the wide rear seat is a small figure with long hair and aviator shades. Above the left breast of his denim jacket is a red and white button. It says 'Back to Mono'. That's where the limo is heading.

24

May Pang Interview by Kingsley Abbott

After Phil Spector's initial work with the Beatles with the famed Let It Be *controversy, and his work with John Lennon's initial solo projects such as 'Instant Karma', there followed a lull of activity. In 1973, during what was to become known as Lennon's 'lost weekend' period, he and Phil collaborated on the* Rock'N'Roll *album. The story of these sessions has been told sketchily in various places, sometimes with Lennon being painted very much as the villain, but now May Pang who, as well as being John's constant companion at the time and intimately involved in the sessions, tells the full story from their point of view in an exclusive interview for this book.*

Can you tell me a bit about how the idea for the Rock'N'Roll *album came about?*
John and I would often talk about oldies that we loved. Even though he was 10 years older, we liked the same music. More than the hit, he loved the B-sides. I still have all the 45s, and nowadays I get a chance to tell artists like Carla Thomas that John loved 'I Can't Take It' [Editor's note: the B-side of Carla's fifth Atlantic single 'I'll Bring It On Home To You' from 1962]. Carla was so thrilled when I told her. John wanted to cut an album where he was just the artist, just the voice, singing all the old songs he loved. John had worked with Phil before, co-producing, on *Plastic Ono Band* and *Imagine*. John loved echo, so it was a natural progression to have Phil do this album.

How did you approach Phil?
When we first began to court Phil for the album in LA, he would say things like 'Oh, I'm not sure.' We would go out to restaurants, where Phil would move two or three times on whims – starters here, main course there, somewhere else after – John didn't want to do this sort of star trip. We thought we were coaxing Phil, but it was his game. Once he realised that he would have complete control – that John just wanted to be the voice, Phil said yes. Phil kept asking 'Do I have final control?' He was on very good behaviour up to that point!

What was it like when the sessions began?
Things were always a bit different with Phil! It was always kinda
scary – which is what he wanted. When he had been co-producer
with John, he was calmer, but now he was in total control. He knew
what he wanted, but achieving it was something different. You have
to remember that John was used to working with at most five others
in a studio. On that first session at the big room at A&M, I think
we counted 27 musicians – everybody was there! People on those
sessions included Leon Russell, Hal Blaine, Dr John, Jeff Barry
(on tambourine), Barry Mann, Nino Tempo and his sax group, Jose
Feliciano, Jesse Ed Davis, Michael Hazelwood, Barney Kessel and
his two sons David and Danny, and even Steve Cropper. They were
not necessarily all playing at one time; for instance I don't think Dr
John and Leon were there together, but it was always a huge number,
never less than twenty. Phil's standard set-up was three acoustic
guitars, three electric guitars, two pianos, two basses, two drummers
and a horn section of at least four, but sometimes up to six or eight.
John was a Johnny Carson fan, and he was thrilled that Pete C, the
horn player from that show, was on the sessions. Phil would hear
things in his head, and had some players just playing one note. It
was all done on 16 tracks on 2" tapes. One problem with Phil's set
up was that, if John wanted to change any one thing, it was very
difficult with everybody playing in the same room at the same time
– the room leakage was tough.

Communication via the media

John's work ethics were very tight – he was used to working from
a particular time, perhaps about 7pm through to midnight, and then
having smokes and drinks afterwards. On that first day, we arrived
and all the musicians were there, but Phil doesn't turn up for three

hours. Then it seemed all the microphones needed re-configuring. Each night Phil would come dressed differently: in karate gear one day, as a surgeon another and so on. He would also get through a bottle of Courvoisier each night, and this sort of set the tone for the sessions. Everybody was ordering stuff, and it became wild. At the beginning it was okay, and we had a good time, but it soon got out of hand. And then there were the visitors: Joni Mitchell came with Warren Beatty, Cher, Harry Nilsson, David Geffen... everybody wanted to hang out. The band was ready for 7 pm, but we wouldn't roll until 9 or 10 pm and then go on through until 2 or 3 am. I warned that they shouldn't drink, but Phil set the pace. John succumbed to it, as he was with his pals. Harry introduced John to Brandy Alexanders, which were like milkshakes. I tried to keep John on the straight and narrow, as I was in the role of production assistant, and I would fight with Phil. Phil knew I was protecting John, and I didn't mind taking the flak. Though I was only 22, I didn't take any of Phil's nonsense. He was afraid of me. He kept telling John he shouldn't trust me. I think I intimidated him, as I was straight-laced. It was one thing to drink at the end of a session, but not during. However, Phil loved drama, and he wanted to keep us all in there. He seemed to think that we were all there to entertain him. One night he threatened to swallow the studio key to keep us in, so I just left at that time. At one point I checked with Capitol to see how much money we had spent, and they told me some really small amount. It appeared that, because Phil had a production deal with Warners that they were supposedly paying for it all. Each night Phil would take home all the masters. It was a circus with Phil. John trusted him, and had never anticipated difficulties. It was fun at first as far as John was concerned, but I was worried. John could be chameleon-like and would go with the flow. At that time he was the biggest name working in LA, which was part of the trouble perhaps – had we been back home in NY it may have been very different. Phil was in his territory in LA. John wanted to get back on track. He thought that the sessions were okay, not brilliant.

The sessions were thrown out of A&M, weren't they?
Yes. One of the musicians, I don't know who, poured a bottle of drink all over the console. It certainly wasn't John, he would have had much more respect for equipment or instruments than to ever do anything like that. It was then that we moved over to Record Plant.

How did John react musically in the studio?
John was subservient to Phil in the studio, which is, as you remember, how he wanted it for this album. He would comment and express preferences, which Phil would note. John gave up his right in this case, although he had insisted on using his own engineer, Roy Cicala, from Record Plant. John never saw the need for all the drama. John's dramas were emotional; he didn't need them physically.

How was John emotionally during this period?
A lot of things have been taken out of context. John was in good spirits and that was the reason he wanted to go back into the studio. He had just finished *Mind Games*. John was feeling bad at that time only for the things that might have gotten into the press. For instance, if he went out and something happened it seemed he always got the blame. He was the new kid on the block in LA and made good copy. Subsequently, Yoko has said that he was always drunk, but this is not true. Sometimes yes, but not as often as people write. In my opinion, Yoko would like for the public to think that if John stayed at home in NY he wouldn't have been like this and that he was calling her all the time to try and go back. It was actually the opposite – she would call John up to 20 times a day! Yoko would also call Phil. During his time with me, John was more productive than any other time in his solo career. He completed three albums, reconnected with Julian, and worked with Elton and Bowie among others. When we were recording the Harry Nilsson album, we lived with Keith Moon, Harry, Ringo and others – all under one roof. Yoko thought that John and me would last for maybe two weeks and then it would be over, but at the time John never intended to go back. No one knew the situation, but John and I did keep talking and seeing each other secretly after he went back to the Dakota.

How were the sessions for the album planned with Phil?
Phil's work ethics were odd. He would come to the house and discuss the numbers and the arrangements. He'd come at night and leave before dawn. My girlfriend Arlene and I thought this was weird and that he was some sort of vampire! Phil would come with his bodyguard, George, and talk just to John. We'd leave them, and John was pretty happy at first. On one occasion, the day after he tied John up when he was drunk, Phil turned up at the studio sporting a black eye created by a make-up artist. He wanted to blame John for hitting

him the night before. At these planning sessions, John had a good idea of the feel he wanted for each song, and he was sure Phil would know what he meant. John wasn't looking for any sort of perfection, but wanted certain feels. In fact he liked records with imperfections. Who could have guessed it would turn out so differently? One trouble was that Phil would never tell us who would play what. A lot of it was decided on the spur of the moment in the studio.

What was your view of the finished product?
There were a few wonderful musical times – a couple of terrific things, like the Chuck Berry song. Here and there it was great. It could have been a terrific album. You recall that Phil had taken the master tapes and we had to battle to get them back. Eventually Al Coury, (the head of A&R and Promotion), made a deal with Phil and his reps, but by that time John was already onto *Walls And Bridges*. When we heard the tapes, it was awful. You could hear studio noise, and you could hear the difference between Phil's productions and John's more succinct basis. We kept what John could salvage, which was four tracks, and gave a couple of songs back to Phil in the deal. I think that maybe Cher and Harry Nilsson eventually did them. Phil was just so full of himself that he felt no one could touch him. John was a better producer for himself in the end with *Walls And Bridges*. It was a question of confidence. John was insecure about things like his voice, but he was brilliant. His forte in life was as a singer/ songwriter who knew the feel of what he wanted. It took a long time for him to realise he could do it.

How would you sum up Phil as a person from that time?
He was very controlling. I admired him as a producer, but he came into my home and created havoc. He took advantage of the situation. John would have been very happy if it had gone okay, but he was very sad with the result. One occasion sums up the whole time. One night, John just wanted to run through some songs, but Phil said that we had to come to his house for a surprise. It was a strange, big house, with barbed wire, fences and dogs. So we wondered what it would be. We knew Chuck Berry was in town, so we thought maybe... So we got there, and soon after Phil's butler announces from the top of the stairs – 'Mr Charles Berry.' And there is Chuck with two women, including a blonde that I already knew. Phil then turns out the lights! It was dark in there already, so there was only the light from an

aquarium. John rushed up to help Chuck come down the stairs. It was all so strange. Finally Phil puts the lights back on, and we were all sitting around on a L-shaped couch, and there was the sort of chat with Chuck and John talking about doing something musically together. Chuck asks John if he'd like to, and then Phil stands over us saying to John, 'Don't answer him! Don't answer him!' And he's kicking John on the shins to try and keep control of the situation! At that point I went into another room, as I was so embarrassed. It was a music/billiards room, and soon they all came in. Phil puts Chuck between two big speakers and puts on some of his (Phil's) biggest songs, saying 'I made this for you Chuck'. It was deafening! John eventually said to Phil to turn it down. Phil said that he didn't get it, and John simply said that he thought it was a wasted night, and that he would rather have worked.

25
Quotes 2

Rather than develop his artists' careers, Phil developed himself; rather than serve the artist, the artist served Phil.
Jerry Wexler, Atlantic Records

Well, in the beginning I made a lot of records that I didn't put names on and nobody knows about, and it's better that way. But of those that you know of, I would imagine 'Be My Baby' and 'Lovin' Feelin'' are the most satisfying. 'River Deep' is a satisfying record. I mean, I could tell you how 'Lovin' Feelin'' was made. I could tell you I'm the greatest fuckin' record producer who ever lived and that I'll eat up all these cats in the studio if they want to put their mouths right there and their money right there. 'He's A Rebel', it's fine; the 'Da Doo Ron Ron' is fine.
Phil Spector

He (Spector) wanted to write with us. He had been writing with Jeff Barry and Ellie Greenwich. For some reason he wanted to change. He said he had this new group from Orange County called the Righteous Brothers. He said he'd love us to write something for them with him. At the time, we loved 'Baby I Need Your Loving' by the Four Tops. We just loved that record and we thought it was great. We wanted to write something like it. Cynthia and I started alone without Phil. I remember we used 'You've Lost That Loving Feeling' as a dummy title. We wrote a verse and a chorus. I didn't know how to end it. 'Gone, gone, gone, whoa, whoa, whoa' wasn't in there yet. We played Phil the verse and the chorus and told him it was a dummy title. He ended up coming up with the 'Gone, gone, gone, whoa, whoa, whoa,' but he also came up with the concept of that middle part – the 'bomp, do, do-do' which for the time was very, very different. He also said 'Hey man, "You've Lost That Lovin' Feelin'" is the title.' So we ended up using that, and it ended up becoming the most played song of the last century.
Barry Mann

Phil heard us and thought he could do us justice. We just knew this was it, we had arrived. We were 15-year-olds, so you can imagine the excitement. We got to know Phil quite well and worked at his studio in his apartment in Manhattan. Phil was a genius in the studio, a perfectionist for sure. He was demanding, but not abusive, or anything. There are some stories, believe me that I don't feel comfortable sharing. Let's just say that Phil Spector was a colourful character. We worked with him for about a year and a half. We met Phil when we went down to do background recordings for one of his groups. He asked, 'Do you know any songs?' I said I could sing 'Why Do Fools Fall In Love'. When I sang that, Phil said 'This is it! That's it!' We didn't know what the hell he was talking about – what was 'it'? He said, 'that's the voice I have been looking for.'
Ronnie Spector

I don't ever get tired of singing our songs, like 'Be My Baby', because it's always a different audience. When you hear the audience getting revved up to see you, you just don't think that you sang it a thousand times. I never, ever get tired of it. I love 'Be My Baby', but 'Walking In The Rain' is my favourite.
Ronnie Spector

One day George Harrison and Phil Spector were doing something in Studio 3, and they needed a rough mix of 'My Sweet Lord'. I therefore went into Room 4 – which was a little remix suite – with Spector, and although I'd done virtually nothing up to that point engineering-wise, over the course of twenty minutes he dictated to me how to achieve his famous 'Wall of Sound'. It was like 'Put on the tape. Lift the fader. Run that tape echo. Spin the echo around... a bit more, bit more, bit more... that's it. Now let's bring in this track...' I did everything, but I was like a puppet as he dictated the whole process step by step. In terms of the delays, and the kinds of reverbs he was using, I think there was a formula, but in all other respects he did it by ear. It was amazing. Within twenty minutes he had dictated how to turn a very dry eight-track recording into his trademark sound.
John Kurlander – Abbey Road engineer for 30 years

After the Wrecking Crew made its mark on the music scene, Phil Spector went off to do his own thing. No one really knew what he was up to until we realised that some of the big Beatles hits were his

productions... and then I got a call from Donna, his Girl Friday, asking me to do some dates. The old band was reassembled for some special sessions for Leonard Cohen at Gold Star and at Whitney Studios in Glendale. They were incredible dates. There was one major change though – we had the Kessel brothers (Barney's sons). Phil was now hiring the second generation of Hollywood musicians.
Hal Blaine

A new Wall of Sound was assembled at A&M. We were in the big studio, and the lot was buzzing with the name of John Lennon. We worked there for about a week and then moved to the Record Plant for a few nights. Everyone was totally immersed in the project. This was Phil Spector at his greatest. The material and the band were synched beautifully.
Hal Blaine

At our next recording session, on 4th February 1964, with Andrew producing and Bill Farley engineering again, there were some surprise guests. We'd become friendly with Phil Spector and attended a star-studded party in his honour thrown at Decca a week earlier, so he continued the friendship by dropping in on our recording. Graham Nash and Allan Clarke of the Hollies also came and later Gene Pitney arrived direct from the airport, with duty-free cognac. It was his birthday, and his family custom was that everyone had to drink a whole glass. Pitney played piano while Spector and the Hollies played tambourine and maracas and banged coins on empty bottles. We recorded three songs, 'Little By Little', 'Can I Get A Witness' and 'Now I've Got A Witness', which we invented on the spot. The session then degenerated into silliness, but everybody had a great time cutting 'Andrew's Blues' and 'Spector And Pitney Came Too' – both of which were very rude. It's often said that we recorded 'Not Fade Away' at this session, with Phil Spector playing maracas, but Andrew used this as publicity, although he was more impressed than the media were.
Bill Wyman [Editor's note: as well as playing maracas on 'Little By Little', Phil also later played acoustic guitar on 'Play With Fire', along with just Mick, Keith and Jack Nitzsche on guitar and harpsichord.]

The Phil Spector experience was... (very long pause)... I don't know. Phil – I can't really talk too much about that. It was a bit of a dirge.

I left it in his hands. He wanted full reign. Looking back, I think he wasn't where he had been when he recorded that album.
Dion

I don't remember Phil Spector being fun. The sessions were fun, and so was everyone else: Sonny Bono, Jack Nitzsche, Nino, Leon Russell, Jim Horn, all those guys. They were fun people. Bobby Sheen. But Phil wasn't fun to me. He was sneaky, and sneaky people make me nervous. Now he never did anything to me. He paid me. Fine. Goodbye. We never passed two or three words. I'm the type who jokes around, but with him I was not comfortable. He probably doesn't remember my name. I didn't like the creep.
Gloria Jones, of the Blossoms who masqueraded as the Crystals on 'He's A Rebel'

All I remember thinking is, oh, that voice. Certain singers make me go crazy. Darlene was definitely one of them. Dusty Springfield was another. When I put this record on I was laid out on the floor crying. It's still one of my all-time favourites.
Ellie Greenwich, recalling Darlene Love's '(Today I Met) The Boy I'm Gonna Marry'

The third Darlene Love single might have been the best of them all: 'A Fine Fine Boy', which was as close to pure R&B as Phil ever got.
Darlene Love

Darlene started to sing and the hair stood up all over my body. It was a performance that made time stop. When she finished, Fanita fell over with both her hands up in the air.
Cher, recalling Darlene Love recording 'Christmas (Baby Please Come Home)'

The Christmas album, I would later realise, was Phil Spector at his best and worst. The work itself was clearly his masterpiece, and everyone attached to it felt a hem-of-the-garment thrill. I could almost forget – almost – all the double crosses and disappointments of the preceding months and forgive Phil. That's how great the Christmas album was.
Darlene Love

Appendix I
Most Popular Phil Spector Productions

During the preparation of this book, I placed internet requests asking for people's top ten favourite Phil Spector productions, with an additional request for their most popular Christmas album tracks. There are perhaps the expected most popular songs, but also some surprising less usual high scorers. There are some surprising low scorers as well. I scored 12 points for a first place vote, 10 for a second, followed by 8 down to 1 for third down to tenth. Songs followed by an asterisk were songs that received at least one first place vote. Read on and peruse the list, and see if your favourites are there. The voting for the Christmas album showed a runaway winner with Darlene Love's 'Christmas (Baby Please Come Home)'. Only 'Sleigh Ride' showed above the rest as a second choice. Thanks to everyone who responded to my requests, especially those on www.spectropop.com.

Phil with the Righteous Brothers

01   You've Lost That Lovin' Feelin' – Righteous Bros – 662 *
02   Be My Baby – Ronettes – 461*
03   River Deep Mountain High – Ike & Tina Turner – 450 *
04   Then He Kissed Me – Crystals – 356*
05   Baby, I Love You – Ronettes – 318*
06   He's A Rebel – Crystals – 305*
07   I'll Never Need More Than This – Ike & Tina Turner – 277*
08   This Could Be The Night – Modern Folk Quartet – 260*

09   Walking In The Rain – Ronettes – 202
10   Da Doo Ron Ron – Crystals – 201
11   I Wonder – Crystals – 178*
12   Is This What I Get For Loving You – Ronettes – 165
13   Just Once In My Life – Righteous Bros – 157
14   Hung On You – Righteous Bros – 147*
15   Instant Karma – Plastic Ono Band – 140*
16   Do I Love You – Ronettes – 138
17   Born To Be Together – Ronettes – 136*
18   Little Boy – Crystals – 131
19   I Love How You Love Me – Paris Sisters – 117*
20   Corrine Corrina – Ray Peterson – 112*
21   You Baby – Ronettes – 106
22   Black Pearl – Checkmates Ltd – 102
23   Love Is All I Have To Give – Checkmates Ltd – 100*
24   Paradise – Ronettes – 96*
25   Hold Me Tight – Treasures – 85*
26   To Know Him Is To Love Him – Teddy Bears – 73
27   I Wish I Never Saw The Sunshine – Ronettes – 66*
28   Fine Fine Boy – Darlene Love – 60
29   Strange Love – Darlene Love – 52
30   The Boy I'm Gonna Marry – Darlene Love – 41
31   Every Breath I Take – Gene Pitney – 39
32   Let It Down – George Harrison – 36
33   The Best Part Of Breakin' Up – Ronettes – 35*
34   I Really Do – Spectors Three – 33*
35   All Grown Up – Crystals – 32
36   There's No Other (Like My Baby) – Crystals – 28
37   Heartbreaker – Crystals – 22
38   Puddin' 'N' Tain – Alley Cats – 21
39= Good Lovin' Man – Dion – 20
39= Raincoat In The River – Sammy Turner – 20
41= Zip-A-Dee-Doo-Dah – Bob B. Soxx & the Blue Jeans – 18
41= Isn't It A Pity – George Harrison – 18
43= A Love Like Yours – Ike & Tina Turner – 17
43= You Said Goodbye – Teddy Bears – 16
43= Stumble And Fall – Darlene Love – 15
46= Uptown – Crystals – 14
46= Pretty Little Angel Eyes – Curtis Lee – 14
46= Memories – Leonard Cohen – 14

46= Born To Be With You – Dion – 14
50= Make The Woman Love Me – Dion – 13
50= Imagine – John Lennon – 13
52   Oh Baby – Harvey & Doc with the Dwellers – 12*
53   What Is Life – George Harrison – 11
54= Spanish Harlem – Ben E King – 10
54= Under The Moon Of Love – Curtis Lee – 10
54= A Nice Way To Turn Seventeen – Crystals – 10
57   A Long Way To Be Happy – Darlene Love – 9
58   Try Some, Buy Some – Ronnie Spector – 8
59   A Woman's Story – Cher – 7
60= Why Don't They Let Us Fall In Love – Veronica – 6
60= He Knows I Love Him Too Much – Paris Sisters – 6
60= Jimmy Baby – Bob B. Soxx & the Blue Jeans – 6
60= (Let's Dance) The Screw – Crystals – 6
60= Baby, I Love You – Cher – 6
60= When I Saw You – Ronettes – 6
60= He's Sure The Boy I Love – Darlene Love – 6
67= Angel Baby – John Lennon – 5
67= Why Do Lovers Break Each Other's Hearts – Bob B. Soxx &
       the Blue Jeans – 5
67= He Hit Me (And It Felt Like A Kiss) – Crystals – 5
67= Everyday I Have To Cry – Ike & Tina Turner – 5
67= Awaiting On You All – George Harrison – 5
67= Happy Xmas (War Is Over) – John Lennon & Yoko Ono – 5
73= (He's A) Quiet Guy – Darlene Love – 4
73= Save The Last Dance For Me – Ike & Tina Turner – 4
73= Chapel Of Love – Ronettes – 4
76= My Heart Beat A Little Bit Faster – Bob B. Soxx & the Blue Jeans – 3
76= Be My Baby – John Lennon – 3
76= Stand By Me – John Lennon – 3
76= Another Country, Another World – Crystals – 3
76= Ebb Tide –Righteous Bros – 3
81   Here It Comes (And Here I Go) – Jerri Bo Keno – 2
82= God – John Lennon – 1
82= Twist And Shout – Top Notes – 1
82= Beware Of Darkness (live) – George Harrison – 1
82= Baby Let's Stick Together– Dion – 1

The Modern Folk Quartet

One of the lesser known acts that scores highly in the preceding poll is the Modern Folk Quartet whose sole known outing under Spector's wing is the wonderful 'This Could Be The Night', which is well known as one of Brian Wilson's long standing faves. The MFQ began back in 1962/3 during the US folk boom of that period as a two guitar, banjo and upright bass line-up consisting of Cyrus Faryer, Henry Tad Diltz (aka the famed rock photographer), Chip Douglas and Jerry Yester. They issued an album in '63 on Warner Brothers, which was very much a set of folk adaptations of older songs. They looked very clean, with suits, ties and broad smiles. In 1964 they released a beat boom inspired single on Warner Bros called 'The Love Of A Clown', with an harmonically interesting and melodic B-side 'If All You Think', both sides being written by future Lovin' Spoonful member Yester.

Two years later came another obscure single on RCA that was more obviously within the folk rock mould: 'Night Time Girl', written by Al Kooper and Irwin Levine, and its group-penned flip 'Lifetime' were both arranged and produced by Jack Nitzsche, giving the likely connection to Spector who had already shown interest in producing the Lovin' Spoonful. The TCBTN session came and went, unreleased until the *Seventies Rare Masters Volume 2* album, and the group stayed together with the same line-up for several later albums including *Moonlight Serenade* and *Bamboo Saloon*, which highlight their fine harmonic and arranging skills, and are highly rated by the fans who know them. Spector's brief association with them is perhaps one of the most unfulfilled episodes of his career given the class of the one track that we do know.

Appendix II
The Case For Mono With Reference To
Brian Wilson And Phil Spector

This short piece was posted by Joe Nelson to the Spectropop *discussion board (find it at www.spectropop.com). It certainly provokes thought...*

A couple of weeks back I noted an old *Goldmine* article ('Brian Wilson: Unknown For A Very Long Time', Vol 14, No. 24, November 18, 1988) in which Brian Wilson was quoted in a statement that suggested that his avoidance of stereo wasn't just about his partial deafness. I finally got the chance to go over the article with a fine-toothed comb and locate the quote. The context was a note about Brian's work habits around the time of *Smile* – recording every snatch of song that came to his head, then assembling them into finished songs later. It was a move being compared to the dada artists, but the writer Neal Umphred noted that unlike the dadas Brian wasn't a fan of letting things happen by chance. Everything was carefully considered in how the 'collages' were put together:

Brian: I look at sound like a painting... the balance is conceived in (the artist's) mind. You finish the sound, you dub it down, and you've stamped out a picture of your balance with that mono dub-down. But in stereo – you leave the dub-down to the listener – to his speaker balance and placement. It just doesn't seem complete to me. Umphred: That may be his belief, but in fact the wide stereo common in 60s mixes invites the participation of the listener's mind. Contemporary stereo mixes are too polished, too perfect; many of today's finest recordings are, in the long run, boring. They do not invite your mind into the process; they ask nothing in return. Hence the continued attractiveness of older, imperfect recordings...

Huh???????

Is it my imagination, or did Umphred miss something? From what I've always gathered, Brian wanted you to see his art, and that the

way he saw it. If you could or would change anything, you weren't getting his vision. Mono was what it was, that mix was set in stone. In Brian's monaural world, stereo was just another way to hear mono. It's like my mother's old stereo console system – from my vantage point of some corner of the room I neither knew nor cared that different sounds came out of the two speakers. Perhaps this is why Phil Spector preferred mono – he didn't spend ages perfecting the balance on 'You've Lost That Lovin' Feelin'' just to have some nerd with a stereo phonograph and a copy of the stereo LP decide to can the string build-up with a twist of the balance knob during the bridge.
Joe Nelson

Brian Wilson's Early Spectorised Productions

For many years everyone from Brian himself down has pointed to the influences that Spector had on Wilson's work with the Beach Boys. Indeed two tracks have been included on the recent Ace Records' *Phil's Spectre* issues: 'Why Do Fools Fall In Love' on the first volume and 'I Do' on the second. Generally it can be said that the best of the influences were heard on the arrangement subtlety and instrumental blends on *Pet Sounds*, but before this there were several more obvious copy attempts, not all of which were entirely successful. With the Honeys girl group, Brian cut 'He's A Doll' and 'The One You Can't Have', the original issues of which seemed to have lost all the intended power that didn't emerge out of the murky mix until a late-nineties re-issue. Certainly Spector-isms can be heard on 'Don't Worry Baby', a song that Brian had pitched for the Ronettes, and other isms can be heard in many other Beach Boy places. An interesting recent find has been an outtake from the *Surfer Girl* album, an early unreleased attempt at the later Beach Boys song 'Back Home'. Recorded on June 14th, 1963, it has a Spector feel all over it, though without the massive rumble, and is thought to be Brian's first visit to Gold Star. Musicians were Spector regulars Hal Blaine, David Gates, Jay Migliori, Steve Douglas and Carol Kaye alongside Brian. No other Beach Boys appear to have been present, certainly not as players. Also recorded that day with the same musicians was a tune called 'Black Wednesday', which was the working title for the Sharon Marie record 'Runaround Lover'.
Kingsley Abbott

Appendix III
Phil's Humour

'Two Japanese businessmen are enjoying a geisha bath when one says to the other, "Akido, I regret having to say this, but I must tell you that your wife is dishonouring you. Worse – she is dishonouring you with a gentleman of the Jewish persuasion." Akido calmly finishes bathing, and over dinner that night he says, "Honourable wife, I have heard that you are dishonouring me with a man of the Jewish persuasion." And Akido's wife lowers her eyes and says, "Ah, honourable husband, who tells you that meshugoss?"'

'My mother, when I told her "I'm interested in sex, drugs and rock'n'roll" as a child, she figured I was going to be a politician.'

'I hate Michael Bolton so much that I had to send a letter to Barry Manilow, apologising for hating him so much as I used to hate him.'

'Albert Einstein invented the bomb, invented nuclear fission, invented the theory of relativity, and you look at every picture of him, the man couldn't invent a hair conditioner.'

'You have a lot of people in the recording industry who have difficulty in spelling IQ.'

'I prefer to be accurately rude than hypocritically polite.'

'The difference between a Madonna video and a porno film – some porno films have got pretty good music.'

And to finish... the *Abbey Road* book by Brian Southall has a picture captioned:
'A star for a day! Abbey Road studio technician Eddie Klein was signed up by producer Phil Spector, as a joke, to make a tap dancing record with this star-studded line-up: George Harrison, Billy Preston, Klaus Voormann, Phil Spector, Ringo Starr and Gary Wright.'

Appendix IV
Quotes 3

Philip was always strange – always a very strange man. But he was really young at the time. I was 16, so Philip must have been maybe 22. I remember the first time I met Philip, he'd been taking French lessons and when we were first introduced, he said to me in French, 'Will you go to bed with me?' And I said to him in French, 'For money.' I was really taken aback that he could be that condescending. It pissed me off. So we had a very strange relationship from that moment on. But we always liked each other. I didn't always approve of his behaviour because he could be a real dick, really treacherous and a complete megalomaniac. But he was weird; he would fuck with the people he could and wouldn't with the people who wouldn't stand for it. He was like a child in that he would push you to see what the boundaries were.

But it was such a different time. It was nothing like now. It was like living on the earth and being brought up on the moon. The record business, rock'n'roll, wasn't an industry then. I remember being with Brian Wilson and the Byrds – we hung out at Gold Star Studios – and it was like, the music was made by the young people and the older people just didn't get involved because they really didn't know what it was. They didn't get it. And the young people didn't know how much they were worth or how important they were as artists...

I started on 'Be My Baby' and finished on 'You've Lost That Lovin' Feelin'', and I did everything in between, including the Christmas album... I have a distinctive voice. You can hear it if you listen closely. I had to stand five feet behind everybody else when we were recording because my voice just wouldn't blend – it kind of cut through. It got to be a joke in the studio. One more step back Cher! But Yeah, I can always hear my harmonies.
Cher

When asked why he doesn't write songs anymore: 'Because I'm not as good as Irving Berlin.'
Phil Spector

Real American music – Louis Armstrong. He never played a wrong note. He never sang a wrong note. Everything he did was perfect. You know what Dizzy Gillespie said when someone asked him about Louis? – 'No Louis, No Diz.'
Phil Spector

I did meet Spector once. He was sitting up on a big chair looking like a little Buddha, answering yes and no to questions. Later on I asked producer Bumps Blackwell what he thought of Spector's 'genius', and he grinned and answered, 'Genius is knowing what to steal.'
Charles White – Little Richard biographer and BBC York DJ

We would rehearse for hours and hours, and no one could even go to the toilet for fear of moving a mic... Phil had positioned the mics himself, and the placement was sacred... Finally, after endless run-throughs, Phil would call a 'ten' and scream, 'Don't touch the mics!' And no one did.
Hal Blaine

I give Phil full credit for everything he did musically. He was certainly a frontrunner, a brilliant kid... Phil had his finger on the pulse of what kids wanted better than anybody I ever knew. He just knew what would be a hit, he just absolutely knew. It is great stuff, he made some great, great records.
Nino Tempo

I was always flattered when Phil would call up and say, 'Come on down, I need an extra pair of ears.' He always valued my reaction. He would look at me and if I had a pained look he would say, 'What don't you like? What's wrong?' And I would tell him. Very often, not always, he would say, 'Let's see if we can't change that.'
Nino Tempo

I learnt a lot by being in the Teddy Bears. I learnt I didn't want to be a singer. I learnt about payola and distributors and manufacturing. I learnt about the Mafia.
Phil Spector

I wanted to be in the background, but I wanted to be important in the background. I wanted to be the focal point. I knew about

Toscanini. I knew that Mozart was more important than the operas: that Beethoven was more important than whoever was playing or conducting his music. That's what I wanted to be.
Phil Spector

A Phil Spector session was a party session. Phil would have a notice on the door of the studio, 'Closed Session', and anyone who stuck their head in he'd grab them and give them a tambourine or a cowbell. There'd sometimes be more percussionists than orchestra. I used to call it the Phil-harmonic. It was an absolute ball.
Hal Blaine

I think Irving Berlin had an ego. I think he wanted to be number one. And so did I.
Phil Spector

Timing is the key to everything.
Phil Spector

Timing... That's all it is, a feeling. I never thought about anything I did before. I didn't think, why the Ronettes, why the Righteous Brothers, why John Lennon? I just did it. So I don't think, why Starsailor? Why Coldplay? It just feels okay. And I haven't had that instinct in me for years and years and years.
Phil Spector

One night I'll never forget... We'd spent the evening in George's flat with Paul McCartney and Ringo. It was 4 am. We were in Curzon Street. Suddenly Phil 'stole' his Rolls from his chauffeur and nearly rammed the front of a bank in his efforts to reverse. Drove down the Mall at 70 mph. Out of the blue, he made a huge U-turn in the private road leading to Clarence House, before the stunned astonished eyes of two policemen. We finished up in a self-service in Leicester Square. We spent some ten minutes selecting a mountain of food. Then arrived at the cash desk... to discover that we didn't have a penny between us. Meekly we had to replace the food, dish by dish. Under the eyes of incredulous waiters. Exit Spector and Hall helpless with laughter. And believe it or not, we were stone cold sober!
Tony Hall – DJ & columnist

Oh my God, there's a story there! In the industry then, if you got a hit with an artist, you would always follow it up with a similar-sounding one. Then, on the third one, you would change things a little. We heard that Phil wanted something for the Paris Sisters. I had a ballad called 'It Was Me Yesterday', and Phil came over to hear it. We played it for him, but he just kept talking. He was very rude, so I said to him, 'Why did you bother to come over if you weren't going to listen to the song?', and I suggested that he leave. He went mad, and stormed out!

A little later, he got to hear 'Today I Met The Boy I'm Gonna Marry', which had got to him in a roundabout sort of way, and he liked it. When we got together, he looked at me and must have thought, 'Uh-oh, it's that woman'. But he stayed with the song and used it. Then he took 'Why Do Lovers Break Each Other's Hearts', and we were on our way to a writing partnership.

When we worked together, Phil did contribute. He would edit the songs. He always had his input, and some of them were completely three-way efforts. Phil is very musically talented, although I hear that Celine Dion couldn't work with him. I guess Phil finds it hard to live up to being Phil.
Ellie Greenwich – on meeting and working with Phil

As much as an influence as Philip was he didn't have an orchestra... my orchestral influence was Jack Nitzsche's '63 'Lonely Surfer'.
Andrew Loog Oldham – on *Spectropop* website, via Al Kooper

The studio is where I feel comfortable, where I feel reasonable.
Phil Spector

I believed I was the best in the world.
Phil Spector, 2003

I knew.
Phil Spector

Appendix V
A Selection Of Phil Spector Collectibles (US & UK)

Singles
The Crystals: '(Let's Dance) The Screw Pts 1 & 2' (1963) Philles 111DJ – $ 6000+ (Light blue (rarest) or white labels; beware, this has been bootlegged with some minor variations)

Phil Spector: 'Thanks For Giving Me The Right Time!' (1965) Philles – no cat. no. – $1000+ (Actually plays the Righteous Brothers' 'Ebbtide'/'For Sentimental Reasons')

Darlene Love: 'Stumble and Fall'/'He's A Quiet Guy' (Yellow/red stock copy) (1964) Philles 123 – $800 (Yellow/red DJ copies $300, white label DJ copies $150)

Darlene Love: 'Christmas (Baby Please Come Home)'/'X-Mas Blues' (1964) Philles 125 – $ 400+

The Ronettes: 'Is This What I Get For Loving You?' (1965) Philles 128 (Picture sleeve) – $150 (Similar price for picture sleeves of 'Walking In The Rain' and 'Born To Be Together')

Veronica: 'Why Don't They Let Us Fall In Love' (1964) Phil Spector Records 2 – $200 (A rarer mistitled version with 'Can't' instead of 'Don't' fetches $600)

Veronica: 'So Young' (1964) Phil Spector Records 1 – $200

The Blossoms: 'Things Are Changing' (1966) Equal Employment Opportunities Campaign T4LM-8172-1 (An edition of approx 4000 DJ copies that went to radio stations only – it features Spector's track for Brian Wilson's 'Don't Hurt My Little Sister' that was aimed at the Ronettes, and that features Brian playing piano) – $150 (NB Bootlegs that play at 45 rather than the original 33 exist)

EPs And LPs
The Crystals: *Crystals Twist Uptown* (1962) Philles PHLP 4000 – $600+

The Crystals: *He's A Rebel* (1963) Philles PHLP 4001 – $ 600+

The Crystals: *Sing The Greatest Hits Volume 1* (1963) Philles PHLP 4003 – $600+

Bob B. Soxx & The Blue Jeans: *Zip-A-Dee-Doo-Dah* (1963) Philles PHLP 4002 – $500

The Ronettes: *Presenting The Fabulous Ronettes* (1964) Philles
PHLP 4006 (Blue & black label – $800+ – yellow and red version
- $400)
The Crystals: *He's A Rebel* (1963) London HA-U 8120(LP) – £160
The Crystals: *Da Doo Ron Ron* (1963) London RE-U 1381 (EP)
– £100
Bob B. Soxx & The Blue Jeans: *Zip-A-Dee-Doo-Dah* (1963) London
HA-U 8121(LP) – £120
The Ronettes: *Presenting The Fabulous Ronettes* (1964) London
HA-U 8212 (LP Plum label) – £160
Various Artists: *A Christmas Gift To You* (1963) London HA-U 8141
(Original issue LP plum label) – £100
Various Artists: *Rare Masters Vols 1&2* (1976) Phil Spector
International 2307 008/9 (LPs) – £35 each

Plus two never released albums:
Ike & Tina Turner: *River Deep Mountain High* Philles 4011 (1967)
– $8000 (Only pressed in very limited numbers in the US on red &
yellow Philles – approx 6 copies known – value is for record only, as
sleeves not known to have been printed)
Various Artists: *The Phil Spector Spectacular* Philles PHLP 100
(1972) – $1500 (DJ copies only – no cover – originally intended to
follow the Christmas album on the Apple label)

And Finally...

As this musical reader is finally being completed in May 2011, Phil Spector remains behind bars following the failure of his appeal against conviction. It has been a deliberate decision not to dwell on trial details or outcomes. This book has been about Phil Spector the record producer and the wonderful singers, musicians, writers and arrangers that he worked with above all else, although it is of course impossible to totally separate personality aspects from his musical story. We end with some brief thoughts on the subject from Mark Wirtz.

Man and talent are two entirely different energies, and we shouldn't judge one because of the other. There have been some extraordinary talents in history that have touched human beings all over the world that were despicable human beings. As mortals we are merely vessels for our talents. Talking about Phil Spector now... regardless of the man and his foibles, I don't think we should confuse that with the beauty and magnificence of his talent, and especially now that he's probably going to go down in history as somewhat of a... we accept the fact that the man as a man screwed up or whatever, that in no way impedes upon his talent and the beauty of it and what he has given us. We should continue to respect it as we continue to respect Beethoven and other... sometimes maniacs... I think it would be nice if people were to keep that in mind.
Mark Wirtz

Copyrights

'Nik Cohn Visits Mr Spector' by Nik Cohn, from *Creem* magazine #19, December, 1972. © Nik Cohn 1972. Reproduced by kind permission of the author.

'To Know Him Is To Love Him' by Greg Shaw, from *History Of Rock* magazine #26, Orbis Publishing, 1982. Reproduced by kind permission of the publishers.

'Phil Spector's Wall Of Sound' by Rob Finnis, from *Radio One: Story Of Pop* magazine #14, 1973. Reproduced by kind permission of the author.

'A Producer's View Of The Wall Of Sound' by Tony Hatch, written especially for this book. Reproduced by kind permission of the author.

'Spector Soundalikes' by Mick Patrick, written especially for this book. Reproduced by kind permission of the author.

'Phil Spector: The Pre-Philles Years' by Mike Callahan, from *Goldmine* magazine, March 1980. Reproduced by kind permission of the publisher Greg Loescher.

'Phil Spector: The Philles Years' by Mike Callahan, from *Goldmine* magazine, April 1980. Reproduced by kind permission of the publisher Greg Loescher.

'Wall Of Sound' by Mike Callahan, from *Goldmine* magazine, December 1980. Reproduced by kind permission of the publisher Greg Loescher.

'He's A Rebel' by Mike Kelly, from *Discoveries* magazine, July 1996. Reproduced by kind permission of the publishers.

'19 + 1 Choices' by Dave Marsh, excerpted from *The Heart And Soul Of Rock & Soul*, Plume, 1989. Reproduced by kind permission of the author.

'Phil's Fillies' by Geoff Brown, from *History Of Rock* magazine #26, Orbis Publishing, 1982. Reproduced by kind permission of the publishers.

'The Crystals' interview by Wayne Jones, from *Goldmine* magazine, December 1980. Reproduced by kind permission of the publisher Greg Loescher.

'Ronnie Spector: Say Goodbye To Hollywood' by John Tobler, from *Hot Wacks* magazine. Reproduced by kind permission of the author.

'End Of The Century' by Dee Dee Ramone, from *Poison Heart: Surviving The Ramones*, Firefly, 1997. Reproduced by kind permission of the publishers.

'Rebuilding The Wall Of Sound' by Richard Williams, from *Long Distance Call: Writings On Music*, by Richard Williams, Aurum Press, 2000. © Richard Williams 2000. Reproduced by kind permission of the author.

Various excerpts from *Spectropop* website by kind permission of the participants.